RISOTTO & RICE

RISOTTO & RICE

150 DELICIOUS RECIPES SHOWN IN 220 INSPIRING PHOTOGRAPHS

CHRISTINE INGRAM

southwater

This edition is published by Southwater an imprint of Anness Publishing Ltd Blaby Road, Wigston, Leicestershire LE18 4SE; info@anness.com

www.southwaterbooks.com; www.annesspublishing.com

If you like the images in this book and would like to investigate using them for publishing, promotions or advertising, please visit our website www.practicalpictures.com for more information.

Publisher: Joanna Lorenz
Recipes: Carla Capalbo, Kit Chan, Roz Denny, Rafi Fernandez, Silvana Franco, Deh-Ta Hsiung, Shehzad Husain, Christine Ingram, Soheila Kimberley, Masaki Ko, Elisabeth Lambert Ortiz, Ruby Le Bois and Sallie Morris
Photography: Dave King (recipes) and David Jordan (cutouts and techniques)
Food for photography: Jennie Shapter (recipes) and Sara Lewis (cutouts and techniques)
Stylist: Jo Harris
Editor: Brian Burns
Designer: Graham Webb
Production Controller: Wendy Lawson

A CIP catalogue record for this book is available from the British Library.

The front cover shows Risotto with Asparagus – for recipe, see page 63.

PUBLISHER'S NOTE
Although the advice and information in this book are believed to be accurate and true at the time of going to press, neither the authors nor the publisher can accept any legal responsibility or liability for any errors or omissions that may have been made nor for any inaccuracies nor for any loss, harm or injury that comes about from following instructions or advice in this book.

NOTES
Bracketed terms are intended for American readers. For all recipes, quantities are given in both metric and imperial measures and, where appropriate, in standard cups and spoons. Follow one set of measures, but not a mixture, because they are not interchangeable.

Standard spoon and cup measures are level. 1 tsp = 5ml, 1 tbsp = 15ml, 1 cup = 250ml/9fl oz. Australian standard tablespoons are 20ml. Australian readers should use 3 tsp in place of 1 tbsp for measuring small quantities. American pints are 16fl oz/2 cups. American readers should use 20fl oz/2.5 cups in place of 1 pint when measuring liquids.

Electric oven temperatures in this book are for conventional ovens. When using a fan oven, the temperature will probably need to be reduced by about 10–20°C/20–40°F. Since ovens vary, you should check with your manufacturer's instruction book for guidance.

The nutritional analysis given for each recipe is calculated per portion (i.e. serving or item), unless otherwise stated. If the recipe gives a range, such as Serves 4–6, then the nutritional analysis will be for the smaller portion size, i.e. 6 servings. The analysis does not include optional ingredients, such as salt added to taste.

Medium (US large) eggs are used unless otherwise stated.

Contents

Introduction

The rice grain has been a favourite ingredient with cooks worldwide for thousands of years and has certainly played a significant part in man's development. Each of the major cuisines has its own way of dealing with rice, and the recipes here include the very best.

Rice has been cultivated in South-east Asia for thousands of years, and in Thailand since 6000BC. It is likely that early humans first grew wild rice, and later began cultivating local species. Certainly, rice is highly adaptable: some varieties tolerate floods and cold nights, while others survive hot weather and relatively little water.

From north-eastern India and Thailand, rice spread first through South-east Asia, and then further afield until it spread out across the rest of the world.

It is believed that rice cultivation began in China in the Yangtze river delta around 4000BC, although it is thought that rice did not become an important part of the Chinese diet until around 800BC.

By the 9th century AD, rice was widely eaten in southern China, but in the north, where it could not be grown, it was food only for the wealthy.

THE REST OF THE WORLD

Rice was probably introduced to the Middle East via northern India and Afghanistan through conquest, expansion and trading. However, even in the 13th century, rice was still regarded as a luxury item in Baghdad.

Rice came to Europe by various routes, its popularity determined by whether or not it could be grown locally, as high transportation costs limited supply and demand. By the middle of the 20th century, thanks to lower transportation costs, rice became affordable to the majority.

In Spain, rice was introduced by the Moors, who ruled that country for about 300 years, from the beginning of the 8th century. They built the irrigation canals around Valencia and in the hills around Murcia, which are still used today for rice growing.

In parts of Europe where cultivation was not an option, rice was often regarded with suspicion and there was some resistance to eating it. In Britain, it took many years for rice to become accepted. However, it was not totally unknown in England; in the 13th century, knights returning from the Crusades brought back rice along with other Arabian products such as sugar and lemons.

LEFT: *Fresh, tasty and filling, salmon and rice gratin is an all-in-one supper that's easy to make in advance and simply reheat.*

ABOVE: *Celebration paella is one of Spain's best-loved dishes.*

ABOVE: *Pancetta and broad bean risotto is healthy, filling and utterly delicious.*

ABOVE: *Colourful, rice-stuffed vegetables make a tasty and popular supper dish.*

In the Americas, maize was the main cereal until the Spanish and Portuguese introduced rice there in the late 16th century. It is now grown in many South American countries, notably Brazil, which grows as much as Japan yet is still the world's second largest rice importer.

Some scholars believe rice came to North America with West African slaves. Another story tells of a ship bearing rice from Madagascar that was blown off course and landed in South Carolina. The reality is probably a mixture of these stories. The United States is now the world's second major rice exporter, and rice is grown far and wide, from Asia to Australia.

A VERY VERSATILE GRAIN

Rice's status as one of the world's most widespread and ancient staple foods is fully reflected in this book. In these pages you will find a stunning collection of recipes reflecting the tastes, flavours and aromas of many different places across the globe, including the Middle East, the Mediterranean and Morocco, Japan, Indonesia and Thailand, the Caribbean and the United States, Africa, India and Turkey, and more.

For ease of use, the chapters are organized into appetizers and soups, vegetarian dishes, fish and shellfish, poultry, meat, side dishes and salads, and, of course, desserts. Explore these recipes and you will soon come to appreciate the importance of this endlessly versatile food. Banish any notion that risotto and rice dishes need be plain and humble. With tastes to suit every palate – sweet, sour, spicy, exotic, rich, savoury, fragrant, aromatic, understated and delicate, meaty and filling – the recipes in this book brim with colour, diversity and tireless invention. Whether you are looking for meals for one, a romantic meal for two, family feasts, light lunches, elegant dinner party suppers, tasty snacks, quick winter warmers or fresh summer salads, the dishes on offer here will leave you spoiled for choice every time.

Appetizers and soups

Whether you are using fish or fowl, cheese or eggs, meat or vegetables, the sheer versatility of rice is immediately evident in the range of tempting first courses in this chapter. From simple yet tasty to spicy and rich, many of these dishes from around the world can also make deliciously satisfying main courses in their own right.

Fried rice balls stuffed with mozzarella

These deep-fried balls of risotto go by the name of suppli al telefono *in their native Italy. Stuffed with mozzarella cheese, they are delicious and make very popular snacks.*

SERVES 4

1 quantity Risotto alla Milanese
   (see page 19) or a mushroom risotto
   of your choice
3 eggs
breadcrumbs, to coat
115g/4oz/²/₃ cup mozzarella cheese,
   cut into small cubes
oil, for deep-frying
plain (all-purpose) flour, to coat
dressed frisée lettuce and cherry
   tomatoes, to serve

1 Put the risotto in a bowl and allow it to cool completely. Beat two of the eggs, and stir them into the cold risotto until well mixed.

2 Use your hands to form the rice mixture into balls the size of a large egg. If the mixture is too moist to hold its shape well, stir in a few tablespoons of breadcrumbs. Poke a hole into the centre of each ball with your finger, then fill it with a few small cubes of mozzarella, and close the hole over again with the rice mixture.

3 Heat the oil for deep-frying until a small piece of bread sizzles as soon as it is dropped in.

4 Spread some flour on a plate. Beat the remaining egg in a shallow bowl. Sprinkle another plate with breadcrumbs. Roll the balls in the flour, then in the egg, and finally in the breadcrumbs.

5 Fry them a few at a time in the hot oil until golden and crisp. Drain on kitchen paper while the remaining balls are being fried. Serve hot, with a simple salad of dressed frisée lettuce and cherry tomatoes.

Nutritional information per portion: Energy 813kcal/3389kJ; Protein 28.9g; Carbohydrate 89.6g, of which sugars 1.9g; Fat 37.9g, of which saturates 22.1g; Cholesterol 233mg; Calcium 464mg; Fibre 0.8g; Sodium 754mg.

Rice cakes with smoked salmon

These elegant rice cakes are made using a risotto base. You could skip this stage and use leftover seafood or mushroom risotto, or use leftover long grain rice and flavour with spring onions.

SERVES 4

15g/¹/₂oz/2 tbsp dried
　　porcini mushrooms
30ml/2 tbsp olive oil
1 medium onion, chopped
225g/8oz/generous 1 cup risotto rice
about 90ml/6 tbsp white wine
about 750ml/1¼ pints/3 cups fish stock
　　or chicken stock
15ml/1 tbsp chopped fresh parsley
15ml/1 tbsp chopped fresh chives
5ml/1 tsp chopped fresh dill
1 egg, lightly beaten
about 45ml/3 tbsp ground rice, plus extra
　　for dusting
oil, for frying
60ml/4 tbsp sour cream
175g/6oz smoked salmon
salt and ground black pepper
radicchio and oak leaf lettuce salad,
　　tossed in French dressing, to serve

1 Soak the mushrooms for 10 minutes, then drain and chop into small pieces. Heat the olive oil in a large pan and fry the onion for 3–4 minutes until soft. Add the rice and cook, stirring, until the grains are thoroughly coated in oil. Pour in the wine and stock, a little at a time, stirring constantly over a gentle heat until each quantity of liquid has been absorbed before adding more.

2 When the rice is tender, and all the liquid absorbed, stir in the mushrooms, parsley, chives, dill and seasoning. Remove from the heat and leave to cool for a few minutes.

3 Add the beaten egg, then stir in enough ground rice to bind the mixture – until it is soft but manageable. Dust your hands with ground rice and shape the mixture into four patties, 13cm/5in in diameter and about 2cm/³⁄₄in thick.

4 Heat the oil in a frying pan and fry the rice cakes, in batches if necessary, for 4–5 minutes until evenly browned on both sides. Drain on kitchen paper and cool slightly. Place each rice cake on a plate and top with 15ml/1 tbsp sour cream. Twist two or three thin slices of smoked salmon on top, and serve with a dressed salad.

Nutritional information per portion: Energy 475kcal/1978kJ; Protein 18.3g; Carbohydrate 55.9g, of which sugars 1.6g; Fat 17.8g, of which saturates 4.1g; Cholesterol 72mg; Calcium 56mg; Fibre 0.6g; Sodium 849mg.

Festive black bean rice

This Spanish dish is traditionally served for the Fiesta de Moros y Cristianos.

SERVES 6

400g/14oz/2 cups black beans, soaked overnight
1 onion, quartered
1 carrot, sliced
1 stalk celery, sliced
1 garlic clove, crushed
1 bay leaf
1.75 litres/3 pints/7½ cups water
5ml/1 tsp paprika
45ml/3 tbsp olive oil
juice of 1 orange
300g/10½oz/1¾ cups long grain rice
salt and cayenne pepper
chopped fresh parsley, sliced orange, sliced red onion,
    and 2 hard-boiled eggs cut into wedges, to garnish

1 Put the beans, onion, carrot, celery, garlic, bay leaf and water in a large pan, bring to the boil and boil for 10 minutes, then simmer for 1 hour, topping up if necessary. Drain, and discard the vegetables.

2 Blend together the paprika, oil and cayenne pepper and put in a clean saucepan with the beans and orange juice. Top up with water, if necessary. Heat until just simmering, cover and cook for 10–15 minutes until tender. Remove from the heat and leave for 15 minutes. Add salt to taste.

3 Cook the rice by boiling or by absorption. Drain, pack into a buttered bowl and leave for 10 minutes. Unmould on to a serving plate. Place the black beans around the edge and garnish with the parsley, orange and onion slices and egg.

Nutritional information per portion: Energy 445kcal/1875kJ; Protein 19.7g; Carbohydrate 77.8g, of which sugars 3.2g; Fat 7g, of which saturates 1.1g; Cholesterol 0mg; Calcium 68mg; Fibre 5.6g; Sodium 12mg.

Alicante omelette rice

If you cannot get butifarra for this dish, use chorizo or any similar Spanish sausage instead.

SERVES 6

45ml/3 tbsp sunflower oil
200g/7oz butifarra or other Spanish sausage, sliced
2 tomatoes, peeled, seeded and chopped
175g/6oz lean pork, cut into bitesize pieces
175g/6oz skinless, boneless chicken breast or rabbit,
    cut into chunks
350g/12oz/1¾ cups Spanish rice or risotto rice
900ml–1 litre/1½–1¾ pints/3¾–4 cups hot chicken stock
pinch of saffron strands, crushed
115g/4oz/⅔ cup cooked chickpeas
6 eggs
salt and ground black pepper

1 Preheat the oven to 190°C/375°F/Gas 5. Heat the oil in a flameproof casserole and fry the sausage for a few minutes. Transfer to a plate.

2 Add the tomatoes and fry for a few minutes until slightly thickened. Stir in the pork and chicken pieces, and cook for 2–3 minutes, stirring, until lightly browned. Add the rice, stir for 1 minute, then add the stock. Add the saffron, with salt and pepper to taste, and stir well. Bring to the boil, lower the heat and add the sausage and chickpeas. Cover tightly with the lid and cook over a low heat for about 15 minutes until the rice is tender.

3 Beat the eggs with a little water and a pinch of salt and pour over the rice. Bake, uncovered, for 10 minutes, until the eggs have set and browned slightly on top.

Nutritional information per portion: Energy 533kcal/2226kJ; Protein 29.1g; Carbohydrate 55.5g, of which sugars 1.7g; Fat 21.7g, of which saturates 6.3g; Cholesterol 242mg; Calcium 72mg; Fibre 1.5g; Sodium 436mg.

Aubergine and rice rolls

As well as making an original appetizer, these little rolls of aubergine wrapped around a filling of ricotta and rice are tasty served as part of a buffet or for a Turkish-style meze.

SERVES 4

2 aubergines (eggplants)
olive oil, for shallow frying
75g/2³/₄oz/scant ¹/₂ cup ricotta cheese
75g/2³/₄oz/scant ¹/₂ cup soft goat's cheese
225g/8oz/2 cups cooked white
    long grain rice
15ml/1 tbsp chopped fresh basil
5ml/1 tsp chopped fresh mint, plus mint
    sprigs, to garnish
salt and ground black pepper

FOR THE TOMATO SAUCE

15ml/1 tbsp olive oil
1 red onion, finely chopped
1 garlic clove, crushed
400g/14oz can chopped tomatoes
125ml/4fl oz/¹/₂ cup chicken stock
    or white wine, or a mixture of both
15ml/1 tbsp chopped fresh parsley

1 Preheat the oven to 190°C/375°F/ Gas 5. To make the sauce, gently heat the olive oil in a small pan. Add the chopped red onion and crushed garlic and fry for 3–4 minutes until slightly softened.

2 Add the chopped tomatoes, then the chicken stock, and/or wine if using, and the chopped fresh parsley. Season to taste.

3 Bring the mixture to the boil, then lower the heat and continue to simmer for 10–12 minutes, stirring frequently, until the tomato mixture has thickened slightly.

4 Cut the aubergines lengthways into four or five slices and shallow fry in olive oil in a large frying pan, in batches, until golden brown on both sides. Drain on kitchen paper. Mix the ricotta, goat's cheese, rice, basil and mint in a bowl. Season well with salt and pepper.

5 Place a generous spoonful of the cheese and rice mixture at one end of each aubergine slice and roll up. Arrange the rolls side by side in a shallow baking dish. Pour over the tomato sauce and bake for 10–15 minutes until heated through. Garnish with mint sprigs and serve.

Nutritional information per portion: Energy 283kcal/1185kJ; Protein 8.9g; Carbohydrate 24.7g, of which sugars 6.7g; Fat 17.3g, of which saturates 6.6g; Cholesterol 25mg; Calcium 56mg; Fibre 3.3g; Sodium 125mg.

Stuffed vegetables

Colourful and utterly delicious, this is a popular supper dish and, with a choice of vegetables included, there are flavours to please everyone.

SERVES 4

45ml/3 tbsp olive oil, plus extra
    for greasing
1 aubergine (eggplant)
1 green (bell) pepper, halved, cored
    and seeded
2 beefsteak tomatoes
1 onion, chopped
2 garlic cloves, crushed
115g/4oz/1–1¹⁄₂ cups button (white)
    mushrooms, chopped
1 carrot, grated
225g/8oz/2 cups cooked white
    long grain rice
15ml/1 tbsp chopped fresh dill
90g/3¹⁄₄oz/scant ¹⁄₂ cup feta
    cheese, crumbled
75g/2³⁄₄oz/³⁄₄ cup pine nuts, toasted
30ml/2 tbsp currants
salt and ground black pepper

1 Heat the oven to 190°C/375°F/Gas 5. Lightly grease a shallow baking dish. Halve the aubergine through the stalk, and scoop out the flesh to leave two hollow "boats". Dice the flesh.

2 Cut the tops off the tomatoes and hollow out the centres. Chop the flesh and add to the aubergine. Drain the tomatoes upside down on kitchen paper.

3 Blanch the aubergine halves in a pan of boiling water for 3 minutes. Add the pepper halves and blanch for 3 minutes. Drain and place, hollow sides up, in the dish.

4 Pour 30ml/2 tbsp olive oil into a large pan, heat gently, then add the chopped onion and crushed garlic. Fry for about 5 minutes.

5 Stir in the aubergine and tomato mixture, chopped mushrooms and grated carrot. Cover and cook for 5 minutes until softened. Mix in the rice, dill, feta cheese, pine nuts and currants. Season with salt and pepper to taste.

6 Divide the mixture among the vegetable shells, drizzle over the remaining olive oil and bake for 20 minutes until the topping has browned. Serve hot or cold.

Nutritional information per portion: Energy 544kcal/2265kJ; Protein 12.9g; Carbohydrate 63.3g, of which sugars 17.2g; Fat 26.8g, of which saturates 5.3g; Cholesterol 16mg; Calcium 134mg; Fibre 4.1g; Sodium 343mg.

Flamenco eggs

This adaptation of a classic Spanish recipe works very well with Camargue red rice, although any long grain rice – brown or white – could be used.

SERVES 4

175g/6oz/scant 1 cup Camargue red rice
chicken stock, vegetable stock or water
45ml/3 tbsp olive oil
1 Spanish onion, chopped
1 garlic clove, crushed
350g/12oz lean minced (ground) beef
75g/2³/₄oz chorizo sausage, cut into
    small cubes
5ml/1 tsp paprika, plus extra for dusting
10ml/2 tsp tomato purée (paste)
15–30ml/1–2 tbsp chopped fresh parsley
2 red (bell) peppers, seeded and sliced
3 tomatoes, peeled, seeded and chopped
125ml/4fl oz/¹/₂ cup passata (bottled
    strained tomatoes) or tomato juice
4 eggs
40ml/8 tsp single (light) cream
salt and ground black pepper

1 Preheat the oven to 180°C/350°F/Gas 4. Cook the rice in a pan of stock or water, following the instructions on the packet. Heat 30ml/2 tbsp of the oil in a frying pan and fry the onion and garlic for 5 minutes until lightly browned, stirring occasionally. Add the minced beef and cook, stirring occasionally, until browned. Stir in the chorizo and paprika and continue cooking over a low heat for 4–5 minutes. Stir in the tomato purée, parsley and seasoning.

2 Heat the remaining oil in a pan and fry the peppers until they begin to sizzle. Cover and cook over a medium heat, shaking the pan occasionally, for 4–5 minutes until the peppers are singed in places. Add the tomatoes and continue cooking for 3–4 minutes until they are very soft. Remove the pan from the heat, stir in the passata or tomato juice and add salt to taste.

3 Drain the rice, and divide it among four shallow ovenproof dishes. Spread the meat mixture over the rice and top with the peppers and tomatoes. Make a hole in the centre of each portion and break in an egg. Spoon 10ml/ 2 tsp of the cream over each egg yolk, dust with paprika, and bake for about 12–15 minutes until the whites of the eggs are set. Serve at once.

Nutritional information per portion: Energy 592kcal/2464kJ; Protein 26.6g; Carbohydrate 30.4g, of which sugars 12g; Fat 41.1g, of which saturates 11.8g; Cholesterol 416mg; Calcium 155mg; Fibre 4.1g; Sodium 1150mg.

Dolmades

Now popular the world over, these stuffed vine leaves originated in Greece. If you can't locate fresh vine leaves, use a packet or can of brined vine leaves.

MAKES 20–24

24–28 fresh young vine leaves, soaked in
　hot water for 20 minutes, then rinsed
　and dried
30ml/2 tbsp olive oil
1 large onion, finely chopped
1 garlic clove, crushed
225g/8oz/2 cups cooked long grain rice,
　or mixed white and wild rice
45ml/3 tbsp pine nuts
15ml/1 tbsp flaked (sliced) almonds
40g/1¹/₂oz/¹/₄ cup sultanas
　(golden raisins)
15ml/1 tbsp chopped fresh chives
15ml/1 tbsp finely chopped fresh mint
juice of ¹/₂ lemon
150ml/¹/₄ pint/²/₃ cup white wine
hot vegetable stock
salt and ground black pepper
fresh mint sprig, to garnish
garlic yogurt and pitta bread,
　to serve (optional)

1 Boil the vine leaves in a pan of water for 2–3 minutes until pliable. If using leaves from a packet or can, place them in a large bowl, cover with boiling water and leave for a few minutes until the leaves can be easily separated. Rinse them under cold water and drain on kitchen paper.

2 Heat the oil in a frying pan and fry the onion and garlic for 3–4 minutes until soft. Spoon into a large bowl. Mix in the rice, 30ml/2 tbsp of the pine nuts, and the almonds, sultanas, chives, mint, lemon juice and seasoning. Set aside four large vine leaves. Lay a vine leaf on a clean work surface, veined side up, add a spoonful of filling near the stem, fold over the lower part of the leaf and roll up, folding in the sides. Stuff the remaining leaves in the same way.

3 Line the base of a deep frying pan with the reserved leaves. Add the dolmades, seam sides down, in one layer. Pour over the wine and enough stock just to cover. Top with a plate, then a lid, and simmer for 30 minutes.

4 Transfer to a plate. Cool, chill, then garnish with the remaining pine nuts and the mint. Serve with a little garlic yogurt and pitta bread, if you like.

Nutritional information per portion: Energy 43kcal/181kJ; Protein 0.7g; Carbohydrate 6.7g, of which sugars 1.7g; Fat 1.1g, of which saturates 0.1g; Cholesterol 0mg; Calcium 12mg; Fibre 0.3g; Sodium 2mg.

Risi e bisi

This is a classic pea and ham risotto from the Veneto. Although traditionally served as a first course in Italy, it also makes an excellent supper dish with hot, crusty bread.

SERVES 4

75g/2³/₄oz/6 tbsp butter
1 small onion, finely chopped
about 1 litre/1³/₄ pints/4 cups simmering
    chicken stock
275g/9¹/₂oz/1¹/₂ cups risotto rice
150ml/¹/₄ pint/²/₃ cup dry white wine
225g/8oz/2 cups frozen petits pois
    (baby peas), thawed
115g/4oz cooked ham, diced
salt and ground black pepper
50g/1³/₄oz/²/₃ cup freshly grated
    Parmesan cheese, to serve

1 Melt 50g/1³/₄oz/4 tbsp of butter in a pan until foaming. Add the onion and cook gently for 3 minutes, stirring frequently, until softened. Have the hot stock ready in another pan.

2 Add the rice to the onion mixture. Stir until the grains start to swell, then pour in the wine. Stir until it stops sizzling and most has been absorbed. Then pour in a little hot stock, with salt and pepper to taste. Stir continuously, over a low heat, until all the stock has been absorbed.

3 Slowly add the remaining stock, allowing the rice to absorb it all before adding more, and stirring constantly. Add the peas after 20 minutes. After 25–30 minutes, the rice should be al dente and the risotto moist and creamy.

4 Stir in the cooked ham and the remaining butter. Heat through until the butter melts. Taste for seasoning. Transfer to a warmed serving bowl. Grate or shave over a little Parmesan and serve the rest separately.

Nutritional information per portion: Energy 545kcal/2268kJ; Protein 19.3g; Carbohydrate 61.9g, of which sugars 1.9g; Fat 21.6g, of which saturates 12.8g; Cholesterol 69mg; Calcium 184mg; Fibre 2.7g; Sodium 597mg.

Risotto alla milanese

This classic risotto is often served with the hearty beef stew called osso buco, *but is filling enough to be served as a delicious first course or light supper dish in its own right.*

SERVES 3–4

about 1.2 litres/2 pints/5 cups simmering
   beef stock or chicken stock
good pinch of saffron strands
75g/2³/₄oz/6 tbsp butter
1 onion, finely chopped
275g/9¹/₂oz/1¹/₂ cups risotto rice
75g/2³/₄oz/1 cup freshly grated
   Parmesan cheese
salt and ground black pepper

1 Ladle a little simmering stock into a small bowl. Add the saffron and leave to infuse. Melt 50g/1³/₄oz/4 tbsp of butter in a large pan until foaming. Add the onion and cook gently for 3 minutes, stirring frequently, until softened but not browned.

2 Add the rice. Stir until the grains start to swell and burst, then add a few ladlefuls of the stock, with the saffron liquid and salt and pepper to taste. Stir over a low heat until the stock has been absorbed.

3 Slowly add the remaining stock, allowing the rice to absorb it all before adding more, and stirring constantly. After 20–25 minutes, the rice should be just tender and the risotto golden yellow, moist and creamy.

4 Stir in two-thirds of the grated Parmesan and remaining butter. Heat until the butter melts. Taste for seasoning. Transfer to a warmed serving bowl or platter. Serve hot, with the remaining grated Parmesan served separately.

Nutritional information per portion: Energy 477kcal/1981kJ; Protein 12.8g; Carbohydrate 56.2g, of which sugars 1g; Fat 21.9g, of which saturates 13.6g; Cholesterol 59mg; Calcium 245mg; Fibre 0.2g; Sodium 319mg.

Risotto with **four cheeses**

This is a very rich dish, containing Gruyère, taleggio, Gorgonzola and Parmesan cheese. Serve it for a special dinner-party first course, with a light, dry, sparkling white wine.

SERVES 4

40g/1¹/₂oz/3 tbsp butter
1 small onion, finely chopped
1.2 litres/2 pints/5 cups chicken stock
    350g/12oz/1³/₄ cups risotto rice
200ml/7fl oz/scant 1 cup dry white wine
50g/1³/₄oz/¹/₂ cup grated
    Gruyère cheese
50g/1³/₄oz/¹/₂ cup diced
    taleggio cheese
50g/1³/₄oz/¹/₂ cup diced
    Gorgonzola cheese
50g/1³/₄oz/²/₃ cup freshly grated
    Parmesan cheese
salt and ground black pepper
chopped fresh flat leaf parsley, to garnish

1 Melt the butter in a large, heavy pan or deep frying pan and fry the onion over a gentle heat for about 4–5 minutes, stirring frequently, until softened and lightly browned. Pour the stock into another pan and heat it to simmering point.

2 Add the rice to the onion mixture, stir until the grains start to swell and burst, then add the wine. Stir until it stops sizzling and most of it has been absorbed by the rice, then pour in a little of the hot stock. Add salt and pepper to taste. Stir over a low heat until the stock has been absorbed.

3 Gradually add the remaining stock, a little at a time, allowing the rice to absorb the liquid before adding more, and stirring constantly. After 20–25 minutes the rice should be *al dente* and the risotto creamy.

4 Remove from the heat, then add the Gruyère, taleggio, Gorgonzola and 30ml/2 tbsp of the Parmesan cheese. Stir gently until the cheeses have melted, then taste for seasoning. Spoon into a serving bowl and garnish with parsley. Serve the remaining Parmesan separately.

Nutritional information per portion: Energy 420kcal/1750kJ; Protein 13.8g; Carbohydrate 47.6g, of which sugars 0.8g; Fat 16.4g, of which saturates 10.4g; Cholesterol 45mg; Calcium 282mg; Fibre 0.2g; Sodium 355mg.

Duck risotto

This makes an excellent appetizer for six or could be served for half that number as a lunch or supper dish. Add a green salad, or serve with green beans and sautéed red (bell) pepper slices.

SERVES 6

2 duck breasts, scored on the fatty sides
    and then rubbed with salt
30ml/2 tbsp brandy
30ml/2 tbsp orange juice
15ml/1 tbsp olive oil (optional)
1 onion, finely chopped
1 garlic clove, crushed
275g/9^1/$_2$oz/1^1/$_2$ cups risotto rice
1–1.2 litres/1^3/$_4$–2 pints/4–5 cups
    simmering duck, turkey or
    chicken stock
5ml/1 tsp chopped fresh thyme
5ml/1 tsp chopped fresh mint
10ml/2 tsp grated orange rind
40g/1^1/$_2$oz/^{1}/$_2$ cup freshly grated
    Parmesan cheese
salt and ground black pepper
strips of thinly pared orange rind,
    to garnish

1 Dry-fry the duck, fat side down, in a heavy frying pan over a medium heat for 6–8 minutes to render the fat. Transfer to a plate. Pull away and discard the fat. Cut the flesh into strips 2cm/^{3}/$_4$in wide. Pour all but 15ml/1 tbsp of the rendered duck fat into a cup or jug (pitcher), then reheat the fat in the pan. Fry the duck slices for 2–3 minutes over a medium high heat until evenly brown but not overcooked. Add the brandy, heat to simmering point, then ignite, either by tilting the pan or using a taper. When the flames have died down, add the orange juice and seasoning. Remove from the heat and set aside.

2 In a large pan, heat 15ml/1 tbsp of the remaining duck fat or use olive oil. Gently fry the onion and garlic until soft but not browned. Add the rice and cook, stirring, until coated in oil and slightly translucent around the edges. Slowly ladle in the stock, stirring constantly, allowing each quantity to be absorbed before adding the next. Just before the final ladleful, stir in the duck, thyme and mint. Cook until the rice is tender but still firm to the bite.

3 Add the orange rind and Parmesan and season. Remove from the heat, cover and leave for a few minutes. Serve garnished with strips of orange rind.

Nutritional information per portion: Energy 171kcal/715kJ; Protein 8.6g; Carbohydrate 18.7g, of which sugars 0.9g; Fat 7g, of which saturates 2.3g; Cholesterol 48mg; Calcium 34mg; Fibre 0.4g; Sodium 99mg.

Thai-style rice and seafood pasties

Thai-style food is hugely popular in many parts of the world, especially along the American West Coast, where rice is one of the most important crops.

MAKES 18

500g/1lb 2oz puff pastry, thawed if frozen
1 egg, beaten with 30ml/2 tbsp water
fresh coriander (cilantro) leaves and lime
   twists, to garnish

FOR THE FILLING
275g/9½oz skinned white fish fillets,
   such as cod or haddock
plain (all-purpose) flour seasoned
   with salt and ground black pepper,
   for dusting

8–10 large raw prawns (shrimp)
15ml/1 tbsp sunflower oil
about 75g/2¾oz/6 tbsp butter
6 spring onions (scallions), finely sliced
1 garlic clove, crushed
4cm/1½in piece of fresh root ginger
225g/8oz/2 cups cooked Thai fragrant rice
10ml/2 tsp finely chopped fresh
   coriander (cilantro)
5ml/1 tsp finely grated lime rind

1 Preheat the oven to 190°C/375°F/Gas 5. For the filling, cut the fish into 2cm/¾in pieces and dust with seasoned flour. Peel and devein the prawns and cut each one into four pieces.

2 Heat half of the oil and 15g/½oz/1 tbsp of the butter in a frying pan and add the spring onions. Fry gently for 2 minutes. Add the garlic and fry for 5 minutes, until the onions are very soft. Transfer to a large bowl.

3 Heat the remaining oil and a further 25g/1oz/2 tbsp of the butter in a clean pan. Fry the fish pieces briefly. As soon as they begin to turn opaque, use a slotted spoon to transfer them to the bowl with the spring onions. Cook the prawns in the fat remaining in the pan. When they begin to change colour, lift them out and add them to the bowl. Grate the ginger, then add to the bowl with the cooked rice, coriander and lime rind. Mix carefully, taking care not to break up the fish.

4 Dust the work surface with a little flour. Roll out the pastry and cut into 10cm/4in rounds. Place spoonfuls of filling just off centre on the pastry rounds. Dot with a little butter. Dampen the edges of the pastry with a little of the egg wash, then fold one side of the pastry over the filling and press the edges together firmly. Place these on a lightly greased baking sheet. Decorate the pasties with pastry trimmings, if you like. Brush them with egg wash and bake for 12–15 minutes or until golden. Transfer to a plate and garnish with fresh coriander leaves and lime twists.

Nutritional information per pasty: Energy 171kcal/715kJ; Protein 8.6g; Carbohydrate 18.7g, of which sugars 0.9g; Fat 7g, of which saturates 2.3g; Cholesterol 48mg; Calcium 34mg; Fibre 0.4g; Sodium 99mg.

Spicy peanut and rice balls

Tasty rice balls, rolled in chopped peanuts and deep-fried, make a delicious snack. Serve them as they are, or with a chilli sauce for dipping.

MAKES 16

1 garlic clove, crushed
1cm/¹/₂in piece of fresh root ginger,
    peeled and finely chopped
1.5ml/¹/₄ tsp ground turmeric
5ml/1 tsp sugar
2.5ml/¹/₂ tsp salt
5ml/1 tsp chilli sauce
10ml/2 tsp fish sauce or soy sauce
30ml/2 tbsp chopped fresh
    coriander (cilantro)
juice of ¹/₂ lime
225g/8oz/2 cups cooked white
    long grain rice
115g/4oz peanuts, chopped
vegetable oil, for deep-frying
lime wedges and chilli dipping sauce,
    to serve (optional)

1 Process the crushed garlic, chopped root ginger and ground turmeric in a food processor to form a paste. Add the sugar, salt, chilli sauce, fish sauce or soy sauce, the chopped fresh coriander and the lime juice. Process briefly to mix.

2 Add three-quarters of the cooked rice to the paste in the food processor, and then process until it is smooth and sticky. Scrape the mixture into a mixing bowl and stir in the remainder of the rice. Wet your hands and shape the mixture into thumb-sized balls.

3 Spread the chopped peanuts out on a plate, then roll the rice balls in the chopped peanuts, making sure they are evenly coated.

4 Pour enough vegetable oil into a deep-fryer or wok to cover the peanut balls, and heat to the required temperature. Deep-fry the balls, in batches, until crisp and golden.

5 When they are cooked, lift out the peanut balls, drain them on kitchen paper, then pile them on to a platter. Serve hot with lime wedges and a chilli dipping sauce, if using.

Nutritional information per ball: Energy 123kcal/512kJ; Protein 2.9g; Carbohydrate 12.4g, of which sugars 0.8g; Fat 6.8g, of which saturates 1g; Cholesterol 0mg; Calcium 7mg; Fibre 0.4g; Sodium 45mg.

Rice omelettes

A popular supper dish, rice omelettes are a favourite with Japanese children, who usually top them with a liberal helping of tomato ketchup.

SERVES 4

1 skinless, boneless chicken thigh, about
   115g/4oz, cubed
40g/1¹/₂oz/3 tbsp butter
1 small onion, chopped
¹/₂ carrot, diced
2 shiitake mushrooms, stems removed
   and chopped
15ml/1 tbsp finely chopped fresh parsley
225g/8oz/2 cups cooked white
   long grain rice
30ml/2 tbsp tomato ketchup
6 eggs, lightly beaten
60ml/4 tbsp milk
5ml/1 tsp salt, plus extra to season
ground black pepper
tomato ketchup, to serve

1 Season the chicken with salt and pepper. Melt 10ml/2 tsp butter in a frying pan and fry the onion for 1 minute. Add the chicken and fry until white and cooked. Add the carrot and mushrooms, stir-fry over a medium heat until soft, then add the parsley. Set aside, and wipe the frying pan with kitchen paper.

2 Melt 10ml/2 tsp butter in the pan, add the rice and stir well. Mix in the fried ingredients, ketchup and pepper. Stir well, adding salt if necessary. Keep it warm. Beat the eggs and milk in a bowl. Stir in the measured salt, with pepper to taste.

3 Melt 5ml/1 tsp of the remaining butter in an omelette pan. Pour in a quarter of the egg mixture and stir it briefly with a fork, then allow it to set for 1 minute. Top with a quarter of the rice mixture, placed to one side.

4 Fold the omelette over to enclose the filling and then slide it to the edge of the pan to shape it into a curve. Slide it on to a warmed plate, cover with kitchen paper and press neatly into a rectangular shape. Keep it hot while cooking three more omelettes from the remaining ingredients. Serve immediately, with tomato ketchup.

Nutritional information per portion: Energy 429kcal/1796kJ; Protein 24.1g; Carbohydrate 30.4g, of which sugars 6.5g; Fat 24.6g, of which saturates 10.8g; Cholesterol 450mg; Calcium 106mg; Fibre 1.4g; Sodium 433mg.

Sushi

Once barely known outside Japan, these tasty rolls of flavoured rice and paper-thin seaweed have become very popular, partly due to the proliferation of sushi bars in many major cities.

SERVES 4–6

FOR THE TUNA SUSHI
2–3 baby carrots, blanched
3 sheets nori
115g/4oz fresh tuna fillet,
    cut into fingers
5ml/1 tsp thin wasabi paste (Japanese
    horseradish mustard)

FOR THE SALMON SUSHI
2 eggs
10ml/2 tsp sugar
2.5ml/$^1/_2$ tsp salt
10ml/2 tsp butter
3 sheets nori
150g/5$^1/_2$oz fresh salmon fillet,
    cut into fingers

$^1/_2$ small cucumber, cut into strips
5ml/1 tsp thin wasabi paste

FOR THE SUSHI RICE
450g/1lb/4 cups sushi rice, rinsed
about 650ml/1$^1/_4$ pints/2$^3/_4$ cups water

FOR THE SUSHI DRESSING
60ml/4 tbsp rice vinegar
15ml/1 tbsp sugar
2.5ml/$^1/_2$ tsp salt

TO SERVE
sliced pickled ginger, cut in strips
wasabi paste, thinned with water
Japanese sushi soy sauce

1 For the sushi rice, place the rice in a heavy pan and pour in the measured water or enough water according to the instructions on the packet. Bring the rice to the boil, then cover the pan tightly and cook over a very low heat for 15 minutes. Increase the heat to high for 10 seconds, then remove from the heat and leave to stand for 10 minutes.

2 Meanwhile, to make the sushi dressing, blend together the rice vinegar, sugar and salt.

3 Stir the sushi dressing into the rice, then cover with a damp cloth and leave to cool. Do not put it in the refrigerator, as this will make the rice go hard.

4 To make the tuna sushi, cut the carrots into thin strips. Lay one nori sheet, shiny side down, on a bamboo rolling mat. Lay strips of tuna across the length of the nori and spread with a little wasabi. Place a line of carrots next to the tuna and, using the mat as a guide, roll up tightly. Repeat with the other sheets of nori.

5 Place a square of baking parchment on the bamboo mat and spread with a little of the cooled sushi rice, leaving a 1cm/$^1/_2$in edge at the top and bottom.

6 Put the tuna-filled nori roll on top, about 2.5cm/1in from the edge of the rice, and roll up, using the paper as a guide. Wrap in baking parchment. Repeat with the other nori roll. Chill for 10 minutes.

7 To make the salmon sushi, beat the eggs with 30ml/2 tbsp water and the sugar and salt. Melt about one-third of the butter in a small frying pan and add one-third of the egg mixture to make an omelette. Repeat until you have three small omelettes.

8 Place a nori sheet, shiny side down, on the mat, cover with an omelette and spread with sushi rice, leaving a 1cm/$\frac{1}{2}$in edge at the top and bottom. Lay strips of salmon across the width and lay cucumber strips next to the salmon. Spread a little wasabi paste over the salmon. Roll the nori around the filling. Wrap in clear film (plastic wrap) and chill for 10 minutes. Repeat to make three rolls.

9 When the rolls are cool, remove the baking parchment and clear film. Using a wet knife, cut the rolls into six slices. Serve with pickled ginger, wasabi and Japanese sushi soy sauce.

Nutritional information per portion: Energy 183kcal/768kJ; Protein 10.2g; Carbohydrate 28.7g, of which sugars 2.1g; Fat 2.9g, of which saturates 0.5g; Cholesterol 13mg; Calcium 25mg; Fibre 0.4g; Sodium 17mg.

Spinach and rice soup

Use very young spinach leaves to prepare this light and fresh-tasting soup. The added flavours of garlic and chilli are delicious and the rice makes this a satisfying meal in a bowl.

SERVES 4

675g/1¹/₂lb fresh spinach leaves, washed
45ml/3 tbsp extra virgin olive oil
1 small onion, finely chopped
2 garlic cloves, finely chopped
1 small fresh red chilli, seeded and
    finely chopped

225g/8oz/generous 1 cup risotto rice
1.2 litres/2 pints/5 cups vegetable stock
salt and ground black pepper
shavings of pared Parmesan or pecorino
    cheese, to serve

1 Place the spinach in a large pan with just the water that clings to its leaves after washing. Add a large pinch of salt. Heat gently until the spinach has wilted, then remove from the heat and drain, reserving any liquid.

2 Either chop the spinach finely using a large kitchen knife or place in a food processor and process the leaves to a fairly coarse purée.

3 Heat the oil in a large pan and gently cook the onion, garlic and chilli for 4–5 minutes until softened. Stir in the rice until well coated, then pour in the stock and reserved spinach liquid. Bring to the boil, lower the heat and simmer for 10 minutes.

4 Add the spinach, with salt and pepper to taste. Cook for 5–7 minutes, until the rice is tender. Check the seasoning. Serve in heated bowls, topped with the shavings of cheese.

Nutritional information per portion: Energy 293kcal/1215kJ; Protein 13g; Carbohydrate 26.8g, of which sugars 3.4g; Fat 14.7g, of which saturates 4.4g; Cholesterol 15mg; Calcium 476mg; Fibre 3.8g; Sodium 400mg.

Pumpkin, rice and chicken soup

To make this warm, comforting soup into an even more substantial meal, just add a little more rice and make sure you use all the chicken from the stock.

SERVES 4

15ml/1 tbsp sunflower oil
25g/1oz/2 tbsp butter
6 green cardamom pods
2 leeks, chopped
1 wedge of pumpkin, about 450g/1lb,
    skinned, seeded, and cut into
    2.5cm/1in cubes
115g/4oz/generous 1/2 cup basmati rice,
    soaked for 30 minutes
350ml/12fl oz/11/2 cups milk
salt and ground black pepper
strips of pared orange rind, to garnish
wholemeal (whole-wheat) bread, to serve

FOR THE CHICKEN STOCK

2 chicken quarters
1 onion, quartered
2 carrots, chopped
1 celery stalk, chopped
6–8 peppercorns
900ml/11/2 pints/33/4 cups water

1 Put the stock ingredients in a pan and bring to the boil. Skim the surface, lower the heat, cover and simmer for 1 hour. Strain into a clean bowl. Discard the vegetables. Skin and bone one or both chicken pieces. Cut the flesh into strips.

2 Heat the oil and butter in a large pan and fry the cardamom pods for 2–3 minutes until slightly swollen. Add the leeks and pumpkin. Cook, stirring, for 3–4 minutes over a medium heat. Lower the heat, cover and sweat for 5 minutes more or until the pumpkin is quite soft, stirring once or twice. Add 600ml/1 pint/ 21/2 cups of the stock. Bring to the boil, lower the heat, cover and simmer gently for 10–15 minutes, until the pumpkin is soft. Remove the cardamoms, then process the soup in a food processor until smooth. Pour into a clean pan.

3 Pour the remaining stock into a measuring jug (cup) and make up with water to 300ml/1/2 pint/11/4 cups. Drain the rice and put it into a pan. Pour in the stock, bring to the boil, then simmer for 10 minutes until tender. Season to taste. Stir into the vegetables, with the milk, chicken and remaining stock. Heat until simmering, put into bowls and garnish with orange rind and black pepper. Serve with wholemeal bread.

Nutritional information per portion: Energy 336kcal/1406kJ; Protein 25.4g; Carbohydrate 33.9g, of which sugars 7.8g; Fat 11g, of which saturates 5g; Cholesterol 71mg; Calcium 168mg; Fibre 2.9g; Sodium 122mg.

Avgolemono

This Greek favourite is a fine example of how a few carefully chosen ingredients can make a marvellous dish. Use a well-flavoured stock and as little or as much rice as you like.

SERVES 4

900ml/1½ pints/3¾ cups chicken stock
50g/1¾oz/generous ⅓ cup
    long grain rice, soaked for 30 minutes
3 egg yolks
30–60ml/2–4 tbsp lemon juice
30ml/2 tbsp finely chopped fresh parsley
salt and ground black pepper
lemon slices and parsley sprigs,
    to garnish

1 Pour the stock into a pan, bring to simmering point, then add the drained rice. Half-cover and cook for about 12 minutes until the rice is just tender. Season with salt and pepper.

2 Whisk the egg yolks in a bowl, then add about 30ml/2 tbsp of the lemon juice, whisking constantly until the mixture is smooth and bubbly. Add a ladleful of soup and whisk again.

3 Remove the soup from the heat and slowly add the egg mixture, whisking all the time. The soup will turn a pretty lemon colour and will thicken slightly.

4 Taste and add more lemon juice if necessary. Stir in the parsley. Serve at once, without reheating, garnished with lemon slices and parsley sprigs.

Nutritional information per portion: Energy 488kcal/2050kJ; Protein 46g; Carbohydrate 36.2g, of which sugars 11.3g; Fat 18.7g, of which saturates 9.6g; Cholesterol 127mg; Calcium 163mg; Fibre 3.4g; Sodium 771mg.

Seafood and rice chowder

Like most chowders — the word comes from chaudière, *the French word for cauldron – this is a substantial dish, which could easily be served with crusty bread for a lunch or supper.*

SERVES 4–6

200g/7oz/generous 1 cup drained, canned
   corn kernels
600ml/1 pint/2¹/₂ cups milk
15g/¹/₂oz/1 tbsp butter
1 small leek, sliced
1 small garlic clove, crushed
2 rindless smoked streaky (fatty) bacon
   rashers(strips), finely chopped
1 small green (bell) pepper, seeded
   and diced
1 celery stalk, chopped
115g/4oz/generous ¹/₂ cup white
   long grain rice

5ml/1 tsp plain (all-purpose) flour
about 450ml/³/₄ pint/scant 2 cups hot
   chicken stock or vegetable stock
4 large scallops, preferably with corals
115g/4oz white fish fillet, such as monkfish
   or plaice, cut into bitesize chunks
15ml/1 tbsp finely chopped fresh parsley
good pinch of cayenne pepper
30–45ml/2–3 tbsp single (light)
   cream (optional)
salt and ground black pepper

1 Process half the corn kernels and a little milk in a food processor or blender until creamy. Melt the butter in a large pan and gently fry the leek, garlic and bacon for 4–5 minutes until the leek has softened but not browned. Add the green pepper and celery and sweat over a very gentle heat for 3–4 minutes more, stirring frequently. Stir in the rice and cook for a few minutes until the grains begin to swell. Sprinkle over the flour. Cook, stirring, for about 1 minute, then gradually stir in the remaining milk and the stock.

2 Bring the mixture to the boil over a medium heat, then lower the heat and stir in the creamed corn mixture, whole corn kernels and seasoning. Cover the pan and simmer the chowder very gently for 20 minutes or until the rice is tender, stirring occasionally, and adding a little more stock or water if the mixture thickens too quickly or the rice begins to stick to the bottom of the pan.

3 Pull the corals away from the scallops, slice the white flesh into 5mm/¹/₄in pieces, then stir them into the chowder with the white fish chunks. Cook for 4 minutes, then stir in the corals, parsley and cayenne. Cook for a few more minutes to heat through, then stir in the cream, if using. Adjust the seasoning and serve.

Nutritional information per portion: Energy 488kcal/2050kJ; Protein 46g; Carbohydrate 36.2g, of which sugars 11.3g; Fat 18.7g, of which saturates 9.6g; Cholesterol 127mg; Calcium 163mg; Fibre 3.4g; Sodium 771mg.

Vegetarian dishes

With ingredients as varied as pumpkin,

squash and asparagus, dill, basil, rosemary

and saffron, artichokes and champagne,

here is proof – if any were needed – that

vegetarian rice dishes need never lack

taste, piquancy or colour. Whether you're

looking for appetizers or main courses,

you'll find flavours to delight, from

the Middle East and Mediterranean to the

United States.

Vegetable and rice tarte tatin

This upside-down tart combines Mediterranean vegetables with a medley of rice, garlic, onions and olives in a delicious appetizer for four, or light lunch for two.

SERVES 4 AS AN APPETIZER

30ml/2 tbsp sunflower oil

about 25ml/1½ tbsp olive oil

1 aubergine (eggplant), sliced lengthways

1 large red (bell) pepper

5 tomatoes

2 red shallots, finely chopped

1–2 garlic cloves, crushed

150ml/¼ pint/²⁄₃ cup white wine

10ml/2 tsp chopped fresh basil

225g/8oz/2 cups cooked white or brown long grain rice

40g/1½oz/²⁄₃ cup pitted black olives, chopped

350g/12oz puff pastry, thawed if frozen

ground black pepper

green salad to serve

1 Preheat the oven to 190°C/375°F/Gas 5. Heat the sunflower oil with 15ml/1 tbsp of the olive oil in a frying pan and fry the aubergine slices for 4–5 minutes on each side until golden brown. Lift out and drain on kitchen paper.

2 Seed the pepper and cut it into strips. Add the strips to the oil remaining in the pan, turning them to coat. Cover the pan with a lid or foil and sweat the peppers over a moderately high heat for 5–6 minutes, stirring occasionally, until the pepper strips are soft and flecked with brown.

3 Slice two of the tomatoes and set them aside. Plunge the remaining tomatoes briefly into boiling water, then peel them, cut them into quarters and remove the cores and seeds. Chop them roughly.

4 Heat the remaining oil in the frying pan and fry the shallots and garlic for 3–4 minutes until softened. Add the chopped tomatoes and cook for a few minutes until softened. Stir in the wine and basil, with black pepper to taste. Bring to the boil, then remove from the heat and stir in the cooked rice and black olives. Arrange the tomato slices, aubergine slices and peppers in a single layer over the bottom of a heavy, 30cm/12in, shallow ovenproof dish. Spread the rice mixture on top.

5 Roll out the pastry to a circle slightly larger than the diameter of the dish and place on top of the rice, tucking the overlap down inside the dish. Bake for 25–30 minutes, until the pastry is golden and risen. Cool slightly, then invert the tart on to a large, warmed serving plate. Serve in slices, with a leafy green salad.

Nutritional information per portion: Energy 536kcal/2242kJ; Protein 8.2g; Carbohydrate 59.1g, of which sugars 8.8g; Fat 29.5g, of which saturates 1.2g; Cholesterol 0mg; Calcium 89mg; Fibre 2.6g; Sodium 522mg.

Greek picnic pie

This marvellous pie is ideal for picnics. It can be served warm or cold and makes a good vegetarian dish for a buffet lunch.

SERVES 6

375g/13oz shortcrust pastry, thawed
    if frozen
45–60ml/3–4 tbsp olive oil
1 large aubergine (eggplant), sliced
    into rounds
1 onion, chopped
1 garlic clove, crushed
175g/6oz spinach, washed
4 eggs

75g/2³/₄oz/¹/₂ cup crumbled feta cheese
40g/1¹/₂oz/¹/₂ cup freshly grated
    Parmesan cheese
60ml/4 tbsp natural (plain) yogurt
90ml/6 tbsp creamy milk
225g/8oz/2 cups cooked white or brown
    long grain rice
salt and ground black pepper

1 Preheat the oven to 180°C/350°F/Gas 4. Roll out the pastry thinly and line a 25cm/10in flan ring. Prick all over. Bake for 10–12 minutes until golden (or bake blind, lined with baking parchment and weighted with baking beans).

2 Heat 30–45ml/2–3 tbsp of oil in a frying pan and fry the aubergine for 6–8 minutes on each side until golden. You may need a little more oil at first, but this will be released as the flesh softens. Lift out and drain on kitchen paper.

3 Add the onion and garlic to the oil remaining in the pan and fry over a gentle heat for 4–5 minutes until soft, adding a little extra oil if necessary.

4 Chop the spinach finely, by hand or in a food processor. Beat the eggs in a large mixing bowl, then add the spinach, feta, Parmesan, yogurt, milk and the onion mixture. Season well with salt and pepper and stir well.

5 Spread the rice in an even layer over the bottom of the cooled, part-baked pie. Reserve a few aubergine slices for the top, and arrange the rest in an even layer over the rice. Spoon the spinach mixture over the aubergines and place the remaining slices on top. Bake for 30–40 minutes until lightly browned. Serve warm, or cool completely before transferring to a serving plate or wrapping and packing for a picnic.

Nutritional information per portion: Energy 554kcal/2309kJ; Protein 16.6g; Carbohydrate 53.3g, of which sugars 4.3g; Fat 31.4g, of which saturates 15.5g; Cholesterol 185mg; Calcium 299mg; Fibre 2.7g; Sodium 473mg.

Wild rice with grilled vegetables

The mixture of wild rice – which is not really rice at all but a grass – and long grain rice in this dish works very well, and makes an extremely tasty vegetarian meal.

SERVES 4

225g/8oz/generous 1 cup mixed wild and
    long grain rice
1 red, 1 yellow and 1 green (bell) pepper
1 large aubergine (eggplant),
    thickly sliced
2 red onions, sliced
225g/8oz/generous 3 cups brown cap
    (cremini) or shiitake mushrooms
2 small courgettes (zucchini), cut in
    half lengthways
olive oil, for brushing
45ml/3 tbsp chopped fresh thyme
salt and ground black pepper

FOR THE DRESSING

90ml/6 tbsp extra virgin olive oil
30ml/2 tbsp balsamic vinegar
2 garlic cloves, crushed

1 Put the mixed wild and long grain rice in a large pan of cold salted water. Bring to the boil, then lower the heat, cover the pan and cook gently for 30–40 minutes (or cook according to the instructions on the packet) until all the rice grains are tender.

2 To make the dressing, whisk the extra virgin olive oil, the balsamic vinegar, crushed garlic and seasoning together in a bowl or shake in a screw-top jar until thoroughly blended. Set the dressing aside. Preheat the grill (broiler).

3 Seed and quarter the peppers, then arrange them with the other vegetables on the grill rack. Brush with olive oil. Grill for about 5 minutes. Turn the vegetables over, brush them with more olive oil and grill for 5–8 minutes more, or until tender and charred in places.

4 Drain the rice, turn into a bowl with the thyme and toss in half the dressing. Spoon on to individual plates and arrange the grilled vegetables on top. Pour over the remaining dressing, garnish with more chopped thyme and serve.

Nutritional information per portion: Energy 296kcal/1237kJ; Protein 7.8g; Carbohydrate 59.3g, of which sugars 13.5g; Fat 3g, of which saturates 0.5g; Cholesterol 0mg; Calcium 39mg; Fibre 4.7g; Sodium 460mg.

Courgette roulade

This makes a really impressive buffet supper or dinner party dish, or can be wrapped and served chilled as the pièce de résistance *at a picnic. You can serve it with a herb and green leaf salad.*

SERVES 6

40g/1¹/₂oz/3 tbsp butter
50g/1³/₄oz/¹/₂ cup plain
   (all-purpose) flour
300ml/¹/₂ pint/1¹/₄ cups milk
4 eggs, separated
3 courgettes (zucchini), grated
55g/2oz/²/₃ cup grated Parmesan cheese
salt and ground black pepper
herb and green leaf salad, to serve

FOR THE FILLING

75g/2³/₄oz/²/₃ cup soft goat's cheese
60ml/4 tbsp fromage frais or ricotta
225g/8oz/2 cups cooked rice, such as Thai
   fragrant rice or Japanese short grain
15ml/1 tbsp chopped mixed fresh herbs
15ml/1 tbsp olive oil
15g/¹/₂oz/1 tbsp butter
75g/2³/₄oz/generous 1 cup button (white)
   mushrooms, very finely chopped

1 Preheat the oven to 200°C/400°F/ Gas 6. Line a 33 x 23cm/13 x 9in Swiss roll tin (jelly roll pan) with baking parchment. Melt the butter in a pan, stir in the flour and cook for 1–2 minutes, stirring all the time.

2 Gradually add the milk, stirring to form a smooth sauce. Remove from the heat and cool for a few minutes.

3 Stir the egg yolks into the sauce, one at a time. Add the courgettes and half the Parmesan and season. Whisk the egg whites until stiff, fold into the courgette mixture and scrape into the prepared tin. Spread evenly.

4 Bake for 10–15 minutes until golden. Turn out on to a sheet of baking parchment sprinkled with the remaining Parmesan. Peel off the paper. Use the paper as a guide to roll up the roulade. Leave to cool.

5 Mix the cheeses, rice, herbs and seasoning in a bowl. Pan-fry the mushrooms in the oil and butter until browned. Unwrap the roulade, spread with the rice filling and lay mushrooms along the centre. Roll up. Put on a baking sheet, cover with foil and bake for 15–20 minutes at 190°C/375°F/ Gas 5. To serve cold, wrap in clear film (plastic wrap) and chill.

Nutritional information per portion: Energy 322kcal/1343kJ; Protein 14g; Carbohydrate 22.3g, of which sugars 4.2g; Fat 20.2g, of which saturates 10.5g; Cholesterol 166mg; Calcium 194mg; Fibre 1g; Sodium 250mg.

Rice with dill and broad beans

This is a favourite rice dish in Iran, where it is called Baghali Polo. The combination of broad beans, dill and warm spices works very well, and the saffron rice adds a splash of bright colour.

SERVES 4

275g/9¹/₂oz/1¹/₂ cups basmati rice, soaked and drained
750ml/1¹/₄ pints/3 cups water
40g/1¹/₂oz/3 tbsp melted butter
175g/6oz/1¹/₂ cups frozen baby broad (fava) beans, thawed and peeled
90ml/6 tbsp finely chopped fresh dill, plus 1 fresh dill sprig, to garnish
5ml/1 tsp ground cinnamon
5ml/1 tsp ground cumin
2–3 saffron strands, soaked in 15ml/ 1 tbsp boiling water
salt

1 Put the rice into a pan with the water and a little salt. Bring to the boil, lower the heat and simmer gently for 5 minutes. Drain, rinse in warm water and drain again.

2 Melt the butter in a non-stick pan. Pour two-thirds of the melted butter into a small jug (pitcher) and set aside. Spoon enough rice into the pan to cover the bottom. Add a quarter of the beans and a little dill. Spread over another layer of rice, then a layer of beans and dill.

3 Repeat the layers, ending with a rice layer. Cook gently for 8 minutes until nearly tender. Pour over the reserved melted butter, and add the cinnamon and cumin. Cover with a dish towel and tight-fitting lid; lift the cloth corners over the lid. Cook over a low heat for 25–30 minutes.

4 Mix 45ml/3 tbsp cooked rice with the saffron water. Mound the remaining rice on a large plate and spoon the saffron rice on one side. Serve garnished with a dill sprig.

Nutritional information per portion: Energy 363kcal/1516kJ; Protein 9.2g; Carbohydrate 60.6g, of which sugars 1.1g; Fat 9.1g, of which saturates 5.3g; Cholesterol 21mg; Calcium 77mg; Fibre 3.8g; Sodium 70mg.

Roasted squash

Gem squash has a sweet, subtle flavour that contrasts well with olives and sun-dried tomatoes in this recipe. The rice adds substance without changing any of the flavours.

SERVES 2

4 whole gem squashes
225g/8oz/2 cups cooked white
    long grain rice
75g/2³⁄₄oz/1¹⁄₂ cups sun-dried
    tomatoes, chopped
50g/1³⁄₄oz/¹⁄₂ cup stoned black
    olives, chopped
60ml/4 tbsp soft goat's cheese
30ml/2 tbsp olive oil
15ml/1 tbsp chopped fresh basil leaves,
    plus extra basil sprigs, to garnish
yogurt and mint dressing, or green salad,
    to serve (optional)

1 Preheat the oven to 180°C/350°F/ Gas 4. Trim away the base of each gem squash, slice off the top and then use a spoon to scoop out and discard the seeds.

2 Mix the cooked white long grain rice, sun-dried tomatoes, black olives, cheese, half the olive oil and the chopped basil in a bowl.

3 With the remaining oil, oil a shallow baking dish just large enough to hold the squash side by side.

4 Divide the rice and sun-dried tomato mixture among the squashes and then arrange them carefully in the dish.

5 Cover the squashes with foil and bake for 45–50 minutes until the squashes are tender when pierced with a skewer.

6 Remove the squashes from the oven. Garnish with basil sprigs. Serve with a yogurt and mint dressing or a green salad, if you like.

Nutritional information per portion: Energy 560kcal/2340kJ; Protein 17.4g; Carbohydrate 47.2g, of which sugars 10g; Fat 34.8g, of which saturates 12.6g; Cholesterol 46mg; Calcium 250mg; Fibre 6.2g; Sodium 868mg.

Provençal rice

This vividly coloured dish from the south of France is traditionally made with white rice, but brown rice adds an extra, nutty flavour.

SERVES 3

2 onions, finely chopped
90ml/6 tbsp olive oil
175g/6oz/1 cup brown long grain rice
10ml/2 tsp mustard seeds
475ml/17fl oz/2 cups vegetable stock
1 large or 2 small red (bell) peppers
1 small aubergine (eggplant),
    cut into cubes
2–3 courgettes (zucchini), sliced
about 12 cherry tomatoes
5–6 fresh basil leaves,
    torn into pieces

2 garlic cloves, finely chopped
60ml/4 tbsp white wine
60ml/4 tbsp passata (bottled strained
    tomatoes) or tomato juice
2 hard-boiled eggs, cut into wedges
8 stuffed green olives, sliced
15ml/1 tbsp capers
3 drained sun-dried tomatoes
    in oil, sliced
butter
salt and ground black pepper

1 Preheat the oven to 200°C/400°F/Gas 6. Heat 30ml/2 tbsp of the oil in a pan and fry the onion over a gentle heat for 5–6 minutes until softened.

2 Add the rice and mustard seeds. Cook, stirring, for 2 minutes, then add the stock and a little salt. Bring to the boil, lower the heat, cover and simmer for 35 minutes until the rice is tender.

3 Meanwhile, cut the remaining onion into wedges. Seed the red peppers and cut into chunks. Put these in a roasting pan with the aubergine, courgettes and cherry tomatoes. Sprinkle over the torn basil leaves and chopped garlic.

4 Pour over the remaining olive oil and sprinkle with salt and black pepper. Roast for 15–20 minutes until the vegetables begin to char, stirring halfway through. Reduce the temperature to 180°C/350°F/Gas 4.

5 Spoon the rice into a casserole. Put the roasted vegetables on top, with the vegetable juices from the pan, then pour over the wine and passata or tomato juice. Arrange the egg wedges on top of the vegetables, with the olives, capers and sun-dried tomatoes. Dot with butter, cover and bake for 15–20 minutes until heated through.

Nutritional information per portion: Energy 478.6kcal/2014.6kJ; Protein 12.6g; Carbohydrate 78.9g, of which sugars 16.1g; Fat 13.3g, of which saturates 2.4g; Cholesterol 64mg; Calcium 98.6mg; Fibre 7.6g; Sodium 152mg.

Pumpkin and pistachio risotto

Vegetarians will love this combination of creamy, golden rice and orange pumpkin, and so will everyone else. It would look particularly impressive served in the hollowed-out pumpkin shell.

SERVES 4

1.2 litres/2 pints/5 cups vegetable stock
  or water
generous pinch of saffron strands
30ml/2 tbsp olive oil
1 onion, chopped
2 garlic cloves, crushed
900g/2lb/7 cups pumpkin, peeled, seeded
  and cut into 2cm/³⁄₄in cubes
400g/14oz/2 cups risotto rice
200ml/7fl oz/scant 1 cup dry white wine
30ml/2 tbsp freshly grated
  Parmesan cheese
50g/1³⁄₄oz/¹⁄₂ cup pistachio nuts,
  roughly chopped
45ml/3 tbsp chopped fresh marjoram
  or oregano, plus leaves to garnish
salt, freshly grated nutmeg and ground
  black pepper

1 Bring the stock or water to the boil and reduce to a low simmer. Ladle a little of it into a small bowl. Add the saffron strands and leave to infuse.

2 In a large, heavy pan or deep frying pan, gently fry the onion and garlic in the oil for 5 minutes until soft. Add the rice and pumpkin and stir to coat everything in oil. Cook for a few more minutes until the rice looks transparent.

3 Pour in the wine and let it bubble hard. When absorbed, add a quarter of the hot stock or water and all the saffron liquid. Cook, stirring, until it is all absorbed. Gradually add the remaining stock or water, stirring constantly, allowing it to be absorbed before adding more. After 20–30 minutes the rice should be golden-yellow, creamy and *al dente*. Remove from the heat.

4 Stir in the Parmesan cheese, cover the pan and leave for 5 minutes. Stir in the pistachio nuts and marjoram or oregano. Season with a little salt, nutmeg and pepper, sprinkle over a few marjoram or oregano leaves and serve.

Nutritional information per portion: Energy 585kcal/2441kJ; Protein 14.4g; Carbohydrate 87.3g, of which sugars 5.7g; Fat 15.9g, of which saturates 3.5g; Cholesterol 8mg; Calcium 196mg; Fibre 3.2g; Sodium 151mg.

Risotto with ricotta and basil

This is a well-flavoured and satisfying risotto of pleasingly contrasting flavours, with the distinctive pungency of basil mellowed by the smooth ricotta.

SERVES 3–4

45ml/3 tbsp olive oil
1 onion, finely chopped
275g/9¹/₂oz/1¹/₂ cups risotto rice
1 litre/1³/₄ pints/4 cups hot
**   vegetable stock**
175g/6oz/³/₄ cup ricotta cheese
50g/1³/₄oz/generous 1 cup fresh basil
**   leaves, finely chopped, plus extra**
**   to garnish**
75g/2³/₄oz/1 cup freshly grated
**   Parmesan cheese**
salt and ground black pepper

1 Heat the oil in a large, heavy pan and fry the onion over a gentle heat until soft but not browned.

2 Add the rice. Cook for a few minutes, stirring, until the rice is coated with oil and is slightly translucent.

3 Pour in about a quarter of the stock. Cook, stirring, until all the stock has been absorbed, then add another ladleful. Continue in this manner, adding more stock when the previous ladleful has been absorbed, until the risotto has been cooking for about 20 minutes and the rice is just tender.

4 Spoon the ricotta into a bowl and break it up a little with a fork. Stir into the risotto along with the basil and Parmesan. Taste and adjust the seasoning, then cover the pan and leave to stand for 2–3 minutes before serving, garnished with basil leaves.

Nutritional information per portion: Energy 373kcal/1557kJ; Protein 16.1g; Carbohydrate 57.9g, of which sugars 2.7g; Fat 8.8g, of which saturates 4.6g; Cholesterol 21mg; Calcium 213mg; Fibre 0.8g; Sodium 305mg.

Risotto with Parmesan

This traditional risotto, simply flavoured with grated Parmesan cheese and golden, fried chopped onion, proves that cooking doesn't have to be elaborate to be satisfying.

SERVES 3–4

1 litre/1³/₄ pints/4 cups vegetable stock
65g/2¹/₂oz/5 tbsp butter
1 small onion, finely chopped
275g/9¹/₂oz/1¹/₂ cups risotto rice
125ml/4fl oz/¹/₂ cup dry white wine
75g/2³/₄oz/1 cup freshly grated
   Parmesan cheese, plus Parmesan
   shavings to garnish
basil leaves, to garnish
salt and ground black pepper

1 Heat the stock in a pan, and leave to simmer until needed.

2 Melt two-thirds of the butter in a large, heavy pan or deep frying pan. Stir in the onion, and cook gently until soft and golden.

3 Add the rice and stir to coat the grains with butter. After 1–2 minutes, pour in the white wine. Raise the heat slightly, and cook, stirring, until the wine evaporates. Add one small ladleful of the hot stock. Cook until the stock has been absorbed, stirring constantly.

4 Gradually add the remaining stock, a little at a time, allowing the rice to absorb the liquid each time before adding more, and stirring constantly. After 20–30 minutes the rice should be creamy and *al dente*.

5 Remove the pan from the heat. Season the risotto with salt and ground black pepper. Stir in the remaining butter and the grated Parmesan cheese. Taste the risotto again for seasoning. Allow the risotto to rest for 3–4 minutes before serving, then garnish with basil leaves and Parmesan shavings.

Nutritional information per portion: Energy 479kcal/1991kJ; Protein 12.8g; Carbohydrate 56.3g, of which sugars 1.1g; Fat 19.9g, of which saturates 12.3g; Cholesterol 53mg; Calcium 248mg; Fibre 0.2g; Sodium 305mg.

Porcini and Parmesan risotto

The success of a good risotto depends on both the quality of the rice used and the technique.
Add the stock gradually and stir constantly to coax a creamy texture from the starch grains.

SERVES 4

15g/¹/₂oz/2 tbsp dried
    porcini mushrooms
150ml/¹/₄ pint/²/₃ cup warm water
1 litre/1³/₄ pints/4 cups vegetable stock
generous pinch of saffron strands
30ml/2 tbsp olive oil
1 onion, finely chopped
1 garlic clove, crushed
350g/12oz/1³/₄ cups arborio
    or carnaroli rice
150ml/¹/₄ pint/²/₃ cup dry white wine
25g/1oz/2 tbsp butter
50g/1³/₄oz/²/₃ cup freshly grated
    Parmesan cheese
salt and freshly ground black pepper
pink and yellow oyster mushrooms,
    to garnish (optional)

1 Put the dried porcini in a bowl and pour over the warm water. Leave to soak for 20 minutes, then lift out with a slotted spoon. Filter the soaking water through a layer of kitchen paper in a sieve (strainer), then place it in a pan with the stock. Bring the liquid to a gentle simmer.

2 Spoon about 45ml/3 tbsp of the hot stock into a cup and stir in the saffron strands. Set aside. Finely chop the porcini. Heat the oil in a separate pan and lightly sauté the onion, garlic and mushrooms for 5 minutes. Gradually add the rice, stirring to coat the grains in oil. Cook for 2 minutes, stirring constantly. Season with salt and pepper.

3 Pour in the white wine. Cook, stirring, until it has been absorbed, then ladle in a quarter of the stock. Cook, stirring, until the stock has been absorbed. Gradually add the remaining stock, a little at a time, allowing the rice to absorb the liquid before adding more, and stirring constantly.

4 After approximately 20 minutes, when all the stock has been absorbed and the rice is cooked but still firm to the bite, stir in the butter, saffron water (with the strands) and half of the Parmesan. Garnish with pink and yellow oyster mushrooms, if using, and serve sprinkled with the remaining Parmesan.

Nutritional information per portion: Energy 497kcal/2069kJ; Protein 11.7g; Carbohydrate 71.3g, of which sugars 1.1g; Fat 15.2g, of which saturates 6.6g; Cholesterol 26mg; Calcium 175mg; Fibre 0.2g; Sodium 176mg.

Leek, mushroom and lemon risotto

Leeks and lemon go together beautifully in this light risotto, while delicious brown cap mushrooms add texture and extra flavour to the dish.

SERVES 4

225g/8oz trimmed leeks
225g/8oz/2–3 cups brown cap
   (cremini) mushrooms
30ml/2 tbsp olive oil
3 garlic cloves, crushed
75g/2³⁄₄oz/6 tbsp butter
1 large onion, roughly chopped
350g/12oz/1³⁄₄ cups risotto rice
1.2 litres/2 pints/5 cups simmering
   vegetable stock

grated rind of 1 lemon
45ml/3 tbsp lemon juice
50g/1³⁄₄oz/²⁄₃ cup freshly grated
   Parmesan cheese
60ml/4 tbsp mixed chopped fresh chives
   and flat leaf parsley
salt and ground black pepper

1 Slice the leeks in half lengthways, wash them well and then slice them evenly. Wipe the mushrooms with kitchen paper and chop them roughly.

2 Heat the oil in a large pan and cook the garlic for 1 minute. Add the leeks, mushrooms and seasoning and cook over a medium heat for about 10 minutes, or until the leeks have softened and browned. Spoon into a bowl and set aside.

3 Add 25g/1oz/2 tbsp of the butter to the pan. As soon as it has melted, add the onion and cook over a medium heat for 5 minutes until it has softened and is golden.

4 Stir in the rice and cook for about 1 minute until the grains begin to look translucent and are coated in the fat. Add a ladleful of stock and cook gently, stirring constantly, until the liquid has been absorbed.

5 Continue to add stock, a ladleful at a time, stirring constantly, until all of it has been absorbed. This should take about 25–30 minutes. The risotto will turn thick and creamy and the rice should be tender but not sticky.

6 Just before serving, add the leeks and mushrooms, with the remaining butter. Stir in the lemon rind and juice. Add the grated Parmesan and the herbs. Adjust the seasoning and serve immediately.

Nutritional information per portion: Energy 442kcal/1844kJ; Protein 11.8g; Carbohydrate 77.6g, of which sugars 5.6g; Fat 9g, of which saturates 3.8g; Cholesterol 14mg; Calcium 128mg; Fibre 2.9g; Sodium 97mg.

Champagne risotto

It may seem rather extravagant to include champagne in a risotto, but it makes a beautifully flavoured dish, one that is just perfect for that special anniversary dinner.

SERVES 3–4

25g/1oz/2 tbsp butter
2 shallots, finely chopped
275g/9¹/₂oz/1¹/₂ cups risotto rice,
    preferably carnaroli
¹/₂ bottle or 300ml/¹/₂ pint/1¹/₄
    cups champagne
750ml/1¹/₄ pints/3 cups simmering light
    vegetable stock

150ml/¹/₄ pint/²/₃ cup double
    (heavy) cream
40g/1¹/₂oz/¹/₂ cup freshly grated
    Parmesan cheese
10ml/2 tsp very finely chopped
    fresh chervil
salt and ground black pepper
black truffle shavings,
    to garnish (optional)

1 Melt the butter in a pan and fry the shallots for 2–3 minutes until softened. Add the rice and cook, stirring all the time, until the grains are evenly coated in butter and are beginning to look translucent around the edges.

2 Pour in about two-thirds of the champagne and cook over a high heat so that the liquid bubbles fiercely. Cook, stirring, until all the liquid has been absorbed before beginning to add the hot stock.

3 Add the stock, a ladleful at a time, making sure that each addition has been completely absorbed before adding the next. The risotto should gradually become creamy and velvety and all the stock should be absorbed.

4 When the rice is tender but still firm to the bite, stir in the remaining champagne and the double cream and Parmesan. Adjust the seasoning. Remove from the heat, cover and leave to stand for a few minutes. Stir in the chervil. If you want to gild the lily, garnish with a few truffle shavings.

Nutritional information per portion: Energy 468kcal/1941kJ; Protein 8g; Carbohydrate 48.3g, of which sugars 4.2g; Fat 23.1g, of which saturates 14.3g; Cholesterol 60mg; Calcium 130mg; Fibre 0.2g; Sodium 128mg.

Roasted pepper risotto

This makes an excellent vegetarian supper dish. Roasting and peeling the peppers releases their full flavour and sweetness, providing a delicious contrast to the pungent garlic.

SERVES 3–4

1 red (bell) pepper
1 yellow (bell) pepper
15ml/1 tbsp olive oil
25g/1oz/2 tbsp butter
1 onion, chopped
2 garlic cloves, crushed
275g/9¹/₂oz/1¹/₂ cups risotto rice

1 litre/1³/₄ pints/4 cups simmering
    vegetable stock
50g/1³/₄oz/²/₃ cup freshly grated
    Parmesan cheese
salt and ground black pepper
freshly grated Parmesan cheese,
    to serve (optional)

1 Preheat the grill (broiler) to high. Cut the peppers in half, remove the seeds and pith and arrange, cut sides down, on a baking sheet. Place under the grill for 5–6 minutes until the skin is charred. Put the peppers in a plastic bag, tie the ends and leave for 4–5 minutes.

2 Peel the peppers when they are cool enough to handle and the steam has loosened the skin. Cut into thin strips.

3 Heat the oil and butter in a large pan and fry the onion and garlic for 4–5 minutes over a low heat until the onion begins to soften. Add the peppers and cook the mixture for 3–4 minutes more, stirring occasionally.

4 Stir in the rice. Cook over a medium heat for 3–4 minutes, stirring all the time, until the rice is evenly coated in oil and the outer part of each grain has become translucent.

5 Add a ladleful of stock. Cook, stirring, until all the liquid has been absorbed. Continue to add the stock, a ladleful at a time, making sure each quantity has been absorbed before adding the next.

6 When the rice is tender but still firm to the bite, stir in the freshly grated Parmesan cheese, and add salt and ground black pepper to taste. Cover and leave to stand for 3–4 minutes, then serve, with extra Parmesan, if using.

Nutritional information per portion: Energy 555kcal/2312kJ; Protein 16.1g; Carbohydrate 80.1g, of which sugars 10g; Fat 18g, of which saturates 8.4g; Cholesterol 34mg; Calcium 238mg; Fibre 2.6g; Sodium 241mg.

Risotto-stuffed aubergines
with spicy tomato sauce

Aubergines are a challenge to the creative cook and allow for some unusual recipe ideas. Here, they are filled with a rice stuffing and baked with a cheese and pine nut topping.

SERVES 4

4 small aubergines (eggplants)
105ml/7 tbsp olive oil
1 small onion, chopped
175g/6oz/scant 1 cup risotto rice
750ml/1¼ pints/3 cups hot
    vegetable stock
15ml/1 tbsp white wine vinegar
25g/1oz/⅓ cup grated Parmesan cheese
15g/½oz/2 tbsp pine nuts

FOR THE TOMATO SAUCE

300ml/½ pint/1¼ cups thick
    passata (bottled strained tomatoes)
    or puréed tomatoes
5ml/1 tsp mild curry paste
salt and ground black pepper

1 Preheat the oven to 200°C/400°F/Gas 6. Cut the aubergines in half lengthways, and remove the flesh with a small knife. Brush the shells with 30ml/2 tbsp of the oil and bake on a baking sheet, supported by crumpled foil, for 6–8 minutes, until soft.

2 Chop the aubergine flesh. Heat the remaining oil in a medium pan. Add the aubergine flesh and the onion, and cook over a gentle heat for 3–4 minutes until soft. Add the rice and stock, bring to the boil, then leave to simmer, uncovered, for about 15 minutes. Add the vinegar and season to taste.

3 Increase the oven temperature to 230°C/450°F/Gas 8. Spoon the rice mixture into the aubergine skins, top with the cheese and pine nuts, return to the oven and brown for 5 minutes.

4 To make the sauce, mix the passata or puréed tomatoes with the curry paste in a pan. Heat through and add salt to taste. Spoon the sauce on to four individual serving plates and arrange two aubergine halves on each one.

Nutritional information per portion: Energy 478kcal/1985kJ; Protein 13g; Carbohydrate 41.3g, of which sugars 5.8g; Fat 28.9g, of which saturates 7g; Cholesterol 19mg; Calcium 255mg; Fibre 3.5g; Sodium 214mg.

Jerusalem artichoke risotto

Although this warming risotto is a very simple dish, the delicious and distinctive flavour of Jerusalem artichokes turns it into something special.

SERVES 3–4

400g/14oz Jerusalem artichokes
40g/1¹/₂oz/3 tbsp butter
15ml/1 tbsp olive oil
1 onion, finely chopped
1 garlic clove, crushed
275g/9¹/₂oz/1¹/₂ cups risotto rice
125ml/4fl oz/¹/₂ cup fruity white wine
1 litre/1³/₄ pints/4 cups simmering
  vegetable stock
10ml/2 tsp chopped fresh thyme
40g/1¹/₂oz/¹/₂ cup freshly grated
  Parmesan cheese, plus extra to serve
salt and ground black pepper
fresh thyme sprigs, to garnish

1 Peel the artichokes, cut them into pieces and immediately add them to a pan of lightly salted water. Simmer them for 10–2 minutes, until tender, then drain and mash with 15g/¹/₂oz/1 tbsp of the butter. Add a little more salt, if needed.

2 Heat the oil and the remaining butter in a pan and fry the onion and garlic for 5–6 minutes until soft. Add the rice and cook over a medium heat for about 2 minutes until the grains are translucent around the edges.

3 Pour in the wine, stir until it has been absorbed, then start adding the simmering stock, a ladleful at a time, stirring constantly and making sure each quantity has been absorbed before adding more.

4 With the last ladleful of stock, stir in the mashed artichokes and the chopped thyme. Season with salt and pepper. Continue cooking until the risotto is creamy and the artichokes are hot. Stir in the Parmesan. Remove from the heat, cover the pan and leave the risotto to stand for a few minutes. Spoon into a serving dish, garnish with thyme sprigs and serve with Parmesan cheese.

Nutritional information per portion: Energy 418kcal/1741kJ; Protein 9.6g; Carbohydrate 56g, of which sugars 1.2g; Fat 14.8g, of which saturates 7.7g; Cholesterol 31mg; Calcium 179mg; Fibre 1.1g; Sodium 231mg.

Rosemary risotto with borlotti beans

This is a classic Italian risotto with a subtle and complex flavour, from the heady aroma of rosemary to the savoury beans, tangy mascarpone and tasty Parmesan.

SERVES 3–4

400g/14oz can borlotti beans
30ml/2 tbsp olive oil
1 onion, chopped
2 garlic cloves, crushed
275g/9¹/₂oz/1¹/₂ cups risotto rice
175ml/6fl oz/³/₄ cup dry white wine
900ml–1 litre/1¹/₂–1³/₄ pints/3³/₄–4 cups
simmering vegetable stock
60ml/4 tbsp mascarpone cheese
65g/2¹/₂oz/scant 1 cup freshly
grated Parmesan cheese,
plus extra to serve (optional)
5ml/1 tsp chopped fresh rosemary
salt and ground black pepper

1 Drain the beans, rinse under cold water and drain again. Purée about two-thirds of the beans fairly coarsely in a food processor or blender. Set the remaining beans aside.

2 Heat the olive oil in a large pan and gently fry the onion and garlic for 6–8 minutes until very soft. Add the rice and cook over a medium heat for a few minutes, stirring constantly, until the grains are thoroughly coated in oil and are slightly translucent. Pour in the wine. Cook over a medium heat for 2–3 minutes, stirring all the time, until the wine has been absorbed. Add the stock gradually, a ladleful at a time, waiting for each quantity to be absorbed before adding more, and continuing to stir until about three-quarters of the stock has been added.

3 When the rice is three-quarters cooked, stir in the bean purée. Continue to cook the risotto, adding the remaining stock, until it is creamy and the rice is tender but still firm to the bite. Stir in the reserved beans, with the mascarpone, Parmesan and rosemary, then season to taste. Cover and leave to stand for about 5 minutes. Serve with extra Parmesan.

Nutritional information per portion: Energy 419kcal/1752kJ; Protein 15.1g; Carbohydrate 68.8g, of which sugars 3.9g; Fat 6.2g, of which saturates 2.7g; Cholesterol 12mg; Calcium 198mg; Fibre 4.5g; Sodium 412mg.

Risotto with four vegetables

This is one of the prettiest risottos, with the contrasting green vegetables and orange-fleshed squash. It makes a delicious vegetarian lunch for three to four people, or an appetizer for six. You can use any risotto rice for this dish, such as arborio or carnaroli.

SERVES 3–4

115g/4oz/1 cup shelled fresh peas
115g/4oz/1 cup green beans, cut into
   short lengths
30ml/2 tbsp olive oil
75g/2³/₄oz/6 tbsp butter
1 acorn squash, skin and seeds removed,
   flesh cut into matchsticks
1 onion, finely chopped

275g/9¹/₂oz/1¹/₂ cups risotto rice
125ml/4fl oz/¹/₂ cup Italian dry
   white vermouth
1 litre/1³/₄ pints/4 cups boiling
   vegetable stock
75g/2³/₄oz/1 cup freshly grated
   Parmesan cheese
salt and freshly ground black pepper

1 Bring a pan of lightly salted water to the boil, add the peas and beans and cook for 2–3 minutes, until the vegetables are just tender. Drain, refresh under cold running water, drain again and set aside.

2 Heat the oil with 25g/1oz/2 tbsp of the butter in a medium pan until foaming. Add the squash and cook gently for 2–3 minutes or until just softened. Remove with a slotted spoon and set aside. Add the onion to the pan and cook gently for about 3 minutes, stirring frequently, until softened.

3 Stir in the rice until the grains start to swell and burst, then add the vermouth. Stir until the vermouth stops sizzling and most of it has been absorbed by the rice, then add a few ladlefuls of the stock, with salt and pepper to taste. Stir over a low heat until the stock has been absorbed.

4 Gradually add the remaining stock, a few ladlefuls at a time, allowing the rice to absorb the liquid before adding more, and stirring all the time.

5 After about 20 minutes, when all the stock has been absorbed and the rice is cooked and creamy but still firm to the bite, gently stir in the vegetables, the remaining butter and about half the grated Parmesan. Heat through, then taste for seasoning and serve with the remaining grated Parmesan served separately.

Nutritional information per portion: Energy 836kcal/3472kJ; Protein 22.1g; Carbohydrate 79.4g, of which sugars 6g; Fat 42.7g, of which saturates 22.1g; Cholesterol 89mg; Calcium 379mg; Fibre 3.9g; Sodium 463mg.

Risotto with asparagus

Fresh farm asparagus has only a short season, so it is best to make the most of it while it's available. This elegant risotto is absolutely delicious.

SERVES 3–4

225g/8oz fresh asparagus
750ml/1¼ pints/3 cups vegetable stock
65g/2½oz/5 tbsp butter
1 small onion, finely chopped
275g/9½oz/1½ cups risotto rice, such
   as arborio or carnaroli

75g/2¾oz/1 cup freshly grated
   Parmesan cheese
salt and ground black pepper

1 Bring a pan of water to the boil. Cut off any woody pieces from the ends of the asparagus stalks, peel the lower portions, then cook in the boiling water for 5 minutes. Drain the asparagus, reserving the cooking water, refresh under cold water and drain again. Cut the asparagus diagonally into 4cm/1½in pieces. Keep the tips and next-highest sections separate from the stalks.

2 Place the stock in a pan and add 450ml/¾ pint/scant 2 cups of the asparagus cooking water. Heat to simmering point, and keep it hot.

3 Melt two-thirds of the butter in a large, heavy pan or deep frying pan. Add the onion and fry until it is soft and golden. Stir in all the asparagus except the top two sections. Cook for 2–3 minutes. Add the rice and cook for 1–2 minutes, mixing well to coat it with butter. Stir in a ladleful of the hot liquid. Cook, stirring constantly, until the stock has been absorbed.

4 Gradually add the remaining stock, a little at a time, allowing the rice to absorb the liquid before adding more, and stirring all the time.

5 After 10 minutes, add the remaining asparagus sections. Continue to cook as before, for about 15 minutes, until the rice is *al dente* and the risotto is creamy. Off the heat, stir in the remaining butter and the Parmesan. Grind in a little black pepper, and taste again for salt. Serve at once.

Nutritional information per portion: Energy 629kcal/2616kJ; Protein 20.1g; Carbohydrate 71.9g, of which sugars 2.7g; Fat 27.9g, of which saturates 16.5g; Cholesterol 71mg; Calcium 344mg; Fibre 1.6g; Sodium 408mg.

Persian rice with a tahdeeg

Persian or Iranian cuisine is exotic and delicious, and the flavours are rich and intense. A tahdeeg is the glorious, golden rice crust or "dig" that forms on the bottom of the pan as the rice cooks.

SERVES 6–8

450g/1lb/2¹/₃ cups basmati rice, soaked
150ml/¹/₄ pint/²/₃ cup sunflower oil
2 garlic cloves, crushed
2 onions, 1 chopped, 1 finely sliced
150g/5¹/₂oz/²/₃ cup green lentils, soaked
600ml/1 pint/2¹/₂ cups vegetable stock
50g/1³/₄oz/¹/₃ cup raisins
10ml/2 tsp ground coriander

45ml/3 tbsp tomato purée (paste)
a few saffron strands
1 egg yolk, beaten
10ml/2 tsp natural (plain) yogurt
75g/2³/₄oz/6 tbsp melted ghee or
   clarified butter
salt and freshly ground black pepper

1 Drain the rice, then cook in boiling salted water for 10–12 minutes or until tender. Drain again. Heat 30ml/2 tbsp of the oil in a large pan and fry the garlic and the chopped onion for 5 minutes. Stir in the lentils, stock, raisins, coriander and tomato purée. Season to taste. Bring to the boil, lower the heat, cover and simmer for 20 minutes.

2 Soak the saffron strands in a little hot water. Mix the egg yolk and yogurt in a bowl. Spoon in 120ml/4 fl oz/¹/₂ cup of the cooked rice and mix thoroughly. Season well. Heat about two-thirds of the remaining oil in a large pan. Sprinkle the egg and yogurt rice evenly over the bottom of the pan.

3 Sprinkle the remaining rice into the pan, alternating it with the lentil mixture. Build up in a pyramid shape away from the sides of the pan, finishing with a layer of plain rice. With a wooden spoon handle, make three holes down to the bottom of the pan; drizzle over the melted ghee or butter. Bring to a high heat, then wrap the pan lid in a clean, wet dish towel and place firmly on top. When a good head of steam appears, turn the heat down to low. Cook slowly for about 30 minutes.

4 Fry the onion slices in the remaining oil until browned and crisp. Drain well. Remove the rice pan from the heat, keeping it covered, and plunge the base briefly into a sink of cold water to loosen the rice on the bottom. Strain the saffron water into a bowl and stir in a few spoons of the white rice.

5 Toss the rice and lentils together in the pan and spoon out on to a serving dish, mounding the mixture. Sprinkle the saffron rice on top. Break up the rice crust on the bottom of the pan and place pieces of it around the mound. Sprinkle over the onions and serve.

Nutritional information per portion: Energy 500kcal/2082kJ; Protein 10.1g; Carbohydrate 62.8g, of which sugars 8g; Fat 23.3g, of which saturates 6.2g; Cholesterol 25mg; Calcium 45mg; Fibre 2.6g; Sodium 23mg.

Fish and shellfish

In this chapter you will find recipes for

risotto and rice dishes from around the

world. With ingredients including haddock,

salmon, prawns and trout, squid, crab,

oysters and lobster, enlivened by a range of

herbs and spices, there is something here

for any occasion.

Fish pie with sweet potato topping

This tasty dish is full of contrasting flavours – the sweet potato making an interesting partner for the mild fish. It looks attractive and is delicious with sugar snap peas.

SERVES 4

175g/6oz/scant 1 cup basmati or Texmati
    rice, soaked
450ml/³⁄₄ pint/scant 2 cups good stock
175g/6oz/1¹⁄₂ cups shelled broad
    (fava) beans
450g/1lb sweet potatoes, peeled
450g/1lb floury white potatoes, such as
    King Edwards, peeled
a little milk and butter, for mashing
10ml/2 tsp chopped fresh parsley
5ml/1 tsp chopped fresh dill

15ml/1 tbsp single (light) cream (optional)
675g/1¹⁄₂lb haddock or cod fillets, skinned
450ml/³⁄₄ pint/scant 2 cups milk
30g/1oz/2 tbsp butter
salt and ground black pepper

FOR THE SAUCE
40g/1¹⁄₂oz/3 tbsp butter
30–45ml/2–3 tbsp plain
    (all-purpose) flour
15ml/1 tbsp chopped fresh parsley

1 Preheat the oven to 190°C/375°F/Gas 5. Drain the rice and put in a pan with the stock. Season if necessary and bring to the boil. Cover the pan, lower the heat and simmer for 10 minutes or until all the liquid has been absorbed. Cook the broad beans in a little lightly salted water until tender. Drain thoroughly. When cool enough to handle, pop the beans out of their skins.

2 Cut all the potatoes into chunks. Cook separately in boiling salted water until tender. Drain, mash with a little milk and butter and spoon into separate bowls. Beat parsley and dill into the sweet potatoes, and the cream, if using. Put the fish in a large frying pan with 350ml/12fl oz/1¹⁄₂ cups milk. Dot with half the butter and season. Heat gently and simmer for 5–6 minutes until just tender. Lift out the fish and break into large pieces. Pour the cooking liquid into a measuring jug (cup) and make up to 450ml/³⁄₄ pint/scant 2 cups with the remaining milk.

3 For the sauce, melt the butter in a pan, stir in the flour and cook, stirring, for 1 minute. Gradually add the cooking liquid and milk mixture, stirring, until a thin white sauce is formed. Stir in the parsley, and taste and season, if necessary.

4 Spread out the cooked rice on the bottom of a large oval gratin dish. Add the broad beans and fish and pour over the white sauce. Spoon the mashed sweet and white potatoes over the top, to make an attractive pattern. Dot with a little extra butter and bake for 15 minutes until lightly browned.

Nutritional information per portion: Energy 604kcal/2545kJ; Protein 41.6g; Carbohydrate 88g, of which sugars 8.6g; Fat 10.7g, of which saturates 5.7g; Cholesterol 99mg; Calcium 94mg; Fibre 6.9g; Sodium 223mg.

Kedgeree

This is a popular Victorian breakfast dish. Kedgeree has its origins in kitchiri, which is an Indian rice and lentil recipe. Kedgeree can be flavoured with curry powder, but this version is mild.

SERVES 4

500g/1lb 2oz smoked haddock
115g/4oz/generous ½ cup basmati rice
50g/1³⁄₄oz/4 tbsp butter, diced, plus extra for greasing
30ml/2 tbsp lemon juice
150ml/¼ pint/²⁄₃ cup single (light) cream or soured cream
pinch of freshly grated nutmeg
pinch of cayenne pepper
2 hard-boiled eggs, peeled and cut into wedges
30ml/2 tbsp chopped fresh parsley
salt and ground black pepper

1 In a shallow pan, just cover the haddock with water, heat to simmering point and poach for 10 minutes, until it flakes easily when tested with a knife tip.

2 Lift it out and remove any skin and bones. Flake the flesh. Pour the cooking liquid into a measuring jug (cup), make up the volume with water to 250ml/9fl oz/1 cup, pour into a pan and bring to the boil. Add the rice, stir, lower the heat, cover and simmer for 10 minutes, until tender and the liquid has been absorbed.

3 Preheat the oven to180°C/350°F/ Gas 4 and butter a baking dish. When the rice is cooked, remove from the heat and stir in the lemon juice, cream, flaked haddock, nutmeg and cayenne. Add the egg wedges to the rice and stir in gently.

4 Turn the mixture into the baking dish. Level the surface and dot with butter. Cover the dish loosely with foil and bake for about 25 minutes.

5 Stir in the chopped parsley and season to taste. Serve immediately.

Nutritional information per portion: Energy 320kcal/1336kJ; Protein 15.6g; Carbohydrate 46.6g, of which sugars 0g; Fat 7.6g, of which saturates 3.3g; Cholesterol 149mg; Calcium 39mg; Fibre 0g; Sodium 357mg.

Baked trout with rice, sun-dried tomatoes and nuts

Trout is very popular in Spain, particularly in the north. If you fillet the trout before you cook it, it cooks more evenly, and is easier to serve because there are no bones to get in the way of the stuffing.

SERVES 4

2 fresh trout, each about 500g/1lb 2oz
75g/2³⁄₄oz/³⁄₄ cup mixed unsalted
 cashew nuts, pine nuts, almonds
 and hazelnuts
25ml/1¹⁄₂ tbsp olive oil, plus extra
 for drizzling
1 small onion, finely chopped
10ml/2 tsp grated fresh root ginger
175g/6oz/1¹⁄₂ cups cooked white
 long grain rice
4 tomatoes, peeled and very
 finely chopped
4 sun-dried tomatoes in oil, drained
 and chopped
30ml/2 tbsp chopped fresh tarragon
2 fresh tarragon sprigs
salt and ground black pepper
dressed green leaves, to serve

1 If the fishmonger has not done so, fillet the trout with a sharp knife, leaving as little flesh on the bones as possible. Remove any tiny bones from the cavity with tweezers.

2 Preheat the oven to 190°C/375°F/Gas 5. Spread out the nuts on a baking sheet and bake for 3–4 minutes until golden, shaking occasionally. Chop the nuts roughly.

3 In a small frying pan, fry the onion in oil for 3–4 minutes until soft. Stir in the ginger, cook for 1 minute more, then spoon into a mixing bowl.

4 Stir in the rice, chopped tomatoes, sun-dried tomatoes, toasted nuts and tarragon. Season to taste.

5 Place each of the two trout on a large piece of oiled foil and spoon the stuffing into the cavity. Add a sprig of tarragon and a drizzle of olive oil.

6 Fold the foil over to enclose each trout completely, and then put the parcels in a large roasting pan. Bake in the oven for 20–25 minutes until the fish is just tender. Cut the fish into thick slices and serve with dressed green leaves.

Nutritional information per portion: Energy 501kcal/2094kJ; Protein 46g; Carbohydrate 27.8g, of which sugars 5g; Fat 22.8g, of which saturates 3.3g; Cholesterol 160mg; Calcium 144mg; Fibre 3.2g; Sodium 161mg.

Trout and Parma ham risotto rolls

This makes a delicious and elegant meal. The risotto, which is made with porcini mushrooms and prawns, is a fine match for the robust flavour of the trout rolls.

SERVES 4

4 trout fillets, skinned
4 slices Parma ham
caper berries, to garnish

FOR THE RISOTTO
30ml/2 tbsp olive oil
8 large raw prawns (shrimp), peeled
   and deveined

1 onion, chopped
225g/8oz/generous 1 cup risotto rice
about 105ml/3½ fl oz white wine
about 750ml/1¼ pints/3 cups
   simmering fish stock or chicken stock
15g/½oz/2 tbsp dried porcini or
   chanterelle mushrooms
salt and ground black pepper

1 First make the risotto. Heat the oil in a heavy pan or deep frying pan and fry the prawns very briefly until flecked with pink. Lift out on a slotted spoon and transfer to a plate.

2 Add the chopped onion to the oil remaining in the pan and fry over a gentle heat for 3–4 minutes until soft. Add the rice and stir for 3–4 minutes until the grains are evenly coated in oil. Add 75ml/ 5 tbsp of the wine and then the stock, a little at a time, stirring over a gentle heat and allowing the rice to absorb the liquid before adding more. Continue for 15 minutes. Soak the mushrooms for 10 minutes in warm water to cover.

3 Drain the mushrooms, reserving the liquid, and cut the larger ones in half. Stir the mushrooms into the risotto with 15ml/1 tbsp of the reserved mushroom liquid. If the rice is not yet *al dente*, add a little more stock or mushroom liquid and cook for 2–3 minutes more. Season to taste with salt and pepper.

4 Remove the pan from the heat and stir in the prawns. Preheat the oven to 190°C/375°F/Gas 5.

5 Take a trout fillet, place a spoonful of risotto at one end and roll up. Wrap each fillet in a slice of Parma ham and place in a greased ovenproof dish.

6 Spoon any remaining risotto around the fish fillets and sprinkle over the rest of the wine. Cover loosely with foil and bake for 15–20 minutes until the fish is tender. Spoon the risotto on to a platter, top with the trout rolls and garnish with caper berries. Serve at once.

Nutritional information per portion: Energy 397kcal/1662kJ; Protein 33g; Carbohydrate 43.6g, of which sugars 1.1g; Fat 7.6g, of which saturates 0.3g; Cholesterol 29mg; Calcium 37mg; Fibre 0.2g; Sodium 202mg.

Salmon in puff pastry

This fish-shaped pie makes an elegant party dish. If time is short, you may prefer to make a simple pie. Line a greased baking dish with pastry, then part-bake it before adding the filling and covering with the top layer of pastry. Seal the edges and return to the oven.

SERVES 6

450g/1lb puff pastry, thawed if frozen
1 egg, beaten
3 hard-boiled eggs
90ml/6 tbsp single (light) cream
200g/7oz/1¾ cups freshly cooked
    long grain rice

30ml/2 tbsp finely chopped fresh parsley
10ml/2 tsp chopped fresh tarragon
675g/1½lb fresh salmon fillets
40g/1½oz/3 tbsp butter
juice of ½ lemon
salt and ground black pepper

1 Preheat the oven to 190°C/375°F/Gas 5. Roll two-thirds of the pastry into a large oval, measuring 35cm/14in in length. Cut into a curved fish shape and place on a lightly greased baking sheet. Use the trimmings to make narrow strips. Brush one side of each strip with beaten egg and secure in place around the rim of the pastry to make a raised edge. Prick the base all over with a fork, then bake for 8–10 minutes until the sides are well risen and the pastry is golden. Leave to cool.

2 In a bowl, mash the hard-boiled eggs with the cream, then stir in the cooked rice. Add the parsley and tarragon, season well and spoon on to the prepared pastry. Cut the salmon into 2cm/¾in chunks. Melt the butter until it sizzles. Add the salmon pieces and turn over in the butter so they begin to colour but do not cook through. Remove from the heat and arrange them on the rice, piled in the centre. Stir the lemon juice into the butter in the pan, then spoon over the salmon pieces.

3 Roll out the remaining pastry and cut out a semi-circle piece to cover the head portion and a tail shape to cover the tail. Brush both pieces of pastry with a little beaten egg and place on top of the fish, pressing down firmly to secure. Score a criss-cross pattern on the tail.

4 Cut the remaining pastry into small circles and, starting from the tail end, arrange the circles in overlapping lines to represent scales. Add an extra one for an eye. Brush the whole fish shape with the remaining beaten egg.

5 Bake for 10 minutes. Reduce the temperature to 160°C/325°F/Gas 3 and cook for 15–20 minutes until golden. Slide on to a serving plate and serve.

Nutritional information per portion: Energy 668kcal/2782kJ; Protein 31g; Carbohydrate 36.6g, of which sugars 0.7g; Fat 45.3g, of which saturates 14g; Cholesterol 209mg; Calcium 98mg; Fibre 1.1g; Sodium 389mg.

Salmon risotto with cucumber and tarragon

This simple risotto is cooked all in one go. If you prefer to cook it the traditional way, add the liquid gradually, and the salmon about two-thirds of the way through cooking.

SERVES 4

small bunch of spring onions (scallions)
¹/₂ cucumber, peeled and seeded
25g/1oz/2 tbsp butter
350g/12oz/1³/₄ cups risotto rice
1.2 litres/2 pints/5 cups hot chicken
    stock or fish stock
150ml/¹/₄ pint/²/₃ cup dry white wine
450g/1lb salmon fillet, skinned and diced
45ml/3 tbsp chopped fresh tarragon
salt and ground black pepper

1 Top and tail the spring onions, cut away and discard the green parts, and then chop the white parts. Chop the cucumber.

2 Put the butter in a large pan, heat it until melted, then add the chopped white parts of the spring onions and the chopped cucumber. Cook for 2–3 minutes without letting the spring onions colour.

3 Stir in the risotto rice, then pour in the hot stock and the dry white wine. Bring to the boil, then lower the heat and simmer, uncovered, for 10 minutes, stirring occasionally.

4 Stir in the diced salmon fillet and then season to taste with salt and black pepper. Continue cooking for a further 5 minutes, stirring occasionally, then remove from the heat. Cover the pan and then leave to stand for 5 minutes.

5 Remove the lid, add the chopped tarragon and mix together lightly. Spoon the risotto into a warmed bowl and serve.

Nutritional information per portion: Energy 597kcal/2492kJ; Protein 30.9g; Carbohydrate 67.1g, of which sugars 1.5g; Fat 19.1g, of which saturates 5.4g; Cholesterol 70mg; Calcium 59mg; Fibre 0.6g; Sodium 96mg.

Salmon and rice gratin

This all-in-one supper dish is ideal for informal entertaining because it can be made ahead of time and reheated for about half an hour before being served with a tossed salad.

SERVES 6

675g/1¹/₂lb fresh salmon fillet, skinned
1 bay leaf
a few parsley stalks
1 litre/1³/₄ pints/4 cups water
400g/14oz/2 cups basmati rice, soaked
30–45ml/2–3 tbsp chopped fresh parsley,
    plus extra to garnish
175g/6oz/1¹/₂ cups Cheddar
    cheese, grated
3 hard-boiled eggs, chopped
salt and ground black pepper

FOR THE SAUCE

1 litre/1³/₄ pints/4 cups milk
40g/1¹/₂oz/¹/₃ cup plain (all-purpose) flour
40g/1¹/₂oz/3 tbsp butter
5ml/1 tsp mild curry paste or
    French mustard

1 Put the salmon in a wide, shallow pan. Add the bay leaf, parsley stalks, seasoning and water and bring to simmering point. Poach for 12 minutes until just tender. Lift out the fish, then strain the liquid into a large pan. Leave to cool, then remove any bones and flake the flesh gently with a fork.

2 Drain the rice and add to the poaching liquid. Bring to the boil, lower the heat, cover and simmer for 10 minutes without lifting the lid. Remove from the heat and, without lifting the lid, leave to stand undisturbed for 5 minutes.

3 Meanwhile, for the sauce, mix the milk, flour and butter in a large pan. Bring to the boil over a low heat, whisking constantly until smooth and thick. Stir in the curry paste or mustard, and season to taste. Simmer for 2 minutes.

4 Preheat the grill (broiler). Remove the sauce from the heat and stir in the chopped parsley and rice, with half the cheese. Using a large metal spoon, fold in the flaked fish and eggs. Spoon into a shallow gratin dish and sprinkle with the rest of the cheese. Heat under the grill until the topping is golden brown and bubbling. Serve in individual dishes, garnished with chopped parsley.

Nutritional information per portion: Energy 752kcal/3137kJ; Protein 44.8g; Carbohydrate 66.5g, of which sugars 8.2g; Fat 33.5g, of which saturates 14.5g; Cholesterol 204mg; Calcium 492mg; Fibre 0.6g; Sodium 411mg.

Celebration paella

This paella is a marvellous combination of some of the finest Spanish ingredients. Chicken and rabbit, seafood and vegetables are mixed with rice to make a colourful party dish.

SERVES 6–8

450g/1lb fresh mussels
90ml/6 tbsp white wine
150g/5½oz French (green) beans,
   cut into 2.5cm/1in lengths
115g/4oz/1 cup frozen broad (fava) beans
6 small skinless, boneless chicken breasts,
   cut into large pieces
30ml/2 tbsp plain (all-purpose) flour,
   seasoned with salt and pepper
about 90ml/6 tbsp olive oil
6–8 large raw prawns (shrimp), tailed
   and deveined
150g/5½oz pork fillet (tenderloin),
   cut into bitesize pieces

2 onions, chopped
2–3 garlic cloves, crushed
1 red (bell) pepper, seeded and sliced
2 ripe tomatoes, peeled, seeded
   and chopped
900ml/1½ pints/3¾ cups well-
   flavoured chicken stock
good pinch of saffron, dissolved in
   30ml/2 tbsp hot water
350g/12oz/1¾ cups Spanish rice or
   risotto rice
225g/8oz chorizo sausage, thickly sliced
115g/4oz/1 cup frozen peas
6–8 stuffed green olives, thickly sliced

1 Scrub the mussels, discarding any that do not close when sharply tapped. Place in a large pan with the wine, bring to the boil, then cover the pan tightly and cook for 3–4 minutes until all the mussels have opened, shaking the pan occasionally. Drain, reserving the liquid and discarding any mussels that have not opened.

2 Briefly cook the French beans and broad beans in separate pans of boiling water for 2–3 minutes. Drain. As soon as the broad beans are cool enough to handle, pop them out of their skins.

3 Dust the chicken with the seasoned flour. Heat half of the olive oil in a paella pan or deep frying pan, add the chicken and fry until evenly brown on all sides. Transfer to a plate.

4 Fry the prawns briefly, adding more oil if needed, then use a slotted spoon to transfer them to a plate. Heat a further 30ml/2 tbsp of the oil in the pan and brown the pork evenly. Transfer to a separate plate.

5 Add the remaining oil to the pan and fry the onions and garlic for 3–4 minutes until golden brown. Add the red pepper, cook for 2–3 minutes, then add the chopped tomatoes and cook until thickened.

6 Stir in the chicken stock, the reserved mussel liquid and the saffron liquid. Season with salt and pepper and bring to the boil. When the liquid is bubbling, throw in all the rice. Stir once, then add the chicken pieces, pork, prawns, beans, chorizo sausage and peas. Cook over a moderately high heat for 12 minutes, then lower the heat and leave to cook for 8–10 minutes more, until all the liquid has been absorbed.

7 Add the mussels and olives and continue cooking for a further 3–4 minutes to heat through. Remove the pan from the heat, cover with a clean, damp dish towel and leave to stand for 10 minutes before serving from the pan.

Nutritional information per portion: Energy 378kcal/1581kJ; Protein 27.4g; Carbohydrate 35.8g, of which sugars 4.6g; Fat 13.4g, of which saturates 3.5g; Cholesterol 80mg; Calcium 77mg; Fibre 2.6g; Sodium 264mg.

Seafood paella

This is a great dish to serve to guests on a special occasion because it looks spectacular. Bring the paella pan to the table and let everyone help themselves.

SERVES 4

60ml/4 tbsp olive oil

225g/8oz monkfish or cod fillets, skinned
   and cut into chunks

3 baby squid, cut into rings,
   tentacles chopped

1 red mullet, filleted, skinned and cut into
   chunks (optional)

1 onion, chopped

3 garlic cloves, finely chopped

1 red (bell) pepper, seeded and sliced

4 tomatoes, peeled and roughly chopped

225g/8oz/generous 1 cup risotto rice

450ml/¾ pint/scant 2 cups fish stock

150ml/¼ pint/⅔ cup white wine

4–5 saffron strands soaked in
   30ml/2 tbsp hot water

115g/4oz cooked, peeled prawns (shrimp)

75g/2¾oz/¾ cup frozen peas

8 fresh mussels, scrubbed

salt and ground black pepper

4 Mediterranean prawns (jumbo shrimp),
   in their shells

fresh parsley and lemon, to garnish

1 Heat half the oil in a paella pan or a large frying pan and add the monkfish or cod, and the squid. Also add the red mullet, if using. Stir-fry for 2 minutes, then turn the contents of the pan into a bowl and set aside.

2 Heat the remaining oil in the pan and add the onion, garlic and red pepper. Fry for 6–7 minutes, stirring frequently, until softened. Stir in the tomatoes and fry for 2 minutes, then add the rice. Stir to coat the grains with oil, then cook for 2–3 minutes. Pour over the fish stock, wine and saffron water. Season with salt and black pepper, and mix well.

3 Gently stir in the reserved cooked fish (and juices), the peeled prawns and peas. Push the mussels into the rice. Cover and cook over a gentle heat for 30 minutes or until the stock has been absorbed but the rice mixture is still relatively moist. All the mussels should have opened; discard any that remain closed.

4 Remove the pan from the heat, and leave the paella to stand, covered, for 5 minutes. Arrange the whole prawns on top. Sprinkle the paella with parsley and serve with the lemon wedges.

Nutritional information per portion: Energy 585kcal/2445kJ; Protein 36.1g; Carbohydrate 60.9g, of which sugars 10.1g; Fat 20.4g, of which saturates 5.6g; Cholesterol 268mg; Calcium 132mg; Fibre 4.2g; Sodium 1055mg.

Shellfish risotto with mixed mushrooms

This is a quick and easy risotto, where all the liquid is added in one go. The method is well suited to this shellfish dish, because it means everything cooks together undisturbed.

SERVES 6

225g/8oz fresh mussels

225g/8oz fresh Venus or carpet
  shell clams

45ml/3 tbsp olive oil

1 onion, chopped

450g/1lb/2¹/₃ cups risotto rice

1.75 litres/3 pints/7¹/₂ cups simmering
  chicken stock or vegetable stock

150ml/¹/₄ pint/²/₃ cup white wine

225g/8oz/2–3 cups assorted wild
  and cultivated mushrooms,
  trimmed and sliced

115g/4oz raw peeled prawns
  (shrimp), deveined

1 medium or 2 small squid, cleaned,
  trimmed and sliced

3 drops truffle oil (optional)

75ml/5 tbsp chopped mixed fresh
  parsley and chervil

celery salt and cayenne pepper

1 Scrub the mussels and clams clean and discard any that are open and do not close when tapped with a knife. Set aside. Heat the oil in a large pan and fry the onion for 6–8 minutes until soft but not browned.

2 Add the rice, stirring to coat the grains in oil, then pour in the stock and wine, bring to the boil and cook for 5 minutes. Add the mushrooms and cook for 5 minutes more, stirring occasionally.

3 Add the prawns, squid, mussels and clams and stir into the rice. Cover the pan and simmer over a low heat for 15 minutes until the prawns have turned pink and the mussels and clams have opened. Discard any of the shellfish that remain closed.

4 Remove from the heat. Add the truffle oil, if using, and stir in the herbs. Cover tightly and leave to stand for 5–10 minutes to allow all the flavours to blend. Season to taste with celery salt and a pinch of cayenne, pile into a warmed dish, and serve immediately.

Nutritional information per portion: Energy 423kcal/1768kJ; Protein 21.4g; Carbohydrate 62.5g, of which sugars 0.8g; Fat 7.5g, of which saturates 1.2g; Cholesterol 136mg; Calcium 64mg; Fibre 0.6g; Sodium 335mg.

Squid risotto with chilli and coriander

Squid needs to be cooked either very quickly or very slowly. Here the squid is marinated in lime and kiwi fruit – a popular method in New Zealand for tenderizing squid.

SERVES 3–4

450g/1lb squid
45ml/3 tbsp olive oil
15g/¹/₂oz/1 tbsp butter
1 onion, finely chopped
2 garlic cloves, crushed
1 fresh red chilli, seeded and finely sliced
275g/9¹/₂oz/1¹/₂ cups risotto rice
175ml/6fl oz/³/₄ cup dry white wine
1 litre/1³/₄ pints/4 cups hot fish stock

30ml/2 tbsp chopped fresh
   coriander (cilantro)
salt and ground black pepper

FOR THE MARINADE
2 ripe kiwi fruit, chopped and mashed
1 fresh red chilli, seeded and finely sliced
30ml/2 tbsp fresh lime juice

1 If not already cleaned, prepare the squid by cutting off the tentacles at the base and pulling to remove the quill. Discard the quill and intestines, if necessary, and pull away the thin outer skin. Rinse the body and cut into thin strips. Cut the tentacles into short pieces, discarding the beak and eyes. Mix all the marinade ingredients in a bowl, then add the squid, stirring to coat. Season, cover with clear film (plastic wrap) and leave in the refrigerator for 4 hours or overnight.

2 Drain the squid. Heat 15ml/1 tbsp of the oil in a frying pan and cook the strips, in batches if necessary, for 30–60 seconds over a high heat. It is important that the squid cooks very quickly. Transfer to a plate and set aside. Don't worry if some of the marinade clings to the squid, but if too much juice accumulates in the pan, pour this into a jug (pitcher) and add more olive oil when cooking the next batch so that the squid fries rather than simmers. Reserve the accumulated juices in the jug.

3 Heat the remaining oil with the butter in a large pan and gently fry the onion and garlic for 5–6 minutes until soft. Add the chilli and fry for 1 minute, then add the rice. Cook for a few minutes, stirring, until the rice is coated with oil and slightly translucent. Stir in the wine until it is absorbed. Gradually add the stock and reserved cooking liquid from the squid, a ladleful at a time, stirring constantly and waiting until each quantity of stock has been absorbed before adding the next.

4 After 15 minutes, stir in the squid and continue cooking the risotto until all the stock has been absorbed and the rice is tender, but still firm to the bite. Stir in the chopped coriander, cover with the lid or a dish towel, and leave to rest for a few minutes before serving.

Nutritional information per portion: Energy 663kcal/2771kJ; Protein 31.9g; Carbohydrate 79g, of which sugars 7.3g; Fat 19.4g, of which saturates 4.8g; Cholesterol 348mg; Calcium 63mg; Fibre 1.5g; Sodium 204mg.

Truffle and lobster risotto

This is a truly luxurious dish for a special occasion. To make the most of the truffle's scent, you can store it with the rice for a few days before cooking it.

SERVES 4

50g/1³⁄₄oz/4 tbsp unsalted
    (sweet) butter
1 onion, chopped
350g/12oz/1³⁄₄ cups risotto rice,
    preferably carnaroli
1 fresh thyme sprig
150ml/¹⁄₄ pint/²⁄₃ cup dry white wine
1.2 litres/2 pints/5 cups simmering
    chicken stock
1 freshly cooked lobster
45ml/3 tbsp chopped mixed fresh parsley
    and chervil
3–4 drops truffle oil
2 hard-boiled eggs
1 fresh black or white truffle
salt and ground black pepper

1 Melt the butter, add the onion and fry until soft. Add the rice and stir to coat in the butter. Add the thyme, then the wine, and cook until the liquid has been absorbed. Add the chicken stock a little at a time, stirring. Let each ladleful be fully absorbed before adding the next.

2 Twist off the lobster tail, cut the underside with scissors and remove the white tail meat. Carefully break open the claws with a small kitchen hammer and remove the flesh. Cut half the meat into big chunks, then roughly chop the remainder.

3 Stir in the chopped lobster meat, half the parsley and chervil, and the truffle oil. Remove the rice from the heat, cover the pan and leave to stand for 5 minutes.

4 Divide the cooked rice between four warmed plates and then centre the lobster chunks on top. Cut the hard-boiled eggs into wedges and then arrange them around the lobster meat.

5 Finally, shave fresh truffle over each portion and sprinkle with the remaining herbs. Serve immediately.

Nutritional information per portion: Energy 520kcal/2172kJ; Protein 19.9g; Carbohydrate 71.3g, of which sugars 1.2g; Fat 14.3g, of which saturates 7.4g; Cholesterol 172mg; Calcium 68mg; Fibre 0.2g; Sodium 263mg.

Crab risotto

This rich risotto makes a wonderful main course or appetizer. It is a good dish to follow a trip to the coast, where crabs are cheap and plentiful.

SERVES 3–4

2 large cooked crabs
15ml/1 tbsp olive oil
25g/1oz/2 tbsp butter
2 shallots, finely chopped
275g/9½oz/1½ cups risotto rice,
    preferably carnaroli
75ml/5 tbsp Marsala or brandy
1 litre/1¾ pints/4 cups simmering
    fish stock
5ml/1 tsp chopped fresh tarragon
5ml/1 tsp chopped fresh parsley
60ml/4 tbsp double (heavy) cream
salt and ground black pepper

1 Hold a crab in one hand. Hit the back underside firmly with the heel of your hand. With your thumbs, push against the body and pull away from the shell. Remove and discard the intestines and grey gills. Break off the claws and legs, and break open with a small hammer. Remove the claw and leg meat, and place on a plate.

2 Pick off the white meat and place on the plate, reserving some. Scoop out the brown meat and add to the plate. Repeat with the other crab.

3 Heat the oil and butter in a large pan and gently fry the shallots until soft but not browned. Add the rice.

4 Cook for a few minutes, stirring, until the rice is slightly translucent. Add the Marsala or brandy, bring to the boil and cook, stirring, until evaporated. Add a ladleful of hot stock and cook, stirring, until all the liquid is absorbed. Continue until two-thirds of the stock has been added, then stir in the crab meat and herbs.

5 Continue cooking, adding the remaining stock. When the rice is almost cooked but firm to the bite, remove from the heat, stir in the cream and adjust the seasoning. Cover and leave for 3 minutes to finish cooking. Serve garnished with the reserved white crab meat.

Nutritional information per portion: Energy 496kcal/2060kJ; Protein 14.1g; Carbohydrate 56.4g, of which sugars 1.1g; Fat 18.7g, of which saturates 8.9g; Cholesterol 65mg; Calcium 25mg; Fibre 0.2g; Sodium 229mg.

Mussel risotto

Fresh root ginger and coriander add a distinctive flavour to this dish, while the green chillies give it a little heat. The chillies could be omitted for a milder taste.

SERVES 3–4

900g/2lb fresh mussels

about 250ml/9fl oz/1 cup dry white wine

30ml/2 tbsp olive oil

1 onion, chopped

2 garlic cloves, crushed

1–2 fresh green chillies, seeded and finely sliced

2.5cm/1in piece of fresh root ginger, grated

275g/9^1/$_2$oz/1^1/$_2$ cups risotto rice

900ml/1^1/$_2$ pints/3^3/$_4$ cups simmering fish stock

30ml/2 tbsp chopped fresh coriander (cilantro)

30ml/2 tbsp double (heavy) cream

salt and ground black pepper

1 Scrub the mussels, discarding any that do not close when sharply tapped. Place in a large pan. Add 125ml/4fl oz/^{1}/$_2$ cup of the wine and bring to the boil. Cover the pan and cook the mussels for 4–5 minutes until they have opened, shaking the pan occasionally. Drain, reserving the liquid and discarding any mussels that have not opened. Remove most of the mussels from their shells, reserving a few in their shells for the garnish. Strain the mussel liquid.

2 Heat the oil in another large pan and fry the onion and garlic for 3–4 minutes until beginning to soften. Add the chillies. Continue to cook over a low heat for 1–2 minutes, stirring frequently, then stir in the ginger and fry gently for 1 minute more.

3 Add the rice and cook over a medium heat for 2 minutes, stirring, until the rice is coated in oil and becomes translucent.

4 Stir in the reserved cooking liquid from the mussels. When this has been absorbed, add the remaining wine and cook, stirring, until this has been absorbed. Add the hot fish stock, a little at a time, making sure each addition has been absorbed before adding the next.

5 After 15 minutes, stir in the mussels. Add the coriander and season with salt and pepper. Continue cooking and adding stock to the risotto until it is creamy and the rice is tender but slightly firm in the centre.

6 Remove the risotto from the heat, stir in the double cream, then cover the pan and leave to rest for a few minutes. Spoon into a warmed serving dish, garnish with the reserved mussels in their shells, and serve immediately.

Nutritional information per portion: Energy 439kcal/1833kJ; Protein 17.2g; Carbohydrate 56.6g, of which sugars 1.4g; Fat 11.3g, of which saturates 3.5g; Cholesterol 37mg; Calcium 159mg; Fibre 0.2g; Sodium 146mg.

Scallop risotto

Try to buy fresh scallops for this dish, as they taste much better than frozen ones. Fresh scallops come with the coral attached, which adds flavour, texture and colour.

SERVES 3–4

about 12 scallops, with their corals
50g/1³⁄₄oz/4 tbsp butter
15ml/1 tbsp olive oil
30ml/2 tbsp Pernod
2 shallots, finely chopped
275g/9¹⁄₂oz/1¹⁄₂ cups risotto rice
1 litre/1³⁄₄ pints/4 cups simmering
    fish stock
generous pinch of saffron strands,
    dissolved in 15ml/1 tbsp warm milk
30ml/2 tbsp chopped fresh parsley
60ml/4 tbsp double (heavy) cream
salt and ground black pepper

1 Separate the scallops from their corals. Cut the white flesh into 2cm/³⁄₄in slices. Melt half the butter with 5ml/1 tsp oil. Fry the white pieces for 2–3 minutes. Pour over the Pernod, heat for a few seconds, then ignite and allow to flame for a few seconds. When the flames have died down, remove from the heat.

2 Heat the remaining butter and oil in a separate, large pan and fry the shallots for 3–4 minutes, until soft but not browned. Add the rice and cook for a few minutes, stirring, until the rice is coated with oil and starting to turn translucent.

3 Add the stock, a ladleful at a time, stirring constantly. Wait for each to be absorbed before adding the next.

4 After 15 minutes, add the scallops with the pan juices, corals, saffron milk, parsley and seasoning. Stir well to mix. Continue cooking, adding the remaining stock and stirring occasionally, until the risotto is thick and creamy.

5 Remove from the heat, stir in the cream and cover. Leave the risotto to rest for about 3 minutes to complete the cooking, then pile it into a warmed bowl and serve.

Nutritional information per portion: Energy 550kcal/2290kJ; Protein 23g; Carbohydrate 58.9g, of which sugars 1.2g; Fat 22.5g, of which saturates 12.2g; Cholesterol 82mg; Calcium 48mg; Fibre 0.2g; Sodium 215mg.

Monkfish risotto

Monkfish is a versatile, firm-textured fish with a superb flavour that is accentuated with lemon grass in this sophisticated risotto.

SERVES 3–4

seasoned flour, for dusting
450g/1lb monkfish, cut into cubes
30ml/2 tbsp olive oil
40g/1¹/₂oz/3 tbsp butter
2 shallots, finely chopped
1 lemon grass stalk, finely chopped
275g/10oz/1¹/₂ cups risotto rice,
    preferably carnaroli
175ml/6fl oz/³/₄ cup dry white wine
1 litre/1³/₄ pints/4 cups simmering
    fish stock
30ml/2 tbsp chopped fresh parsley
salt and white pepper
dressed salad leaves, to serve

1 Sprinkle the seasoned flour over the monkfish cubes in a bowl and toss until coated. Heat 15ml/1 tbsp of the oil with half the butter in a frying pan. Fry the monkfish over a medium-high heat for 3–4 minutes until cooked, turning occasionally. Transfer to a plate and set aside.

2 Heat the remaining oil and butter in a large pan and fry the shallots over a low heat for about 4 minutes until soft but not brown. Add the lemon grass and cook for a further 1–2 minutes.

3 Add the rice and cook for about 2–3 minutes, stirring, until coated with oil and slightly translucent.

4 Gradually add the wine and the hot stock, stirring and waiting until each ladleful has been absorbed before adding the next.

5 After 15 minutes, stir in the monkfish. Continue to cook the risotto, adding the remaining stock and stirring constantly until the grains of rice are tender, but still firm to the bite. Season to taste with salt and white pepper.

6 Remove the pan from the heat, stir in the parsley and cover with the lid. Leave the risotto standing for a few minutes before serving with a garnish of freshly dressed salad leaves.

Nutritional information per portion: Energy 431kcal/1802kJ; Protein 23.1g; Carbohydrate 56.4g, of which sugars 1.2g; Fat 9.1g, of which saturates 5.3g; Cholesterol 37mg; Calcium 37mg; Fibre 0.3g; Sodium 84mg.

Seafood risotto

You can use any shellfish or fish for this risotto, as long as the total weight is similar to that used here. The risotto would also make a very good appetizer for eight people.

SERVES 4–6

450g/1lb fresh mussels

about 250ml/9fl oz/1 cup dry white wine

225g/8oz sea bass fillet, skinned and cut
into pieces

seasoned flour, for dusting

60ml/4 tbsp olive oil

8 scallops with corals separated, white
parts halved or sliced if large

225g/8oz squid, cleaned and cut into rings

12 large raw prawns (shrimp) or
langoustines, heads removed

2 shallots, finely chopped

1 garlic clove, crushed

400g/14oz/2 cups risotto rice,
preferably carnaroli

3 tomatoes, peeled, seeded and chopped

1.5 litres/2³⁄₄ pints/6¹⁄₄ cups simmering
fish stock

30ml/2 tbsp chopped fresh parsley

30ml/2 tbsp double (heavy) cream

salt and ground black pepper

1 Scrub the mussels, discarding any that don't close when sharply tapped. Place in a large pan and add 90ml/6 tbsp of the wine. Bring to the boil, cover and cook for 3–4 minutes, shaking the pan occasionally, until all the mussels are open. Drain, reserving the liquid and discarding any unopened mussels. Set aside a few in their shells for garnish; shell the others. Strain the liquid.

2 Dust the sea bass in seasoned flour. Heat 30ml/2 tbsp of the oil in a frying pan and fry the fish, turning, for 3–4 minutes, until tender. Transfer to a plate. Add a little more oil and fry the white parts of the scallops for 1–2 minutes, both sides. Transfer to a plate. Fry the squid for 3–4 minutes in the same pan, adding a little more oil if needed. Set aside. Lastly, fry the prawns or langoustines for 3–4 minutes until pink, turning frequently. Towards the end of cooking, add 30ml/2 tbsp wine and cook until the prawns are tender, but do not burn. Remove from the pan. When cooled, remove the shells and legs, leaving the tails intact.

3 In a large pan, heat the remaining olive oil and gently fry the shallots and garlic for 3–4 minutes until the shallots are soft but not brown. Add the rice. Cook for a few minutes, stirring, until the rice is coated with oil and the grains slightly translucent. Stir in the tomatoes and the reserved liquid from the mussels.

4 When all the free liquid has been absorbed, add the remaining wine, stirring constantly. When the wine has also been absorbed, gradually add the hot stock, one ladleful at a time, continuing to stir the rice constantly and waiting until each quantity of stock has been fully absorbed before adding the next.

5 After 15 minutes, carefully stir in all the seafood, except the mussels reserved for the garnish. Continue to cook until all the stock has been absorbed and the rice is tender but still firm to the bite.

6 Stir in the parsley and cream and adjust the seasoning. Cover the pan and leave the risotto to stand for 2–3 minutes. Serve in individual bowls, garnished with the reserved mussels in their shells.

Nutritional information per portion: Energy 404kcal/1693kJ; Protein 28.1g; Carbohydrate 56.3g, of which sugars 1.1g; Fat 3.9g, of which saturates 1.9g; Cholesterol 228mg; Calcium 200mg; Fibre 0.2g; Sodium 301mg.

Louisiana seafood gumbo

Gumbo is a soup, but is served over rice as a main course. In Louisiana, oysters are cheap and plentiful, and would be used here instead of mussels.

SERVES 6

450g/1lb fresh mussels
450g/1lb raw prawns (shrimp),
    in their shells
1 cooked crab, about 1kg/2¼lb
small bunch of parsley, leaves chopped
    and stalks reserved
150ml/¼ pint/⅔ cup vegetable oil
115g/4oz/1 cup plain (all-purpose) flour
1 green (bell) pepper, seeded
    and chopped

1 large onion, chopped
2 celery sticks, sliced
3 garlic cloves, finely chopped
75g/2¾oz smoked spiced sausage, skinned
275g/9½oz/1½ cups white
    long grain rice
6 spring onions (scallions), shredded
cayenne pepper, to taste
Tabasco sauce, to taste
salt

1 Wash the mussels in several changes of cold water, pulling away the black "beards". Discard any mussels that are broken or do not close when you tap them firmly.

2 Bring 250ml/9fl oz/1 cup water to the boil in a large pan. Add the mussels, cover the pan tightly and cook over a high heat, shaking frequently, for 3 minutes. As the mussels open, lift them out with tongs into a sieve (strainer) set over a bowl. Discard any that fail to open. Shell the mussels, discarding the shells. Return the liquid from the bowl to the pan and make the quantity up to 2 litres/3½ pints/8 cups with water.

3 Peel the prawns and set them aside. Put the shells and heads into the pan with the cooking liquid. Remove all the meat from the crab, separating the brown and white meat. Add all the pieces of shell to the pan with 5ml/2 tsp salt.

4 Bring the shellfish stock to the boil, skimming it regularly. When there is no more froth on the surface, add the parsley stalks and simmer for 15 minutes. Cool the stock, then strain it into a measuring jug (cup) and make the quantity up to 2 litres/3½ pints/8 cups with water.

5 Heat the oil in a large, heavy pan, add the flour and stir constantly over a medium heat until the roux reaches a golden-brown colour. Immediately add the green pepper, onion, celery and garlic. Continue cooking for 3 minutes until the onion is soft. Slice and stir in the sausage. Reheat the stock.

6 Stir the brown crab meat into the roux, then ladle in the hot stock a little at a time, stirring constantly until it has all been smoothly incorporated. Bring to a low boil, partially cover the pan, then simmer the gumbo for 30 minutes.

7 Meanwhile, cook the rice in plenty of lightly salted boiling water until the grains are tender, then drain.

8 Add the prawns, mussels, white crab meat and spring onions to the gumbo. Return to the boil and season with salt, if necessary, cayenne and a dash or two of Tabasco sauce. Simmer for a further minute, then add the chopped parsley leaves. Serve immediately, ladling the soup over the hot rice in soup plates.

Nutritional information per portion: Energy 559kcal/2336kJ; Protein 31.1g; Carbohydrate 57.6g, of which sugars 3.7g; Fat 23g, of which saturates 3.4g; Cholesterol 183mg; Calcium 145mg; Fibre 1.9g; Sodium 474mg.

North African fish with pumpkin rice

This is a dish of contrasts – the slightly sweet flavour of pumpkin, the mildly spicy fish, and the coriander and ginger mixture that is stirred in at the end – all mixed with well-flavoured rice.

SERVES 4

450g/1lb sea bass or other firm fish fillets
30ml/2 tbsp plain (all-purpose) flour
5ml/1 tsp ground coriander
1.5–2.5ml/$^1/_4$–$^1/_2$ tsp ground turmeric
1 wedge of pumpkin, about 500g/1lb 2oz
30–45ml/2–3 tbsp olive oil
6 spring onions (scallions), sliced diagonally
1 garlic clove, finely chopped
275g/9$^1/_2$oz/1$^1/_2$ cups basmati rice, soaked and drained
550ml/19fl oz/2$^1/_2$ cups fish stock
salt and ground black pepper

fresh coriander (cilantro) sprigs, to garnish
lime or lemon wedges, to serve

FOR THE CORIANDER AND GINGER FLAVOURING
45ml/3 tbsp finely chopped fresh coriander (cilantro)
10ml/2 tsp chopped fresh root ginger
$^1/_2$–1 fresh chilli, seeded and very finely chopped
45ml/3 tbsp lime or lemon juice

1 Remove and discard any skin or stray bones from the fish, and cut into 2cm/$^3/_4$in chunks. Mix the flour, ground coriander, turmeric, and a little salt and pepper in a plastic bag, add the fish and shake for a few seconds so that the fish is evenly coated in the spice mixture. Set aside. Make the coriander and ginger flavouring by mixing all the ingredients in a small bowl.

2 Remove the skin and seeds from the pumpkin. Cut the flesh into 2cm/$^3/_4$in chunks. Heat 15ml/ 1 tbsp oil in a large pan and stir-fry the spring onions and garlic for a few minutes until slightly softened. Add the pumpkin and cook over a fairly low heat, stirring frequently, for 4–5 minutes or until the flesh begins to soften. Add the rice, increase the heat and stir for 2–3 minutes.

3 Stir in the stock, with a little salt. Bring to simmering point, then lower the heat, cover and cook for 12–15 minutes until both the rice and the pumpkin are tender.

4 About 4 minutes before the rice is ready, heat the remaining oil in a frying pan and fry the spiced fish over a moderately high heat for about 3 minutes until lightly browned and crisp and the flesh is cooked but still moist. Stir the coriander and ginger flavouring into the rice.

5 Transfer to a warmed serving dish and lay the fish pieces on top. Serve immediately, garnished with coriander, and lemon or lime wedges for squeezing over the fish.

Nutritional information per portion: Energy 436kcal/1825kJ; Protein 27.9g; Carbohydrate 64.2g, of which sugars 3g; Fat 7.2g, of which saturates 1.1g; Cholesterol 52mg; Calcium 101mg; Fibre 2.3g; Sodium 73mg.

Jamaican fish curry

Although the rice is simply boiled for this classic Jamaican recipe, it, nevertheless, takes on the flavour of the sauce with which it is served.

SERVES 4

2 halibut steaks, total weight about
    550–675g/1¼–1½lb
30ml/2 tbsp groundnut (peanut) oil
2 cardamom pods
1 cinnamon stick
6 allspice berries
4 cloves
1 large onion, chopped
3 garlic cloves, crushed
10–15ml/2–3 tsp grated fresh root ginger
10ml/2 tsp ground cumin
5ml/1 tsp ground coriander

2.5ml/½ tsp cayenne pepper or to taste
4 tomatoes, peeled, seeded and chopped
1 sweet potato, about 225g/8oz,
    cut into 2cm/¾in cubes
475ml/17fl oz/2 cups fish stock or water
115g/4oz creamed coconut or desiccated
    (dry unsweetened shredded) coconut
1 bay leaf
225g/8oz/generous 1 cup white long
    grain rice
salt

1 Rub the halibut steaks well with salt and set aside. Heat the oil in a large, heavy pan and stir-fry the cardamom pods, cinnamon stick, allspice berries and cloves for about 3 minutes in order to release the aromas.

2 Add the onion, garlic and ginger. Continue cooking for 4–5 minutes over a gentle heat until the onion is fairly soft, stirring frequently, then add the cumin, coriander and cayenne pepper and cook briefly, stirring all the time.

3 Stir in the tomatoes, sweet potato, fish stock or water, coconut and bay leaf, then season with salt. Bring the mixture to the boil, lower the heat, cover and simmer for 15–18 minutes until the sweet potato is tender.

4 Cook the rice using your preferred method. Meanwhile, add the fish to the pan and spoon over the sauce. Put on the lid and simmer for 10 minutes until the fish is just tender and flakes easily.

5 Transfer the rice to a warmed serving dish, spoon over the curry sauce and arrange the halibut steaks on top. Serve immediately.

Nutritional information per portion: Energy 639kcal/2669kJ; Protein 34.2g; Carbohydrate 62g, of which sugars 8.3g; Fat 28.4g, of which saturates 18.7g; Cholesterol 44mg; Calcium 74mg; Fibre 2.4g; Sodium 115mg.

Poultry

There is no doubting that poultry,

particularly chicken, is one of the world's

favourite foods. And, as these recipes from

Indonesia, Japan, South Africa, Morocco,

the Caribbean and elsewhere show, there

are so many good ways to cook it in risotto

and rice dishes. Whatever your preference –

sweet, tart, spicy, fruity, savoury or meaty

dishes – there's something here to suit

every palate.

Stuffed chicken rolls

These delicious chicken rolls are simple to make, but sophisticated enough to serve at a dinner party, especially if you arrange slices on a bed of tagliatelle tossed with fried wild mushrooms.

SERVES 4

25g/1oz/2 tbsp butter
1 garlic clove, chopped
150g/5½oz/1¼ cups cooked white
    long grain rice
45ml/3 tbsp ricotta cheese
10ml/2 tsp chopped fresh flat
    leaf parsley
5ml/1 tsp chopped fresh tarragon
4 skinless, boneless chicken breasts
3–4 slices Parma ham
15ml/1 tbsp olive oil
125ml/4fl oz/½ cup white wine
salt and ground black pepper
fresh flat leaf parsley sprigs, to garnish
cooked tagliatelle and sautéed wild or
    cultivated mushrooms, to serve

1 Preheat the oven to 180°C/350°F/ Gas 4. Melt 10g/¼oz/2 tsp butter in a small pan and fry the garlic for a few seconds without browning. Spoon into a bowl. Add the rice, ricotta, parsley and tarragon and season with salt and pepper. Stir to mix.

2 Place each chicken breast between two sheets of clear film (plastic wrap) and beat lightly with a rolling pin.

3 Divide the Parma ham slices between the flattened chicken breasts, trimming the ham to fit. Place a spoonful of the rice stuffing at the wider end of each breast.

4 Roll up carefully and tie in place with kitchen string or secure with a cocktail stick (toothpick).

5 Heat the oil and the remaining butter in a frying pan. Lightly fry the chicken rolls until browned. Place side by side in a shallow baking dish, pour over the wine and cover with baking parchment. Bake for 30–35 minutes until the chicken is tender.

6 Cut the rolls into slices and serve on a bed of tagliatelle with sautéed mushrooms and a generous grinding of black pepper. Garnish with sprigs of flat leaf parsley.

Nutritional information per portion: Energy 329kcal/1375kJ; Protein 30g; Carbohydrate 21.3g, of which sugars 1.3g; Fat 11.5g, of which saturates 5.1g; Cholesterol 95mg; Calcium 65mg; Fibre 1.3g; Sodium 257mg.

Chicken piri-piri

This is a classic Portuguese dish, based on a hot sauce made from Angolan chillies. It is popular wherever there are Portuguese communities, and is often served in South Africa.

SERVES 4

4 chicken breast portions
30–45ml/2–3 tbsp olive oil
1 large onion, finely sliced
2 carrots, cut into thin strips
1 large parsnip or 2 small parsnips,
   cut into thin strips
1 red (bell) pepper, seeded and sliced
1 yellow (bell) pepper, seeded and sliced
1 litre/1¾ pints/4 cups chicken stock
3 tomatoes, peeled, seeded and chopped
generous dash of piri-piri sauce
15ml/1 tbsp tomato purée (paste)
½ cinnamon stick
1 fresh thyme sprig, plus extra to garnish
1 bay leaf
275g/9½oz/1½ cups white
   long grain rice
15ml/1 tbsp lime or lemon juice
salt and ground black pepper

1 Heat the oven to 180°C/350°F/Gas 4. Rub the chicken with salt and pepper. Heat 30ml/2 tbsp of the oil in a large, heavy pan and brown the chicken. Transfer to a plate.

2 Fry the onion for 2–3 minutes until slightly softened. Add the carrots, parsnip and peppers, and stir-fry for a few minutes. Cover and sweat for 4–5 minutes until soft.

3 Add the chicken stock, tomatoes, piri-piri sauce, tomato purée, cinnamon, thyme and bay leaf. Season and bring to the boil. Ladle off 300ml/½ pint/1¼ cups of the liquid and set aside in a small pan.

4 Put the rice in the bottom of a casserole. Using a slotted spoon, lift out the vegetables and spread over the rice. Top with the chicken. Pour over the stock from the pan, cover tightly and bake for 45 minutes, until the rice and chicken are tender.

5 Heat the reserved chicken stock, adding a few more drops of piri-piri sauce, and the lime or lemon juice.

6 To serve, discard the bay leaf, spoon the piri-piri chicken and rice on to warmed serving plates and garnish with thyme sprigs. Serve the remaining sauce separately or poured over the chicken.

Nutritional information per portion: Energy 557kcal/2337kJ; Protein 44.3g; Carbohydrate 75.4g, of which sugars 15.5g; Fat 8.8g, of which saturates 1.5g; Cholesterol 105mg; Calcium 73mg; Fibre 5.8g; Sodium 122mg.

Seville chicken with rice

Oranges and almonds are favourite ingredients in southern Spain, especially around Seville, where the orange and almond trees are a familiar and wonderful sight.

SERVES 4

1 orange
8 chicken thighs
seasoned flour, for dusting
45ml/3 tbsp olive oil
1 large onion, roughly chopped
2 garlic cloves, crushed
1 red (bell) pepper, seeded and sliced
1 yellow (bell) pepper, seeded and sliced
115g/4oz chorizo sausage, sliced
50g/1³/₄oz/¹/₂ cup flaked (sliced) almonds
225g/8oz/generous 1 cup brown
    basmati rice
600ml/1 pint/2¹/₂ cups chicken stock
400g/14oz can chopped tomatoes
175ml/6fl oz/³/₄ cup white wine
generous pinch of dried thyme
salt and ground black pepper
fresh thyme sprigs, to garnish

1 Pare a thin strip of peel from the orange and set it aside. Peel the orange, then cut into segments over a bowl to catch the juice. Dust the chicken thighs with seasoned flour.

2 In a large, heavy pan, fry the chicken pieces in oil on both sides until brown. Transfer to a plate.

3 Add the onion and garlic to the pan and fry for 4–5 minutes until the onion begins to brown. Add the red and yellow peppers and fry, stirring occasionally, until slightly softened.

4 Add the chorizo and stir-fry for a few minutes. Sprinkle over the almonds and rice. Cook for 1–2 minutes.

5 Pour in the stock, tomatoes and wine. Add the orange strip and thyme. Season well. Bring to simmering point, stirring, then return the chicken pieces to the pan.

6 Cover tightly and cook very gently for 1–1¹/₄ hours until the chicken is tender. Just before serving, add the orange segments and heat through. Garnish with thyme and serve.

Nutritional information per portion: Energy 861kcal/3598kJ; Protein 65.3g; Carbohydrate 67.1g, of which sugars 17.1g; Fat 34g, of which saturates 5.6g; Cholesterol 155mg; Calcium 172mg; Fibre 6.3g; Sodium 453mg.

Chicken pilaff

The French marmite *pot is ideal for this recipe. The tall sides slant inwards, reducing evaporation and ensuring that the rice cooks slowly without becoming dry.*

SERVES 3–4

15–20 dried chanterelle mushrooms
about 15–30ml/1–2 tbsp olive oil
15g/¹/₂oz/1 tbsp butter
4 thin rashers (strips) rindless smoked
   streaky (fatty) bacon, chopped
3 skinless, boneless chicken breasts,
   cut into thin slices
4 spring onions (scallions), sliced
225g/8oz/generous 1 cup basmati rice,
   soaked and drained
450ml/³/₄ pint/scant 2 cups hot
   chicken stock
salt and ground black pepper

1 Preheat the oven to 180°C/ 350°F/Gas 4. Soak the mushrooms for 10 minutes in warm water. Drain, reserving the liquid. Slice the mushrooms, discarding the stalks.

2 Heat the olive oil and butter in a frying pan. Fry the bacon for 2–3 minutes. Add the chicken and stir-fry until the pieces are golden brown all over. Transfer to a bowl using a slotted spoon.

3 Quickly fry the mushrooms and spring onions in the fat left in the pan and add to the chicken pieces.

4 Add the rice to the pan, with a little olive oil, if necessary. Stir-fry for 2–3 minutes. Spoon it into an earthenware *marmite* pot or casserole.

5 Pour the hot chicken stock and reserved mushroom liquid over the rice in the *marmite* pot or casserole. Stir in the reserved chicken and mushroom mixture and season to taste with salt and pepper.

6 Cover the pot or casserole with a double piece of foil and secure with a lid. Cook in the oven for 30–35 minutes until the rice is tender.

Nutritional information per portion: Energy 437kcal/1823kJ; Protein 27.2g; Carbohydrate 45.4g, of which sugars 0.4g; Fat 15.9g, of which saturates 5.1g; Cholesterol 77mg; Calcium 24mg; Fibre 0.7g; Sodium 386mg.

Risotto with chicken

This is a classic combination of chicken and rice, cooked with Parma ham, garlic, white wine and Parmesan cheese to produce a filling savoury dish.

SERVES 6

30ml/2 tbsp olive oil

225g/8oz skinless, boneless chicken breasts, cut into 2.5cm/1in cubes

1 onion, finely chopped

1 garlic clove, finely chopped

450g/1lb/2¹/₃ cups risotto rice

125ml/4fl oz/¹/₂ cup dry white wine

1.5ml/¹/₄ tsp saffron threads

1.75 litres/3 pints/7¹/₂ cups simmering chicken stock

50g/1³/₄oz Parma ham, cut into thin strips

25g/1oz/2 tbsp butter, cubed

25g/1oz/ ¹/₃ cup freshly grated Parmesan cheese, plus extra to serve

salt and ground black pepper

flat leaf parsley, to garnish

1 Heat the oil in a large, heavy pan over a moderately high heat. Add the chicken cubes and cook, stirring, until they start to turn white.

2 Reduce the heat to low and add the onion and garlic. Cook, stirring, until the onion is soft. Stir in the rice. Sauté for 1–2 minutes, stirring constantly, until all the rice grains are coated in oil.

3 Add the wine and cook, stirring, until the wine has been absorbed. Stir the saffron into the simmering stock, then add ladlefuls of stock to the rice, allowing each ladleful to be absorbed before adding the next.

4 After 15 minutes, add the Parma ham and continue cooking until the rice is just tender and the risotto creamy.

5 Add the butter and the Parmesan and stir in well. Season with salt and pepper to taste. Serve the risotto hot, garnished with parsley and sprinkled with a little more Parmesan.

Nutritional information per portion: Energy 418kcal/1744kJ; Protein 17.9g; Carbohydrate 60.9g, of which sugars 0.8g; Fat 9.5g, of which saturates 3.8g; Cholesterol 44mg; Calcium 72mg; Fibre 0.1g; Sodium 194mg.

Chicken liver risotto

The combination of chicken livers, bacon, parsley and thyme gives this risotto a wonderfully rich flavour. Serve it as an appetizer for four or a lunch for two or three.

SERVES 2–4

175g/6oz chicken livers
15ml/1 tbsp olive oil
25g/1oz/2 tbsp butter
40g/1¹/₂oz speck or 3 rindless streaky
   (fatty) bacon rashers (strips),
   finely chopped
2 shallots, finely chopped
1 garlic clove, crushed
1 celery stick, finely sliced
275g/9¹/₂oz/1¹/₂ cups risotto rice
175ml/6fl oz/³/₄ cup dry white wine
900ml–1 litre/1¹/₂–1³/₄ pints/
   3³/₄–4 cups simmering chicken stock
5ml/1 tsp chopped fresh thyme
15ml/1 tbsp chopped fresh parsley
salt and ground black pepper
parsley and thyme sprigs, to garnish

1 Clean the chicken livers carefully, removing any fat or membrane. Rinse well, pat dry with kitchen paper and cut into small, even pieces.

2 Heat the oil and butter in a large pan and fry the speck or bacon for 2–3 minutes. Add the shallots, garlic and celery and gently fry for 3–4 minutes until the vegetables are slightly softened. Increase the heat and add the chicken livers, stir-frying for a few minutes until they are brown all over.

3 Add the rice. Cook, stirring, for a few minutes, then pour over the wine. Allow to boil so that the alcohol is cooked off. Stir frequently, taking care not to break up the chicken livers. When all the wine has been absorbed, add the hot stock, a ladleful at a time, stirring constantly.

4 After 10 minutes, add the thyme and season with salt and pepper. Continue to add the stock as before, allowing it to be absorbed each time before adding more. When the risotto is creamy, and the rice tender but firm, stir in the parsley. Taste and adjust the seasoning. Remove from the heat, cover and leave for a few minutes. Serve garnished with parsley and thyme.

Nutritional information per portion: Energy 627kcal/2614kJ; Protein 22g; Carbohydrate 83.7g, of which sugars 1.1g; Fat 17.5g, of which saturates 7.2g; Cholesterol 279mg; Calcium 42mg; Fibre 0.3g; Sodium 306mg.

Lemon grass and coconut rice with green chicken curry

Use one or two fresh green chillies in this dish, according to how hot you like your curry. The mild aromatic flavour of the rice offsets the spiciness of the curry.

SERVES 3–4

4 spring onions (scallions), trimmed and
   roughly chopped
1–2 fresh green chillies, seeded and
   roughly chopped
2cm/³⁄₄in piece of fresh root
   ginger, peeled
2 garlic cloves
5ml/1 tsp Thai fish sauce
large bunch of fresh coriander (cilantro)
small handful of fresh parsley
30–45ml/2–3 tbsp water
30ml/2 tbsp sunflower oil
4 skinless, boneless chicken
   breasts, cubed

1 green (bell) pepper, seeded and
   finely sliced
200ml/7fl oz/scant 1 cup coconut milk
salt and freshly ground black pepper

FOR THE RICE
225g/8oz/generous 1 cup Thai fragrant
   rice, rinsed
7200ml/7fl oz/scant 1 cup water
1 lemon grass stalk, quartered
   and bruised

1 Put the spring onions, chillies, ginger, garlic, fish sauce and fresh herbs in a food processor or blender. Pour in enough water to process to a smooth paste.

2 Heat half the oil in a large frying pan. Fry the chicken cubes until evenly browned. Transfer to a plate.

3 Heat the remaining oil in the pan. Add the sliced green pepper to the pan and stir-fry for about 3–4 minutes, then add the chilli and ginger paste. Continue to fry, stirring, for about 3–4 minutes until the mixture becomes fairly thick.

4 Return the chicken to the pan and add the coconut milk and water. Season with salt and pepper and bring to the boil, then lower the heat. Half-cover the pan and simmer for 8–10 minutes, until the chicken is cooked.

5 Using the slotted spoon, transfer the chicken and the green pepper mixture to a serving plate. Return the cooking liquid remaining in the pan to the heat and boil it for 10–12 minutes until it is well reduced and fairly thick.

6 Meanwhile, put the rice in a large pan. Add the coconut milk, water and bruised pieces of lemon grass. Stir in a little salt, bring to the boil, then lower the heat, cover and simmer very gently for 10 minutes, or for the time recommended on the packet. When the rice is tender, discard the pieces of lemon grass and fork the rice on to a warmed serving plate.

7 Return the chicken and peppers to the green curry sauce, stir well and cook gently for a few minutes to heat through. Spoon the curry over the rice, and serve immediately.

Nutritional information per portion: Energy 682kcal/2843kJ; Protein 43.4g; Carbohydrate 51g, of which sugars 5.9g; Fat 33.6g, of which saturates 23.4g; Cholesterol 105mg; Calcium 59mg; Fibre 1.5g; Sodium 108mg.

Chicken and basil coconut rice

For this dish, the rice is partly boiled so that it absorbs the flavour of the basil and spices.

SERVES 4

350g/12oz/1¾ cups Thai fragrant rice, rinsed
30–45ml/2–3 tbsp groundnut (peanut) oil
1 large onion, finely sliced into rings
1 garlic clove, crushed
1 fresh red chilli, seeded and finely sliced
1 fresh green chilli, seeded and finely sliced
generous handful of basil leaves
3 skinless, boneless chicken breasts, about 350g/12oz, finely sliced
5mm/¼in piece of lemon grass, pounded or finely chopped
150ml/¼ pint/⅔ cup coconut milk
450ml/¾ pint/scant 2 cups water
salt and ground black pepper

1 Boil the rice in lightly salted water for 6 minutes. Drain. Heat the oil in a frying pan and fry the onion rings for 5–10 minutes until crisp. Remove and drain on kitchen paper.

2 Fry the garlic and chillies in the pan for 2–3 minutes. Add the basil leaves, fry briefly until they start to wilt, then lift out a few for the garnish. Add the chicken and lemon grass, fry for 2–3 minutes, then add the rice. Stir-fry for a few minutes, then add the coconut milk and water. Boil for 4–5 minutes, until the rice is tender, adding a little more water if necessary. Season.

3 Pile the rice into a scooped-out coconut shell, sprinkle with fried onion rings and basil leaves, and serve.

Nutritional information per portion: Energy 492kcal/2064kJ; Protein 28.8g; Carbohydrate 83.1g, of which sugars 11.6g; Fat 4.8g, of which saturates 0.9g; Cholesterol 61mg; Calcium 83mg; Fibre 1.1g; Sodium 220mg.

Indonesian pineapple rice chicken

This dish not only looks spectacular, it also tastes so good that it can easily be served solo.

SERVES 4

75g/2¾oz/¾ cup unsalted peanuts, dry-fried in a non-stick frying pan and cooled
1 large pineapple
45ml/3 tbsp groundnut (peanut) or sunflower oil
1 onion, chopped
1 garlic clove, crushed
2 chicken breasts, about 225g/8oz, cut into strips
225g/8oz/generous 1 cup Thai fragrant rice, rinsed
600ml/1 pint/2½ cups chicken stock
1 lemon grass stalk, bruised
2 thick slices of ham, cut into julienne strips
1 fresh red chilli, seeded and very finely sliced
salt

1 Grind one-sixth of the peanuts in a coffee grinder or herb mill and chop the remainder. Halve the pineapple lengthways, then remove the flesh, saving one hollowed-out half for serving. Chop 115g/4oz of the pineapple into cubes, saving the rest for another dish.

2 Heat the oil in a large pan. Fry the onion and garlic for 3–4 minutes. Add the chicken and stir-fry over a medium heat until brown. Add the rice and stir-fry for a few minutes. Add the stock, lemon grass and a little salt. Bring to a simmering point, cover and cook for 10–12 minutes, until the rice and chicken are tender. Stir in the chopped peanuts, pineapple cubes and ham; spoon into the pineapple shell. Top with ground peanuts and sliced chilli and serve.

Nutritional information per portion: Energy 563kcal/2356kJ; Protein 28.9g; Carbohydrate 66.2g, of which sugars 19.8g; Fat 20.5g, of which saturates 2.8g; Cholesterol 56mg; Calcium 62mg; Fibre 3.5g; Sodium 189mg.

Chicken biryani

One of the most popular of all Indian curries, chicken biryani is guaranteed to go down well, whether for a family supper or entertaining guests.

SERVES 4

275g/9¹/₂oz/1¹/₂ cups basmati rice
10 whole green cardamom pods
2.5ml/¹/₂ tsp salt
2–3 whole cloves
5cm/2in cinnamon stick
45ml/3 tbsp vegetable oil
3 onions, sliced
4 chicken breasts, each about 175g/6oz
1.5ml/¹/₄ tsp ground cloves
1.5ml/¹/₄ tsp hot chilli powder
5ml/1 tsp ground cumin
5ml/1 tsp ground coriander
2.5ml/¹/₂ tsp ground black pepper
3 garlic cloves, chopped
5ml/1 tsp chopped fresh root ginger
juice of 1 lemon
4 tomatoes, sliced
30ml/2 tbsp chopped fresh
    coriander (cilantro)
150ml/¹/₄ pint/²/₃ cup natural
    (plain) yogurt
4–5 saffron strands, soaked in 10ml/2 tsp
    hot milk
150ml/¹/₄ pint/²/₃ cup water
toasted flaked (sliced) almonds and fresh
    coriander sprigs, to garnish
natural yogurt, to serve

1 Soak the rice and drain. Preheat the oven to 190°C/375°F/Gas 5.

2 Remove and finely grind the seeds from half the cardamom pods, using a pestle and mortar. Set aside.

3 Bring a pan of water to the boil. Add the rice, salt, whole cardamom pods, cloves and cinnamon stick. Boil for 2 minutes, then drain, leaving the whole spices in the rice.

4 Heat the oil in a frying pan and fry the onions for 8 minutes, until softened and browned. Cut the chicken into cubes then add them to the pan.

5 Add the ground spices, including the ground cardamom seeds. Mix well, then add the garlic, ginger and lemon juice. Stir-fry for 5 minutes.

6 Transfer the mixture to a casserole and arrange the tomatoes on top. Sprinkle on the fresh coriander, spoon the yogurt evenly on top and cover with the drained rice.

7 Drizzle the saffron milk over the rice and pour over the water. Cover tightly and bake for 1 hour. Transfer to a warmed serving platter. Remove the whole spices from the rice. Garnish with the almonds and coriander, and serve with the natural yogurt.

Nutritional information per portion: Energy 562kcal/2354kJ; Protein 45.2g; Carbohydrate 70.3g, of which sugars 12.4g; Fat 11.2g, of which saturates 1.7g; Cholesterol 106mg; Calcium 128mg; Fibre 2.7g; Sodium 380mg.

Chicken and mushroom donburi

"Donburi" means a one-dish meal in a bowl, and takes its name from the eponymous Japanese porcelain food bowl. As in most Japanese dishes, the rice is a plain but integral part of the dish.

SERVES 4

225–275g/8–9¹/₂oz/generous 1–1¹/₂
   cups Japanese rice or Thai fragrant rice
10ml/2 tsp groundnut (peanut) oil
50g/1³/₄oz/4 tbsp butter
2 garlic cloves, crushed
2.5cm/1in piece of fresh root
   ginger, grated
5 spring onions (scallions),
   diagonally sliced
1 fresh green chilli, seeded and finely sliced
3 skinless, boneless chicken breasts,
   cut into thin strips
150g/5¹/₂oz tofu, cut into small cubes
115g/4oz/1³/₄ cups shiitake mushrooms,
   stalks discarded and caps sliced
15ml/1 tbsp Japanese rice wine
30ml/2 tbsp light soy sauce
10ml/2 tsp sugar
400ml/14fl oz/1²/₃ cups chicken stock

1 Cook the rice by the absorption method or by following the instructions on the packet.

2 While the rice is cooking, heat the oil and half the butter in a large frying pan. Stir-fry the garlic, ginger, spring onions and chilli for 1–2 minutes until slightly softened. Add the strips of chicken and fry until all the pieces are evenly browned.

3 Transfer to a plate and add the tofu to the pan. Stir-fry for a few minutes. Add the mushrooms and stir-fry for 2–3 minutes over a medium heat until they are browned.

4 Stir in the rice wine, soy sauce and sugar and cook briskly for 1–2 minutes, stirring all the time. Return the chicken to the pan, toss over the heat for 2 minutes, then pour in the chicken stock. Stir well and cook gently for 5–6 minutes until everything is bubbling nicely.

5 When the rice is cooked, remove from the heat and leave covered for a few minutes. Just before serving, fork through slightly, then spoon the rice into individual serving bowls. Pile the chicken mixture on top, and give each portion a generous amount of chicken sauce.

Nutritional information per portion: Energy 408kcal/1709kJ; Protein 35.2g; Carbohydrate 46.3g, of which sugars 1.1g; Fat 8.8g, of which saturates 1.2g; Cholesterol 79mg; Calcium 216mg; Fibre 0.5g; Sodium 605mg.

Chicken korma with saffron rice

This dish is an old favourite. It is mild and fragrant, and the saffron gives the rice a lovely golden colour that complements the creamy korma beautifully.

SERVES 4

75g/2³/₄oz/³/₄ cup flaked (sliced) almonds
15ml/1 tbsp ghee or butter
about 15ml/1 tbsp sunflower oil
675g/1¹/₂lb skinless, boneless chicken breasts,
    cut into bitesize pieces
1 onion, chopped
4 green cardamom pods
2 garlic cloves, crushed
10ml/2 tsp ground cumin
5ml/1 tsp ground coriander
1 cinnamon stick
good pinch of chilli powder
300ml/¹/₂ pint/1¹/₄ cups canned coconut milk
175ml/6fl oz/³/₄ cup chicken stock

5ml/1 tsp tomato purée (paste) (optional)
75ml/5 tbsp single (light) cream
15–30ml/1–2 tbsp fresh lime or lemon juice
10ml/2 tsp grated lime or lemon rind
5ml/1 tsp garam masala
salt and ground black pepper
poppadums, to serve (optional)

FOR THE SAFFRON RICE
275g/9¹/₂oz/1¹/₂ cups basmati rice, soaked
750ml/1¹/₄ pints/3 cups chicken stock
generous pinch of saffron strands, crushed,
    then soaked in hot water

1 Dry-fry the almonds in a small frying pan until pale golden. Transfer two-thirds to a plate and continue to dry-fry the rest until slightly deeper in colour. Set aside the darker almonds for the garnish. Let the paler almonds cool, then grind in a spice grinder. Heat the ghee or butter and oil in a large frying pan or wok and fry the chicken until evenly brown. Transfer to a plate.

2 Add a little more oil if necessary and fry the onion for 2 minutes. Then add the cardamom and garlic and fry for 3–4 minutes. Stir in the ground almonds, cumin, coriander, cinnamon and chilli powder, and fry for 1 minute. Stir in the coconut milk and chicken stock, and tomato purée, if using. Bring to simmering point, add the chicken and season. Cover and cook gently for 10 minutes until the chicken is tender. Cover and set aside.

3 Drain the rice and put it in a pan. Add the stock, saffron and seasoning. Bring to the boil over a medium heat, cover tightly and cook over a low heat for 10 minutes. Just before the rice is ready, reheat the korma until simmering, and stir in the cream, citrus juice and rind, and garam masala. Season. Pile the rice into a warmed serving dish and spoon the korma into a separate dish. Garnish with the reserved browned almonds. Serve with poppadums, if you like.

Nutritional information per portion: Energy 671kcal/2805kJ; Protein 52.2g; Carbohydrate 62.2g, of which sugars 2.1g; Fat 23.7g, of which saturates 6.1g; Cholesterol 136mg; Calcium 110mg; Fibre 1.6g; Sodium 137mg.

Chicken and vegetable tagine

Moroccan tagines are usually served with couscous, but rice makes an equally delicious accompaniment. Here, couscous is stirred into the rice to create an unusual and tasty dish.

SERVES 4

4 skinless, boneless chicken breasts
30ml/2 tbsp groundnut (peanut) oil
1 large onion, chopped
2 garlic cloves, crushed
1 small parsnip, cut into 2.5cm/1in pieces
1 small turnip, cut into 2cm/³⁄₄in pieces
3 carrots, cut into 4cm/1¹⁄₂in pieces
4 tomatoes, chopped
1 cinnamon stick
4 cloves
5ml/1 tsp ground ginger
1 bay leaf
1.5–2.5ml/¹⁄₄–¹⁄₂ tsp cayenne pepper
1.1 litres/2 pints/4¹⁄₂ cups chicken stock
400g/14oz can chickpeas, drained
225g/8oz/generous 1 cup long grain rice
115g/4oz/²⁄₃ cup couscous
1 red (bell) pepper, seeded and sliced
150g/5¹⁄₂oz green beans, halved
1 piece of preserved lemon peel
20–30 pitted brown or green olives
45ml/3 tbsp chopped fresh
    coriander (cilantro)
salt

1 Cut the chicken into large pieces. Heat half the oil in a large, heavy pan and fry the chicken until evenly browned. Transfer to a plate.

2 Heat the remaining oil and fry the onion, garlic, parsnip, turnip and carrots over a medium heat for 4–5 minutes, stirring frequently. Lower the heat, cover and sweat for 5 minutes, stirring occasionally.

3 Add the tomatoes, cook for a few minutes, then add the cinnamon stick, cloves, ginger, bay leaf and cayenne. Cook for 1–2 minutes.

4 Pour in 350ml/12fl oz/1¹⁄₂ cups of chicken stock, add the chickpeas and chicken pieces, and season with salt. Cover and simmer for 25 minutes.

5 Bring the remaining chicken stock to the boil in another pan. Add the rice and simmer for 5 minutes until almost tender. Remove from the heat, stir in the couscous, cover tightly and leave for 5 minutes.

6 When the vegetables are almost tender, stir in the pepper slices and green beans and simmer for 10 minutes. Thinly peel the preserved lemon and add to the pan with the olives, stir well and cook for 5 minutes more, or until the vegetables are perfectly tender.

7 Stir the chopped coriander into the rice and couscous mixture and pile it on to a plate. Serve the chicken tagine in the traditional dish or in a casserole.

Nutritional information per portion: Energy 450kcal/1891kJ; Protein 46.9g; Carbohydrate 36.2g, of which sugars 16.4g; Fat 14g, of which saturates 2.3g; Cholesterol 105mg; Calcium 131mg; Fibre 10.8g; Sodium 901mg.

Joloff chicken and rice

In West Africa, where it originated, this dish is usually made in large quantities, using jointed whole chickens. This version is somewhat more sophisticated, but retains the traditional flavour.

SERVES 4

2 garlic cloves, crushed
5ml/1 tsp dried thyme
4 skinless, boneless chicken breasts
30ml/2 tbsp palm or vegetable oil
400g/14oz can chopped tomatoes
15ml/1 tbsp tomato purée (paste)
1 onion, chopped
450ml/¾ pint/scant 2 cups
    chicken stock
30ml/2 tbsp dried shrimps or
    crayfish, ground
1 fresh green chilli, seeded and
    finely chopped
350g/12oz/1¾ cups white long grain rice
550ml/18fl oz/2½ cups water
chopped fresh thyme and oregano sprigs,
    to garnish

1 Mix the garlic and thyme in a bowl and rub into the chicken breasts. Heat the oil in a frying pan, brown the chicken, then remove to a plate. Put the tomatoes, tomato purée and onion in the pan and cook over a moderately high heat for 15 minutes until well reduced. Stir occasionally, then more frequently as it thickens.

2 Lower the heat a little, return the chicken pieces to the pan and stir well. Cook for 10 minutes, stirring, then add the stock, dried shrimps and the chilli. Bring to the boil and simmer for 5 minutes or until the chicken is cooked. Stir occasionally.

3 Put the rice in a large pan. Add the water and the chicken sauce. Bring to the boil, lower the heat, cover and cook over a low heat for 12–15 minutes until the rice is tender and the liquid has been absorbed.

4 Pack the rice in four individual moulds and set aside. Lift out the chicken and transfer to a board. If the sauce is runny, cook it over a high heat to reduce it a little. Unmould a rice timbale on each of four serving plates. Spoon the sauce around, slice the chicken breasts and fan them on the sauce. Garnish with the herbs and serve immediately.

Nutritional information per portion: Energy 719kcal/2998kJ; Protein 44.1g; Carbohydrate 76.3g, of which sugars 5.4g; Fat 25.9g, of which saturates 7.4g; Cholesterol 163mg; Calcium 54mg; Fibre 1.3g; Sodium 187mg.

Yogurt chicken and rice cake

This Middle-Eastern speciality is traditionally flavoured with small, dried berries called zereshk, *but is just as delicious with fresh cranberries.*

SERVES 6

40g/1¹/₂oz/3 tbsp butter
1 chicken, about 1.3–1.6kg/3–3¹/₂lb,
    cut into pieces
1 large onion, chopped
250ml/9fl oz/1 cup chicken stock
2 eggs, beaten
475ml/17fl oz/2 cups natural
    (plain) yogurt

2–3 saffron strands, dissolved in 15ml/
    1 tbsp warm water
5ml/1 tsp ground cinnamon
450g/1lb/2¹/₃ cups basmati rice, soaked
1.2 litres/2 pints/5 cups boiling water
75g/2³/₄oz/³/₄ cup *zereshk* or cranberries
50g/1³/₄oz/¹/₂ cup flaked (sliced) almonds
salt and ground black pepper
mixed leaf salad, to serve

1 Melt two-thirds of the butter in a large, heavy pan. Fry the chicken and onion for 4–5 minutes, add the stock and season. Bring to the boil, lower the heat and simmer for 45 minutes, or until the chicken is cooked and the stock has reduced by half. Drain the chicken, reserving the stock. Cut the flesh into large pieces, discarding the skin and bones, and place in a large bowl. In a separate bowl, mix the eggs with the yogurt, saffron water and cinnamon. Season lightly. Add the chicken, stir, cover and leave to marinate for up to 2 hours.

2 Preheat the oven to 160°C/325°F/Gas 3. Grease a large baking dish, about 10cm/4in deep. Drain the rice and put it in a pan. Add the boiling water and a little salt, bring back to the boil, then lower the heat and simmer for 10 minutes. Drain, rinse in warm water and drain once more.

3 Lift the chicken pieces out of the marinade and put them on a plate. Mix half the rice into the marinade and spread on the bottom of the baking dish. Layer the chicken on top, then cover evenly with half the plain rice. If you are using *zereshk*, wash them first and heat them before layering them with the rice. Sprinkle over the *zereshk* or cranberries, then cover with the rest of the rice. Pour over the reserved stock, sprinkle with flaked almonds and dot with the remaining butter. Cover tightly with foil and bake in the oven for 35–45 minutes.

4 Leave the dish to cool for a few minutes, then place it on a cold, damp dish towel to help lift the rice from the bottom of the dish. Run a knife around the inside rim, invert a large plate over the dish and turn out the rice "cake". Cut into six wedges and serve hot, with a mixed leaf salad.

Nutritional information per portion: Energy 682kcal/2843kJ; Protein 43.4g; Carbohydrate 69g, of which sugars 8.2g; Fat 25.7g, of which saturates 10.2g; Cholesterol 220mg; Calcium 198mg; Fibre 0.6g; Sodium 250mg.

Caribbean chicken with pigeon pea rice

Spicy caramelized chicken tops a rich vegetable rice in this delicious supper dish. Pigeon peas are a common ingredient in Caribbean cooking, but if unavailable you can use borlotti beans instead.

SERVES 4

5ml/1 tsp allspice
2.5ml/1/2 tsp ground cinnamon
5ml/1 tsp dried thyme
pinch of ground cloves
1.5ml/1/4 tsp freshly grated nutmeg
4 skinless, boneless chicken breasts
45ml/3 tbsp groundnut (peanut) or
   sunflower oil
15g/1/2oz/1 tbsp butter
1 onion, chopped
2 garlic cloves, crushed
1 carrot, diced
1 celery stick, chopped
3 spring onions (scallions), chopped
1 fresh red chilli, seeded and thinly sliced
400g/14oz can pigeon peas, drained
225g/8oz/generous 1 cup long grain rice
125ml/4fl oz/1/2 cup coconut milk
550ml/19fl oz/21/2 cups chicken stock
30ml/2 tbsp demerara (raw) sugar
salt and cayenne pepper

1 Mix together the allspice, cinnamon, thyme, cloves and nutmeg. Rub the mixture all over the pieces of chicken. Set aside for 30 minutes.

2 Heat 15ml/1 tbsp of the oil with the butter in a large pan. Fry the onion and garlic over a medium heat until soft and beginning to brown. Add the carrot, celery, spring onions and chilli. Sauté for a few minutes, then stir in the pigeon peas, rice, coconut milk and chicken stock. Season with salt and cayenne pepper. Bring to simmering point, cover and cook over a low heat for about 25 minutes.

3 About 10 minutes before the rice mixture is cooked, heat the remaining oil in a heavy frying pan, add the sugar and cook, without stirring, until it begins to caramelize.

4 Carefully add the chicken to the pan. Cook for 8–10 minutes until the chicken has a browned, glazed appearance and is cooked through. Transfer the chicken to a board and slice it thickly. Serve the pigeon pea rice in individual bowls, with the chicken on top.

Nutritional information per portion: Energy 507kcal/2132kJ; Protein 36.8g; Carbohydrate 76.9g, of which sugars 14.7g; Fat 6.4g, of which saturates 2.6g; Cholesterol 78mg; Calcium 128mg; Fibre 6.9g; Sodium 522mg.

Caribbean peanut and rice chicken

Peanut butter is used in many Caribbean dishes. It adds a rich texture, as well as a delicious depth of flavour all of its own.

SERVES 4

4 skinless, boneless chicken breasts,
    cut into thin strips
225g/8oz/generous 1 cup white long
    grain rice
30ml/2 tbsp groundnut (peanut) oil
15g/¹/₂oz/1 tbsp butter, plus extra
    for greasing
1 onion, finely chopped
2 tomatoes, peeled, seeded and chopped
1 fresh green chilli, seeded and sliced
60ml/4 tbsp smooth peanut butter
450ml/³/₄ pint/scant 2 cups chicken stock
lemon juice, to taste
salt and ground black pepper
lime wedges and flat leaf parsley, to garnish

FOR THE MARINADE

15ml/1 tbsp sunflower oil
1–2 garlic cloves, crushed
5ml/1 tsp chopped fresh thyme
25ml/1¹/₂ tbsp medium curry powder
juice of half a lemon

1 Mix all the marinade ingredients in a bowl and stir in the chicken. Cover with clear film (plastic wrap) and leave in a cool place for 2–3 hours. Cook the rice in lightly salted boiling water until tender. Drain and turn into a buttered casserole.

2 Preheat the oven to 180°C/350°F/Gas 4. Heat 15ml/1 tbsp of the oil and the butter in a large, heavy pan and fry the chicken for 4–5 minutes until evenly brown. Add more oil if necessary. Transfer to a plate.

3 Add the onion to the pan and fry for 5–6 minutes until lightly browned, adding more oil if necessary. Stir in the tomatoes and chilli. Cook gently for 3–4 minutes, stirring occasionally. Remove from the heat.

4 Mix the peanut butter with the chicken stock. Stir into the tomato and onion mixture, then add the chicken. Stir in the lemon juice, season to taste, then spoon the mixture over the rice in the casserole.

5 Cover the casserole. Cook in the oven for 15–20 minutes or until piping hot. Use a large spoon to toss the rice with the chicken mixture. Serve at once, garnished with the lime wedges and parsley.

Nutritional information per portion: Energy 606kcal/2532kJ; Protein 46.4g; Carbohydrate 52.6g, of which sugars 5.3g; Fat 23.2g, of which saturates 6.6g; Cholesterol 113mg; Calcium 41mg; Fibre 2.3g; Sodium 202mg.

Chicken fajitas and wild rice

Fajitas are warmed soft tortillas, filled and folded like an envelope. They're always popular, and you can ring the changes by using brown rice or red Camargue rice.

SERVES 4

115g/4oz/generous ½ cup white
   long grain rice
15g/1oz/3 tbsp wild rice
15ml/1 tbsp olive oil
15ml/1 tbsp sunflower oil
1 onion, cut into thin wedges
4 skinless, boneless chicken breasts,
   cut into thin strips
1 red (bell) pepper, seeded and finely sliced
5ml/1 tsp ground cumin
generous pinch of cayenne pepper
2.5ml/½ tsp ground turmeric
175ml/6fl oz/¾ cup passata (bottled
   strained tomatoes)
125–175ml/4–6fl oz/½–¾ cup
   chicken stock
12 small or 8 large wheat tortillas
sour cream, to serve

FOR THE SALSA
1 shallot
1 small garlic clove
½–1 fresh green chilli, seeded
small bunch of fresh parsley
5 tomatoes, peeled, seeded and chopped
10ml/2 tsp olive oil
15ml/1 tbsp lemon juice
30ml/2 tbsp tomato juice
salt and ground black pepper

FOR THE GUACAMOLE
1 large ripe avocado
2 spring onions (scallions), chopped
15–30ml/1–2 tbsp lime or lemon juice
generous pinch of cayenne pepper
15ml/1 tbsp chopped fresh
   coriander (cilantro)

1 Cook the long-grain and wild rice separately, following the packet instructions. Drain and set aside.

2 Salsa: Finely chop the shallot, garlic, chilli and parsley in a food processor. Spoon into a bowl. Stir in the chopped tomatoes, olive oil, lemon juice and tomato juice. Season, cover with clear film (plastic wrap) and chill.

3 Guacamole: Scoop the avocado flesh into a bowl. Mash it lightly with the spring onions, citrus juice, cayenne, coriander and seasoning, so that small pieces still remain. Cover the surface closely with clear film and chill.

4 Preheat the oven to 180°/350°F/Gas 4. Heat the olive and sunflower oils in a frying pan and fry the onion wedges for 4–5 minutes until softened. Add the chicken strips and red pepper slices and fry until evenly browned. Stir in the cumin, cayenne and turmeric. Fry, stirring, for 1 minute, then stir in the passata and chicken stock. Bring to the boil, lower the heat and simmer gently for 5–6 minutes until the chicken is cooked through. Season to taste.

5 Stir the long grain rice and wild rice into the chicken mixture and cook for 1–2 minutes until the rice is warmed through.

6 To warm the tortillas, either wrap them in foil and place them in the preheated oven for 5 minutes, or wrap 4 or 5 at a time in microwave film and microwave for 20 seconds on 100% full power. When you have warmed the tortillas, spoon a little of the chicken and rice mixture on to each tortilla, top with salsa, guacamole and sour cream, and roll up. Alternatively, let everyone assemble their own fajita at the table.

Nutritional information per portion: Energy 398kcal/1670kJ; Protein 23g; Carbohydrate 44.3g, of which sugars 11.8g; Fat 15.5g, of which saturates 4.4g; Cholesterol 60mg; Calcium 76mg; Fibre 2.9g; Sodium 51mg.

Peruvian duck with rice

This is a very rich dish, brightly coloured with tomatoes and fresh herbs. The fresh ginger gives a wonderful, warm flavour and makes a delicious combination with the garlic.

SERVES 4–6

4 boned duck breasts
1 large onion, chopped
2 garlic cloves, crushed
10ml/2 tsp grated fresh root ginger
4 tomatoes (peeled, if desired), chopped
225g/8oz kabocha or onion squash,
    cut into 1cm/1/2in cubes

275g/91/2oz/11/2 cups long grain rice
750ml/11/4 pints/3 cups chicken stock
15ml/1 tbsp finely chopped fresh
    coriander (cilantro)
15ml/1 tbsp finely chopped fresh mint
salt and ground black pepper

1 Heat a large, heavy pan over a medium heat. Using a sharp knife, score the fatty side of the duck breasts in a criss-cross pattern, rub the fat with a little salt, then dry-fry the duck, skin side down, for 6–8 minutes to render some of the fat.

2 Pour all but 15ml/1 tbsp of the fat into a jar or cup, then fry the breasts, meat side down, in the fat remaining in the pan for 3–4 minutes until brown all over. Transfer to a board, slice thickly and set aside in a shallow dish. Deglaze the pan with a little water and pour this liquid over the duck.

3 Fry the onion and garlic in the same pan for 4–5 minutes until the onion is fairly soft, adding a little extra duck fat if necessary. Stir in the ginger, cook for 1–2 minutes more, then add the tomatoes and cook, stirring, for another 2 minutes.

4 Add the squash, stir-fry for a few minutes, then cover and allow to steam for about 4 minutes.

5 Stir in the rice and cook, stirring, until the rice is coated in the tomato and onion mixture. Pour in the stock, return the slices of duck to the pan and season with salt and pepper.

6 Bring to the boil, then lower the heat, cover and simmer gently for 30–35 minutes until the rice is tender. Stir in the coriander and mint and serve.

Nutritional information per portion: Energy 754kcal/3130kJ; Protein 22.5g; Carbohydrate 58.6g, of which sugars 3.3g; Fat 54.1g, of which saturates 13.5g; Cholesterol 90mg; Calcium 53mg; Fibre 1.3g; Sodium 99mg.

Meat

For many, a risotto or rice dish is not

complete without the satisfying textures

of meats such as juicy beef, lamb, rabbit,

pork, bacon, pancetta and ham. Served with

tasty, nutritious vegetables or fresh salad,

these recipes, with their rich flavours and

appetizing aromas of Thailand, Indonesia,

Turkey, India and Africa, won't disappoint.

Leek and ham risotto

This simple risotto makes an easy supper, yet it is also special enough to serve to your guests.

SERVES 3–4

7.5ml/1½ tsp olive oil
40g/1½oz/3 tbsp butter
2 leeks, sliced
175g/6oz Parma ham, torn into pieces
75g/2¾oz/generous 1 cup button (white) mushrooms, sliced
275g/9½oz/1½ cups risotto rice
1 litre/1¾ pints/4 cups simmering chicken stock
45ml/3 tbsp chopped fresh flat leaf parsley
40g/1½oz/½ cup freshly grated Parmesan cheese
salt and ground black pepper

1 Heat the oil and butter in a large, heavy pan and fry the leeks until soft. Set aside a few strips of Parma ham for garnish and add the rest to the pan. Fry for 1 minute, add the mushrooms and stir-fry for 2–3 minutes until lightly browned.

2 Add the rice. Cook, stirring, for 1–2 minutes until the grains are translucent around the edges. Add a ladleful of hot stock. Stir until this has been fully absorbed, then add the next ladleful. Continue in this way until all the stock has been absorbed.

3 When the risotto is creamy and the rice is tender but still firm to the bite, stir in the parsley and Parmesan. Adjust the seasoning, remove from the heat and cover. Allow to rest for a few minutes. Spoon into a bowl, garnish with the reserved Parma ham and serve.

Nutritional information per portion: Energy 444kcal/1853kJ; Protein 18.9g; Carbohydrate 58g, of which sugars 2.5g; Fat 14.8g, of which saturates 8g; Cholesterol 57mg; Calcium 160mg; Fibre 2.1g; Sodium 697mg.

Rabbit and lemon grass risotto

Lemon grass adds a nice tang to this risotto. If rabbit isn't available, use chicken or turkey.

SERVES 3–4

50g/1¾oz/¼ cup butter
15ml/1 tbsp olive oil
225g/8oz rabbit meat, cut into strips and
    dusted with seasoned flour
45ml/3 tbsp dry sherry
1 onion, finely chopped
1 garlic clove, crushed
1 lemon grass stalk, peeled and very finely sliced
275g/9½oz/1½ cups risotto rice, preferably carnaroli
1 litre/1¾ pints/4 cups simmering chicken stock
10ml/2 tsp chopped fresh thyme
45ml/3 tbsp double (heavy) cream
25g/1oz/⅓ cup freshly grated Parmesan cheese
salt and ground black pepper

1 Heat half the butter and olive oil in a frying pan. Fry the rabbit until brown. Add the sherry, boil briefly, season and set aside. Heat the remaining oil and butter in a large pan. Fry the onion and garlic over a low heat for 4–5 minutes. Add the lemon grass and cook for 4 minutes.

2 Stir in the rice. Add a ladleful of stock and cook, stirring, until absorbed. Continue adding stock gradually, stirring constantly. After 15 minutes, stir in three-quarters of the rabbit and the pan juices. Add the thyme and season. Cook until the rice is tender but still firm to the bite. Stir in the cream and Parmesan, remove from the heat, cover and leave to rest. Serve garnished with rabbit strips.

Nutritional information per portion: Energy 537kcal/2233kJ; Protein 20.3g; Carbohydrate 56.5g, of which sugars 1.3g; Fat 23.7g, of which saturates 12.9g; Cholesterol 88mg; Calcium 113mg; Fibre 0.2g; Sodium 186mg.

Loin of pork with cashew and orange stuffing

The oranges and cashew nuts add contrasting flavours and textures to this stuffing, and combine well with the brown rice. Don't worry if the stuffing doesn't bind – the best thing about brown rice is that it retains its texture.

SERVES 6

1.3–1.6kg/3–3¹/₂lb boned loin of pork
15ml/1 tbsp plain (all-purpose) flour
300ml/¹/₂ pint/1¹/₄ cups dry white wine
salt and ground black pepper
fresh rosemary sprigs and orange slices,
   to garnish

FOR THE STUFFING
25g/1oz/2 tbsp butter
1 small onion, finely chopped

75g/2³/₄oz/scant ¹/₂ cup brown basmati
   rice, soaked and drained
350ml/12fl oz/scant 1¹/₂ cups
   chicken stock
50g/1³/₄oz/¹/₂ cup cashew nuts
1 orange
50g/1³/₄oz/¹/₃ cup sultanas
   (golden raisins)

1 First, make the rice for the stuffing. Melt the butter in a large pan and fry the chopped onion for 2–3 minutes until softened but not browned. Add the rice and cook for 1 minute, then pour in the chicken stock and bring to the boil. Stir, then lower the heat, cover and simmer for 35 minutes until the rice is tender and the liquid has been absorbed. Preheat the oven to 220°C/425°F/Gas 7.

2 While the rice is cooking, open out the loin of pork and cut two lengthways slits through the meat, making sure not to cut right through. Turn the meat over. Remove any excess fat, but leave a good layer of it; this will keep the meat moist during cooking.

3 Spread out the cashew nuts for the stuffing on a baking sheet and roast for 2–4 minutes until golden. Allow to cool, then chop roughly in a food processor or blender. Leave the oven on.

4 Grate 5ml/1 tsp of the orange rind into a bowl, then peel the orange. Working over a bowl to catch the juice, cut the orange into segments. Chop them roughly.

5 Add the chopped orange segments to the cooked rice with the orange rind, roast cashew nuts and the sultanas. Season well, then stir in 15–30ml/1–2 tbsp of the reserved orange juice. Don't worry if the rice doesn't bind – it should have a fairly loose consistency.

6 Spread a generous layer of stuffing along the centre of the pork. If you have any stuffing left over, put it in an ovenproof bowl and set aside.

7 Roll up the loin and tie securely with kitchen string. Rub a little salt and pepper into the surface of the meat and place it in a roasting pan. Roast for 15 minutes, then lower the oven temperature to 180°C/350°F/Gas 4. Roast for 2–2¼ hours more or until the meat juices run clear and without any sign of pinkness when tested with a skewer. Heat any extra stuffing in the covered bowl alongside the meat for the final 15 minutes.

8 Transfer the meat to a warmed serving plate and keep warm. Stir the flour into the meat juices remaining in the roasting tin, cook for 1 minute, then stir in the white wine. Bring to the boil, stirring until thickened, then strain into a gravy boat.

9 Remove the string from the meat before carving. Stud the pork with the rosemary and garnish with the orange slices. Serve with the gravy and any extra stuffing.

Nutritional information per portion: Energy 638kcal/2675kJ; Protein 81.9g; Carbohydrate 19.8g, of which sugars 8.5g; Fat 25.8g, of which saturates 8.8g; Cholesterol 224mg; Calcium 37mg; Fibre 0.9g; Sodium 201mg.

Risotto with smoked bacon and tomato

This classic risotto, with plenty of onions, smoked bacon and sun-dried tomatoes, is enriched with white wine and Parmesan cheese. You'll want to keep going back for more.

SERVES 4–6

8 sun-dried tomatoes in olive oil
275g/9¹/₂oz rindless smoked lean back bacon
75g/2³/₄oz/6 tbsp butter
450g/1lb onions, roughly chopped
2 garlic cloves, crushed
350g/12oz/1³/₄ cups risotto rice
300ml/¹/₂ pint/1¹/₄ cups dry white wine
1 litre/1³/₄ pints/4 cups simmering vegetable stock
50g/1³/₄oz/²/₃ cup freshly grated Parmesan cheese
45ml/3 tbsp mixed chopped fresh chives and flat leaf parsley
salt and ground black pepper

1 Drain the sun-dried tomatoes and reserve 15ml/1 tbsp of the oil. Roughly chop the tomatoes and set aside. Cut the bacon into 2.5cm/1in pieces. Heat the oil from the sun-dried tomatoes in a large frying pan. Fry the bacon until cooked and golden. Remove with a slotted spoon and drain on kitchen paper.

2 Heat 25g/1oz/2 tbsp of the butter in a large, heavy pan and fry the onions and garlic over a medium heat for 10 minutes, until soft and golden brown. Stir in the rice. Cook for 1 minute, stirring until the grains turn translucent.

3 Stir the wine into the stock. Add a ladleful of the mixture to the rice and cook gently, stirring constantly, until the liquid has been absorbed. Stir in another ladleful and allow it to be absorbed. Repeat this process until all the liquid has been used up. This should take 25–30 minutes. The risotto will turn thick and creamy, and the rice should be tender but not sticky.

4 Just before serving, stir in the bacon, sun-dried tomatoes, Parmesan, half the herbs and the remaining butter. Adjust the seasoning (remember that the bacon may be quite salty) and serve sprinkled with the remaining herbs.

Nutritional information per portion: Energy 513kcal/2133kJ; Protein 16.9g; Carbohydrate 55.1g, of which sugars 6.8g; Fat 21.3g, of which saturates 11.1g; Cholesterol 59mg; Calcium 159mg; Fibre 2.1g; Sodium 885mg.

Pancetta and broad bean risotto

This delicious risotto makes a healthy and filling meal, served with cooked, fresh seasonal vegetables or a mixed green salad.

SERVES 4

15ml/1 tbsp olive oil
1 onion, chopped
2 garlic cloves, finely chopped
175g/6oz smoked pancetta, diced
350g/12oz/1¾ cups risotto rice
1.5 litres/2½ pints/6¼ cups simmering
  chicken stock
225g/8oz/2 cups frozen baby broad
  (fava) beans
30ml/2 tbsp chopped fresh mixed herbs,
  such as parsley, thyme and oregano
salt and freshly ground black pepper
shavings of Parmesan cheese, to serve

1 Heat the oil in a large, heavy pan. Add the onion, garlic and pancetta and cook gently for about 5 minutes, stirring occasionally. Do not allow the onion and garlic to brown.

2 Add the rice to the pan and cook for 1 minute, stirring. Add a ladleful of stock and cook, stirring all the time, until the liquid has been absorbed.

3 Continue adding the stock, a ladleful at a time, until the rice is tender, and almost all the liquid has been absorbed. This will take 30–35 minutes.

4 Meanwhile, cook the broad beans in a pan of lightly salted, boiling water for about 3 minutes until tender. Drain well and stir into the risotto, with the mixed herbs. Add salt and pepper to taste. Spoon into a bowl and serve, sprinkled with shavings of Parmesan cheese.

Nutritional information per portion: Energy 444kcal/1858kJ; Protein 16.2g; Carbohydrate 77.9g, of which sugars 1.8g; Fat 7.2g, of which saturates 2.1g; Cholesterol 15mg; Calcium 76mg; Fibre 4.4g; Sodium 452mg.

Beef in pastry with wild mushrooms and rice

A tasty layer of rice and juicy wild mushrooms tops each fillet steak before it is wrapped in puff pastry. This cooks to crisp and flaky perfection, the perfect foil for the filling.

SERVES 4

20g/³⁄₄oz/¹⁄₄ cup dried wild mushrooms, soaked for 10 minutes in warm water to cover

115g/4oz/1¹⁄₂–1³⁄₄ cups morel mushrooms

45ml/3 tbsp olive oil

4 shallots, finely chopped

1 garlic clove, crushed

20g/³⁄₄oz/1¹⁄₂ tbsp butter

175g/6oz/1¹⁄₂ cups cooked white long grain rice

10ml/2 tsp chopped fresh marjoram

15ml/1 tbsp finely chopped fresh parsley

275g/9¹⁄₂oz puff pastry, thawed if frozen

4 fillet steaks, each about 90g/3¹⁄₄oz and 2.5cm/1in thick

10ml/2 tsp Dijon mustard

1 egg, beaten with 15ml/1 tbsp water

salt and ground black pepper

roast potatoes and patty pan squash, to serve (optional)

1 Preheat the oven to 220°C/425°F/Gas 7. Drain the dried mushrooms, reserving the soaking liquid, and chop them finely. Trim the morel mushrooms and chop them. Heat 15ml/1 tbsp of the olive oil in a frying pan and fry the chopped shallots and crushed garlic for 2–3 minutes until soft, stirring occasionally. Add the butter to the pan. When it begins to foam, add the mushrooms and then cook for 3–4 minutes more, stirring occasionally. Put the cooked rice into a bowl and stir in the herbs.

2 Scrape the mushroom mixture into the rice and mix well. Season to taste. Cut the pastry into four and roll out each piece into an 18cm/7in circle. Trim the top and bottom edges.

3 Heat the remaining olive oil in the pan and fry the steaks for about 30 seconds on each side until browned. Spread a little mustard over each steak, then place on one side of a piece of pastry. Spoon a quarter of the mushroom and rice mixture on top of each steak.

4 Fold the pastry over to make a pasty, sealing the join with a little of the egg wash. Repeat to make four pasties, then place them on an oiled baking sheet. Slit the top of each pasty, decorate with the pastry trimmings, and glaze with more egg wash. Bake in the oven for about 15 minutes, until the pastry is golden. Serve with roast potatoes and patty pan squash, if you like.

Nutritional information per portion: Energy 576kcal/2401kJ; Protein 26.3g; Carbohydrate 50.2g, of which sugars 2.2g; Fat 31.2g, of which saturates 3.8g; Cholesterol 55mg; Calcium 72mg; Fibre 1g; Sodium 331mg.

Thai crispy rice noodles with beef

Rice vermicelli are very fine, dry, white noodles bundled in large fragile loops and sold in packets.
Before being added to the dish, they are deep-fried and expand to four times their original size.

SERVES 4

450g/1lb rump (round) or sirloin steak
    (beat out the steak, if necessary,
    to about 2.5cm/1in thick)
teriyaki sauce, for brushing
175g/6oz rice vermicelli
groundnut (peanut) oil, for deep-frying and
    stir-frying
8 spring onions (scallions), sliced diagonally
2 garlic cloves, crushed
4–5 carrots, cut into julienne strips
1–2 fresh red chillies, seeded and
    finely sliced
2 small courgettes (zucchini),
    sliced diagonally
5ml/1 tsp grated fresh root ginger
60ml/4 tbsp white or yellow rice vinegar
90ml/6 tbsp light soy sauce
about 475ml/17fl oz/2 cups spicy stock

1 Brush the steak with teriyaki sauce and marinate in a dish for 2–4 hours.

2 Separate the vermicelli into loops. Spread several layers of kitchen paper on a very large plate. Pour 5cm/2in of oil in a large pan or wok, and heat until a vermicelli loop cooks as soon as it is put in the oil.

3 Add a loop of vermicelli to the oil. It should instantly expand and turn opaque. Turn the noodles over to cook on both sides, then transfer to the plate. Repeat until all the noodles are cooked. Transfer to a separate wok or deep serving bowl and keep warm.

4 In a clean pan or wok, heat 15ml/1 tbsp of fresh oil until it sizzles. Fry the steak for 30 seconds on each side. Transfer to a board and cut into thick slices.

5 Add extra oil to the pan. Stir-fry the spring onions, garlic and carrots over a medium heat for 5–6 minutes. Add the chillies, courgettes and ginger and stir-fry for 1–2 minutes. Add the rice vinegar, soy sauce and stock. Boil for 4 minutes, until the sauce thickens. Add the steak and cook for 1–2 minutes, or longer if you like it well done. Toss the steak mixture with the noodles and serve at once.

Nutritional information per portion: Energy 410kcal/1712kJ; Protein 30.7g; Carbohydrate 41.4g, of which sugars 6.6g; Fat 13.5g, of which saturates 3g; Cholesterol 66mg; Calcium 49mg; Fibre 1.9g; Sodium 1687mg.

Nasi goreng

One of the most popular and best-known Indonesian dishes, this is a marvellous way to use up leftover rice, chicken and meats such as pork.

SERVES 4–6

350g/12oz/1¾ cups basmati rice
(dry weight), cooked and cooled
2 eggs
30ml/2 tbsp water
105ml/7 tbsp sunflower oil
225g/8oz pork fillet or fillet of beef
2–3 fresh red chillies
10ml/2 tsp Thai fish paste (or you can use
blachan – a shrimp paste sold in Asian
shops – if preferred)
2 garlic cloves, crushed
1 onion, sliced
115g/4oz cooked, peeled prawns (shrimp)
225g/8oz cooked chicken, chopped
30ml/2 tbsp dark soy sauce
salt and ground black pepper
deep-fried onions, to garnish

1 Separate the grains of the cold, cooked rice with a fork. Cover and set aside until needed.

2 Beat the eggs with the water and a little seasoning. Heat 15ml/1 tbsp of the oil in a frying pan, pour in half the egg mixture and cook until set. Don't stir. Roll up the omelette, slide it on to a plate, cut into strips and set aside. Make another in the same way.

3 Cut the pork or beef fillet into neat strips. Finely shred one of the chillies and set aside. In a food processor, process the Thai fish paste, the remaining chilli, the garlic and onion to a paste.

4 Heat the remaining oil in a wok. Fry the paste, without browning, until it gives off a spicy aroma.

5 Add the strips of pork or beef and toss the meat over the heat, to seal in the juices. Cook the meat in the wok for 2 minutes, stirring constantly.

6 Add the peeled prawns, cook for about 2 minutes, then add the chopped chicken, rice, soy sauce, salt and pepper to taste, stirring constantly, until heated through.

7 Serve in individual bowls topped with the omelette strips, shredded chilli and deep-fried onions.

Nutritional information per portion: Energy 463kcal/1929kJ; Protein 27.3g; Carbohydrate 49.4g, of which sugars 2.1g; Fat 17.1g, of which saturates 2.7g; Cholesterol 151mg; Calcium 49mg; Fibre 0.5g; Sodium 288mg.

Beef biryani

The Moguls introduced this dry, spicy rice dish to central India. The succulent cubes of steak are cooked with a wonderful combination of yogurt, herbs and spices. It is a satisfying meal in itself.

SERVES 4

2 large onions
1/2–1 fresh green chilli, seeded
2 garlic cloves, chopped
2.5cm/1in piece of fresh root ginger,
    peeled and roughly chopped
small bunch of fresh coriander (cilantro)
60ml/4 tbsp flaked (sliced) almonds
30–45ml/2–3 tbsp water
15ml/1 tbsp ghee or butter, plus
    25g/1oz/2 tbsp butter, for the rice
45ml/3 tbsp sunflower oil
30ml/2 tbsp sultanas (golden raisins)
500g/1lb 2oz braising or stewing steak

5ml/1 tsp ground coriander
15ml/1 tbsp ground cumin
2.5ml/1/2 tsp ground turmeric
2.5ml/1/2 tsp ground fenugreek
good pinch of ground cinnamon
175ml/6fl oz/3/4 cup natural
    (plain) yogurt
275g/91/2oz/11/2 cups basmati rice
about 1.2 litres/2 pints/5 cups hot
    chicken stock or water
salt and ground black pepper
2 hard-boiled eggs, quartered, to garnish
Indian bread, to serve (optional)

1 Chop one of the onions and the chilli, put in a food processor with the garlic, ginger, coriander, half the flaked almonds and the water, and process to a smooth paste.

2 Finely cut the remaining onion into rings or half rings. Heat half the ghee or butter with half the oil in a flameproof casserole. Fry the onion over a medium heat for 10–15 minutes until deep golden brown. Transfer to a plate. Fry the remaining flaked almonds briefly until golden and set aside with the onion rings. Quickly fry the sultanas until they swell. Transfer to the plate.

3 Cut the steak into cubes. Heat the remaining ghee or butter in the casserole with 15ml/1 tbsp oil. Fry the meat, in batches, until evenly brown, transfer to a plate and set aside. Clean the casserole with kitchen paper, heat the remaining oil and cook the onion and ginger paste over a medium heat for 2–3 minutes, stirring, until beginning to brown. Add the spices, season and cook for 1 minute.

4 Lower the heat. Gradually stir in the yogurt. When it has all been incorporated, return the meat to the casserole. Stir to coat, cover tightly and simmer over a gentle heat for 40–45 minutes until the meat is tender. Meanwhile, soak the rice in a bowl of cold water for 15–20 minutes.

5 Preheat the oven to 160°C/325°F/Gas 3. Drain the rice, place in a pan and add the hot chicken stock or water, together with a little salt. Bring back to the boil, cover and cook for 5–6 minutes.

6 Drain the rice, and pile it in a mound on top of the meat in the casserole. With a spoon handle, make a hole through the rice and meat mixture, to the bottom of the pan. Spread the fried onions, almonds and sultanas over the top and dot with the butter. Cover the casserole tightly with a double layer of foil and secure with a lid.

7 Cook the biryani in the oven for 30–40 minutes, until the rice is tender, then spoon on to a warmed serving plate and garnish with the quartered hard-boiled eggs. Serve with Indian bread, if you like.

Nutritional information per portion: Energy 778kcal/3240kJ; Protein 40g; Carbohydrate 70.4g, of which sugars 13.4g; Fat 37.4g, of which saturates 11.8g; Cholesterol 94mg; Calcium 164mg; Fibre 2.3g; Sodium 183mg.

Savoury rice with Madras curry

In this dish, bitesize cubes of stewing beef simmer gently with spices until they are tender enough to melt in the mouth. They are served with basmati rice, cooked until light and fluffy.

SERVES 4

225g/8oz/generous 1 cup basmati rice

15ml/1 tbsp sunflower oil

30ml/2 tbsp ghee or butter

1 onion, finely chopped

1 garlic clove, crushed

5ml/1 tsp ground cumin

2.5ml/1/2 tsp ground coriander

4 green cardamom pods

1 cinnamon stick

1 small red (bell) pepper, seeded, diced

1 small green (bell) pepper, seeded, diced

300ml/1/2 pint/1 1/4 cups chicken stock

salt and ground black pepper

mango chutney, to serve (optional)

FOR THE CURRY

30ml/2 tbsp vegetable oil

30ml/2 tbsp ghee or butter

675g/1 1/2lb stewing beef, in bitesize cubes

1 onion, chopped

3 green cardamom pods

2 fresh green chillies, seeded and
    finely chopped

2.5cm/1in piece of fresh root ginger, grated

2 garlic cloves, crushed

15ml/1 tbsp Madras curry paste

5ml/1 tsp ground cumin

5ml/1 tsp ground coriander

150ml/1/4 pint/2/3 cup beef stock

1 To make the curry, heat half the oil and ghee or butter in a frying pan and fry the beef, in batches if necessary, until browned on all sides. Transfer to a plate and set aside. Heat the remaining oil and ghee and fry the onion for 3–4 minutes until softened. Add the cardamom pods and fry for 1 minute, then add the chillies, ginger and garlic and fry for 2 minutes more. Stir in the curry paste, ground cumin and coriander, then add the meat and stock. Season with salt, bring to the boil, then lower the heat and simmer very gently for 1–1 1/2 hours, until the meat is tender.

2 When the curry is almost ready, put the rice in a bowl and cover with boiling water. Set aside for 10 minutes, drain, rinse under cold water and drain again. Heat the oil and ghee or butter in a large, heavy pan and fry the onion and garlic gently for 3–4 minutes until softened and lightly browned. Stir in the ground cumin and coriander, cardamom pods and cinnamon stick. Fry for 1 minute, then add the diced peppers.

3 Add the rice, stirring to coat the grains in the mixture, and pour in the stock. Bring to the boil, then lower the heat, cover the pan tightly and simmer for 8–10 minutes, or until the rice is tender and the stock has been absorbed. Spoon into a bowl. Serve with the curry, and mango chutney, if you like.

Nutritional information per portion: Energy 738kcal/3070kJ; Protein 44.3g; Carbohydrate 56.5g, of which sugars 9.6g; Fat 37.1g, of which saturates 15.3g; Cholesterol 130mg; Calcium 48mg; Fibre 2.5g; Sodium 205mg.

Lamb Parsi

This is similar to biryani, but here the lamb is marinated with the yogurt, a technique that is a Parsi speciality. Serve with a dhal or spiced mushrooms.

SERVES 6

900g/2lb lamb fillet, cut into
    2.5cm/1in cubes
60ml/4 tbsp ghee or butter
2 onions, sliced
450g/1lb potatoes, cut into large chunks
chicken stock (see method)
450g/1lb/2¹/₃ cups basmati rice, soaked
generous pinch of saffron strands,
    dissolved in 30ml/2 tbsp warm milk
fresh coriander (cilantro) sprigs,
    to garnish

FOR THE MARINADE

475ml/17fl oz/2 cups natural
    (plain) yogurt
3–4 garlic cloves, crushed
10ml/2 tsp cayenne pepper
20ml/4 tsp garam masala
10ml/2 tsp ground cumin
5ml/1 tsp ground coriander

1 Mix all the marinade ingredients in a large bowl. Add the meat, stir to coat, cover and leave to marinate for 3–4 hours in a cool place or overnight in the refrigerator.

2 Melt 30ml/2 tbsp of the ghee or butter in a large, heavy pan and fry the onions for 6–8 minutes until lightly golden. Transfer to a plate.

3 Melt a further 25ml/1¹/₂ tbsp of the ghee or butter in the pan. Fry the marinated lamb cubes in batches until evenly brown. Transfer them to a plate. When all the lamb has been browned, return it to the pan and scrape in the remaining marinade.

4 Add three-quarters of the onions and the potatoes. Cover with stock. Bring to the boil, cover and simmer gently for 40–50 minutes. Preheat the oven to 160°C/325°F/Gas 3.

5 Drain the rice and boil in stock for 5 minutes. Meanwhile, spoon the lamb mixture into a casserole. Drain the rice and mound it on top of the lamb. Using the handle of a wooden spoon, make a hole down the centre.

6 Top with the remaining onions and saffron milk. Dot with ghee. Cover with double foil and a lid. Bake for 30–35 minutes, until the rice is tender. Garnish with coriander and serve.

Nutritional information per portion: Energy 764kcal/3193kJ; Protein 41g; Carbohydrate 81.9g, of which sugars 9.8g; Fat 30.6g, of which saturates 16.1g; Cholesterol 147mg; Calcium 196mg; Fibre 1.5g; Sodium 295mg.

Spicy lamb and apricots with pea rice

The slightly dry flavour of the split peas and basmati rice contrasts well with the sweetness of the dried apricots in this wonderfully exotic dish.

SERVES 4

675g/1¹/₂lb lamb leg fillet

175ml/6fl oz/³/₄ cup natural (plain) yogurt

30ml/2 tbsp sunflower oil

30ml/2 tbsp grated fresh root ginger

juice of half a lemon

175g/6oz/¹/₂ cup chana dhal or yellow
    split peas, soaked for 1–2 hours

225g/8oz/generous 1 cup basmati rice,
    soaked and drained

2 onions, 1 sliced and 1 finely chopped

1 garlic clove, crushed

15ml/1 tbsp chopped fresh
    coriander (cilantro)

5ml/1 tsp ground coriander

10ml/2 tsp ground cumin

30ml/2 tbsp ghee or butter

5ml/1 tsp fenugreek

2.5ml/¹/₂ tsp turmeric

pinch of cayenne pepper

1 cinnamon stick

175g/6oz dried apricots

120ml/4fl oz/¹/₂ cup chicken stock

salt and ground black pepper

fresh coriander, to garnish

1 Trim the meat and cut into bitesize pieces. Mix 125ml/4fl oz/¹/₂ cup of yogurt, half the oil and ginger and the lemon juice in a dish. Add the meat, stir to coat, cover and leave in a cool place for 2–4 hours.

2 Boil the chana dhal in water in a large pan for 20–30 minutes until tender, drain and set aside. Cook the drained rice in boiling salted water for 10 minutes. Drain and set aside.

3 Fry the onion rings in the remaining oil until golden. Transfer to a plate. Add the garlic and remaining ginger and fry for a few seconds. Add the remaining yogurt and cook for a few minutes, stirring. Add the dhal, fresh coriander and salt. Stir, remove from the heat and set aside. Preheat the oven to 180°C/350°F/Gas 4.

4 Drain the meat, reserving the marinade. Melt half the ghee in a casserole and fry the chopped onion for 3–4 minutes. Add the spices. Fry over medium heat until sizzling. Add the meat and fry until browned. Halve or quarter the apricots and add to the pan with the stock, remaining marinade and seasoning. Slowly bring to the boil, cover and cook in the oven for 45–55 minutes, until the meat is tender.

5 Meanwhile, spoon the dhal into a casserole. Stir in the rice. Dot with the remaining ghee or butter and sprinkle with onion rings. Cover with a double layer of foil. Secure with the lid. Place in the oven 30 minutes before the lamb is ready. Serve the rice and spiced lamb together, garnished with fresh coriander.

Nutritional information per portion: Energy 765kcal/3192kJ; Protein 58.5g; Carbohydrate 27.5g, of which sugars 23.4g; Fat 47.5g, of which saturates 14.7g; Cholesterol 218mg; Calcium 53mg; Fibre 2.5g; Sodium 181mg.

Turkish lamb on a bed of rice

In Turkey, meat is cooked over hot charcoal or in a wood-burning stove, producing an almost charred exterior enclosing moist, tender meat. In this recipe, the meat juices flavour the rice beneath.

SERVES 6

half leg of lamb, about 1.3–1.6kg/
    3–3¹/₂lb, boned
bunch of fresh parsley
small bunch of fresh coriander (cilantro)
50g/1³/₄oz/¹/₂ cup cashew nuts
2 garlic cloves
15ml/1 tbsp sunflower oil
1 small onion, finely chopped
200g/7oz/1¹/₄ cups cooked white
    long grain rice
75g/2³/₄oz/scant ¹/₂ cup ready-to-eat
    dried apricots, finely chopped
salt and ground black pepper
fresh parsley or coriander (cilantro)
    sprigs, to garnish
tzatziki, black olives and pitta bread,
    to serve (optional)

1 Preheat the oven to 200°C/400°F/Gas 6. Remove excess fat from the lamb. Trim and cut the joint if necessary, so that it lies flat. Finely chop the herbs in a food processor or blender. Add the cashew nuts and pulse until roughly chopped.

2 Crush one of the garlic cloves. Heat the oil in a frying pan. Fry the onion and crushed garlic for 3–4 minutes until softened. Put the rice in a bowl and add the cashew nut mixture, fried onion mixture and apricots. Season, stir well, then spoon into the bottom of a roasting pan just large enough to hold the lamb.

3 Halve the remaining garlic and rub the cut sides over the meat. Season with pepper, then lay the meat on the rice, tucking all the rice under the meat so no rice is visible. Roast for 30 minutes, then lower the oven temperature to 180°C/350°F/Gas 4. Cook for 35–45 minutes more, until done to your taste, then cover with foil and leave to rest for 5 minutes.

4 Slice the lamb thickly. Spoon the rice mixture on to a platter, top with the lamb and garnish with fresh parsley or coriander. Serve at once, with a bowl of tzatziki, black olives and pitta bread, if you like.

Nutritional information per portion: Energy 644kcal/2706kJ; Protein 77.5g; Carbohydrate 17.2g, of which sugars 5.6g; Fat 30.1g, of which saturates 10.7g; Cholesterol 250mg; Calcium 38mg; Fibre 1.2g; Sodium 184mg.

African lamb and vegetable pilau

Lamb and rice are a popular combination in African cooking. In this dish, spicy lamb is mixed with basmati rice and a colourful selection of different vegetables and cashew nuts.

SERVES 4

450g/1lb boned shoulder of lamb, cubed
2.5ml/1/2 tsp dried thyme
2.5ml/1/2 tsp paprika
5ml/1 tsp garam masala
1 garlic clove, crushed
25ml/1 1/2 tbsp vegetable oil
900ml/1 1/2 pints/3 3/4 cups lamb stock
salt and ground black pepper
Savoy cabbage or crisp lettuce, to serve

FOR THE RICE

225g/8oz/generous 1 cup basmati rice
25g/1oz/2 tbsp butter
1 onion, chopped
1 potato, diced
1 carrot, sliced
1/2 red (bell) pepper, seeded and chopped
1 fresh green chilli, seeded and chopped
115g/4oz/1 cup sliced green cabbage
60ml/4 tbsp natural (plain) yogurt
2.5ml/1/2 tsp ground cumin
5 green cardamom pods
2 garlic cloves, crushed
50g/1 3/4oz/1/2 cup cashew nuts

1 Put the lamb cubes in a large bowl and add the thyme, paprika, garam masala and garlic, with plenty of salt and pepper. Stir, cover, and leave in a cool place for 2–3 hours.

2 Heat the oil in a large pan and fry the lamb over a medium heat for 5–6 minutes, until browned. Stir in the stock, cover and cook for 35–40 minutes, until tender. Using a slotted spoon, transfer the lamb to a bowl.

3 Lay kitchen paper on top of the stock to remove excess fat, discard the paper, then pour the stock into a measuring jug (cup). Top it up with water if necessary to make 600ml/ 1 pint/2 1/2 cups.

4 Soak the rice in cold water. Melt the butter in a separate pan and fry the onion, potato and carrot for 5 minutes.

5 Add the chopped red pepper and green chilli and fry for 3 minutes. Stir in the sliced green cabbage, with the yogurt, cumin, cardamom pods, garlic and reserved lamb stock. Stir well, cover and simmer gently for 5–10 minutes until the cabbage wilts.

6 Drain the rice and stir into the stew with the lamb. Cover and simmer over a low heat for 20 minutes or until the rice is cooked. Sprinkle in the cashew nuts and season with salt and pepper. Serve hot, cupped in cabbage or lettuce leaves.

Nutritional information per portion: Energy 636kcal/2655kJ; Protein 31.2g; Carbohydrate 63.2g, of which sugars 10.1g; Fat 28.9g, of which saturates 11g; Cholesterol 99mg; Calcium 80mg; Fibre 2.7g; Sodium 193mg.

Side dishes and salads

Put aside any thoughts of plain boiled rice

or ungarnished salads. As this chapter

amply demonstrates, whether you're after

something simple or elaborate, you can call

on a wide array of ingredients – vegetables,

meat, poultry, fish, all manner of fruits,

herbs and spices – to produce a stunning

range of fragrant, spicy and exotic rice

accompaniments to main dishes.

Wild rice pilaff

This isn't, in fact, a rice at all, but a type of wild grass. Call it what you will, it has a wonderful nutty flavour and combines well with long-grain rice in this fruity mixture.

SERVES 6

200g/7oz/1 cup wild rice
40g/1¹/₂oz/3 tbsp butter
¹/₂ onion, finely chopped
200g/7oz/1 cup long grain rice
475ml/17fl oz/2 cups chicken stock
75g/2³/₄oz/³/₄ cup flaked
    (sliced) almonds
115g/4oz/²/₃ cup sultanas
    (golden raisins)
30ml/2 tbsp chopped fresh parsley
salt and ground black pepper

1 Bring a large pan of water to the boil. Add the wild rice and 5ml/1 tsp salt. Lower the heat, cover and simmer gently for 45–60 minutes, until the rice is tender. Drain well.

2 Meanwhile, melt 15g/¹/₂oz/1 tbsp of the butter in another large pan. Add the onion and cook over a medium heat for about 5 minutes until it is just softened. Stir in the long grain rice and cook for 1 minute more.

3 Stir in the stock and bring to the boil. Cover and simmer gently for about 30–40 minutes, until the rice is tender and the liquid has been absorbed.

4 Melt the remaining butter in a small pan. Add the almonds and cook until they are just golden. Set aside.

5 Put both types of rice in a bowl and add the almonds, sultanas and half the parsley. Stir to mix. Taste and adjust the seasoning if necessary. Transfer to a warmed serving dish, sprinkle with the remaining parsley and serve.

Nutritional information per portion: Energy 424kcal/1769kJ; Protein 8.4g; Carbohydrate 68.3g, of which sugars 14.5g; Fat 13g, of which saturates 4g; Cholesterol 14mg; Calcium 69mg; Fibre 1.7g; Sodium 48mg.

Dirty rice

Contrary to popular belief, this dish doesn't get its name from its appearance but from its association with New Orleans and jazz, which was referred to occasionally as "dirty music".

SERVES 4

60ml/4 tbsp vegetable oil
25g/1oz/¼ cup plain (all-purpose) flour
50g/1¾oz/4 tbsp butter
1 large onion, chopped
2 garlic cloves, crushed
200g/7oz minced (ground) pork
225g/8oz chicken livers, trimmed and
    finely chopped
dash of Tabasco sauce
1 green (bell) pepper, seeded and sliced
2 celery sticks, sliced
300ml/½ pint/1¼ cups chicken stock
225g/8oz/generous 1 cup cooked white
    long grain rice
4 spring onions (scallions), chopped
45ml/3 tbsp chopped fresh parsley
salt and ground black pepper
celery leaves, to garnish

1 Heat half the oil in a large, heavy pan. Stir in the flour and cook over a low heat, stirring constantly, until the roux is smooth and the colour is a rich chestnut-brown. Immediately remove the pan from the heat and place it on a cold surface such as the draining board of a sink.

2 Heat the remaining oil with the butter in a large frying pan and stir-fry the onion for 5 minutes.

3 Add the garlic and pork. Cook for 5 minutes, breaking up the pork and stirring until it is evenly browned, then stir in the chicken livers and fry for 2–3 minutes until they have changed colour all over. Season with salt, pepper and Tabasco sauce. Stir in the green pepper and celery.

4 Stir the roux into the stir-fried mixture, then gradually stir in the stock. When the mixture begins to bubble, cover and cook for 30 minutes, stirring occasionally. Stir in the rice, spring onions and parsley. Toss over the heat until the rice has heated through. Serve garnished with celery leaves.

Nutritional information per portion: Energy 581kcal/2417kJ; Protein 25.7g; Carbohydrate 56.1g, of which sugars 5g; Fat 28.1g, of which saturates 10.1g; Cholesterol 273mg; Calcium 58mg; Fibre 2.1g; Sodium 165mg.

Stir-fried rice and vegetables

Cooking this rice with ginger, lemon and garlic gives it a wonderfully rich flavour.

SERVES 4

115g/4oz/generous 1/2 cup brown basmati rice, rinsed
350ml/12fl oz/1 1/2 cups vegetable stock
2.5cm/1in piece of fresh root ginger, finely sliced
1 garlic clove, halved
5cm/2in piece of pared lemon rind
15ml/1 tbsp groundnut (peanut) oil
15ml/1 tbsp ghee or butter
175g/6oz baby carrots, trimmed
115g/4oz/1 1/2 cups shiitake mushrooms, caps sliced and
    stems discarded
225g/8oz baby courgettes (zucchini), halved
175–225g/6–8oz/about 1 1/2 cups broccoli, broken into florets
6 spring onions (scallions), diagonally sliced
15ml/1 tbsp light soy sauce
10ml/2 tsp toasted sesame oils

1 Put the drained rice, stock, ginger, garlic and lemon rind in a large pan. Bring to the boil, cover and cook gently for 20–25 minutes until the rice is tender. Remove from the heat, discard the flavourings and keep covered.

2 Heat the oil and ghee or butter in a wok and stir-fry the carrots for 4–5 minutes. Add the mushrooms and courgettes, stir-fry for 2–3 minutes, then add the broccoli and spring onions and cook for 3 minutes, until tender but still firm to the bite. Add the cooked rice and toss briefly to heat through. Toss with the soy sauce and sesame oil. Spoon into a bowl and serve immediately.

Nutritional information per portion: Energy 430kcal/1788kJ; Protein 12.5g; Carbohydrate 58.2g, of which sugars 11.2g; Fat 16.2g, of which saturates 2.2g; Cholesterol 0mg; Calcium 127mg; Fibre 6.5g; Sodium 569mg.

Crackling rice paper fish rolls

The rice in this dish is in the rice paper wrappers, which melt in your mouth.

MAKES 12

24 young asparagus spears, trimmed
25ml/1 1/2 tbsp olive oil
6 spring onions (scallions), finely chopped
1 garlic clove, crushed
225g/8oz raw prawns (shrimp), peeled, deveined and chopped
2cm/3/4in piece of fresh root ginger, grated
30ml/2 tbsp chopped fresh coriander (cilantro)
5ml/1 tsp five-spice powder
5ml/1 tsp finely grated lime or lemon rind
12 Vietnamese rice paper sheets (bahn trang), each about
    20 x 10cm/8 x 4in
45ml/3 tbsp plain (all-purpose) flour mixed to a paste with
    45ml/3 tbsp water
vegetable oil, for deep-frying
salt and ground black pepper
fresh herbs, to garnish

1 Boil the asparagus in lightly salted water for about 3–4 minutes, drain, refresh under cold water and drain again. Heat half the oil in a wok and stir-fry the spring onions and garlic gently for 2–3 minutes. Transfer to a bowl. Heat the remaining oil. Stir-fry the prawns briskly for a few seconds, then stir into the bowl with the ginger, coriander, five-spice powder, lime rind and pepper.

2 Brush the rice paper with water, put two asparagus spears and a spoonful of prawn mixture in the centre of each, fold in the sides and roll up. Seal with flour paste. Deep-fry in hot oil until golden. Drain. Garnish with herbs.

Nutritional information per roll: Energy 105kcal/438kJ; Protein 5g; Carbohydrate 8.8g, of which sugars 0.7g; Fat 5.6g, of which saturates 0.7g; Cholesterol 37mg; Calcium 36mg; Fibre 0.8g; Sodium 38mg.

Chinese fried rice

This dish is an elaborate variation on the more familiar egg fried rice. With filling ingredients such as ham, prawns and peas, it is almost a meal in itself.

SERVES 4

50g/1³/₄oz cooked ham
50g/1³/₄oz cooked prawns
   (shrimp), peeled
3 eggs
5ml/1 tsp salt
2 spring onions (scallions), finely chopped
60ml/4 tbsp vegetable oil
115g/4oz/1 cup peas, thawed if frozen
15ml/1 tbsp light soy sauce
15ml/1 tbsp Chinese rice wine or
   dry sherry
450g/1lb/4 cups cooked white long
   grain rice

1 Dice the cooked ham finely. Pat the cooked prawns dry on kitchen paper.

2 In a bowl, beat the eggs lightly with a pinch of the salt and a few pieces of the spring onions.

3 Heat about half the oil in a wok, stir-fry the peas, prawns and ham for 1 minute, then add the soy sauce, and rice wine or sherry. Transfer to a bowl and keep hot.

4 Heat the remaining oil in the wok and scramble the eggs lightly. Add the rice and stir to make sure that the grains are separate. Add the remaining salt, the remaining spring onions and the prawn mixture. Toss over the heat to mix. Serve hot or cold.

Nutritional information per portion: Energy 86kcal/360kJ; Protein 9.8g; Carbohydrate 3.8g, of which sugars 1.2g; Fat 3.7g, of which saturates 1g; Cholesterol 127mg; Calcium 34mg; Fibre 1.4g; Sodium 477mg.

Indonesian coconut rice

This way of cooking rice is very popular throughout the whole of South-east Asia. Coconut rice goes particularly well with fish, chicken and pork.

SERVES 4–6

350g/12oz/1³/₄ cups Thai fragrant rice
400ml/14fl oz can coconut milk
300ml/¹/₂ pint/1¹/₄ cups water
2.5ml/¹/₂ tsp ground coriander
5cm/2in cinnamon stick
1 lemon grass stalk, bruised
1 bay leaf
salt
deep-fried onions, to garnish

1 Put the rice in a strainer and rinse thoroughly under cold water. Drain well, then put in a pan. Pour in the coconut milk and water. Add the coriander, cinnamon stick, lemon grass and bay leaf. Season with salt. Bring to the boil, stirring frequently, then lower the heat, cover and simmer for 8–10 minutes, until all the liquid has been absorbed.

2 Fork the rice through carefully, removing the cinnamon stick, lemon grass and bay leaf. Cover the pan again with a tight-fitting lid and continue to cook over the lowest possible heat for 3–5 minutes more. Alternatively, remove from the heat and leave to stand for 5 minutes.

3 Pile the rice on to a warm serving dish and serve garnished with the crisp, deep-fried onions.

Nutritional information per portion: Energy 226kcal/945kJ; Protein 4.7g; Carbohydrate 49.9g, of which sugars 3.4g; Fat 0.6g, of which saturates 0.1g; Cholesterol 0mg; Calcium 39mg; Fibre 0.2g; Sodium 75mg.

Chinese jewelled rice

*Another fried rice medley, this time with crab meat and water chestnuts,
providing contrasting textures and flavours.*

SERVES 4

350g/12oz/1¾ cups white long grain rice
45ml/3 tbsp vegetable oil
1 onion, roughly chopped
4 dried black Chinese mushrooms, soaked
    for 10 minutes in warm water
115g/4oz cooked ham, diced
175g/6oz drained canned white
    crab meat

75g/2¾oz/½ cup drained canned
    water chestnuts
115g/4oz/1 cup peas, thawed if frozen
30ml/2 tbsp oyster sauce
5ml/1 tsp sugar
salt

1 Rinse the rice, then cook for about 10–12 minutes in a pan of lightly salted
boiling water, until tender. Drain, refresh under cold water, drain again, then
leave until completely cold.

2 Pour half the oil into a hot wok, drizzling it in a "necklace" just below
the rim. As it runs down, it will coat the inner surface as it heats. When very
hot, stir-fry the rice for 3 minutes. Transfer the cooked rice to a bowl and
set aside.

3 Heat the remaining oil in the wok and cook the onion until softened but
not coloured. Drain the mushrooms, cut off and discard the stems, then chop
the caps.

4 Add the chopped mushrooms to the wok, with the diced ham, white crab
meat, water chestnuts, peas, oyster sauce and sugar. Season with salt to
taste. Stir-fry for 2 minutes, then add the rice and stir-fry for a further 3
minutes until heated through. Serve at once.

Nutritional information per portion: Energy 474kcal/1979kJ; Protein 22.5g; Carbohydrate 77.5g, of which sugars 4.3g;
Fat 7.8g, of which saturates 1.1g; Cholesterol 48mg; Calcium 86mg; Fibre 1.9g; Sodium 710mg.

Thai rice

This dish combines the nutty taste of nutritious, fluffy brown rice with mouthwatering aromatic Thai flavourings, such as lemon grass, lime and ginger.

SERVES 4

2 limes
1 lemon grass stalk
225g/8oz/generous 1 cup brown long
    grain rice
15ml/1 tbsp olive oil
1 onion, chopped
2.5cm/1in piece of fresh root ginger,
    peeled and finely chopped
7.5ml/1½ tsp coriander seeds
7.5ml/1½ tsp cumin seeds
750ml/1¼ pints/3 cups vegetable stock
60ml/4 tbsp chopped fresh
    coriander (cilantro)
spring onions (scallions) and toasted
    coconut strips, to garnish
lime wedges, to serve

1 Pare the limes using a canelle knife or a fine grater, taking care to avoid cutting the bitter pith. Set aside the rind. Finely chop the lower portion of the lemon grass stalk and set aside.

2 Rinse the rice in plenty of cold water until the water runs clear. Drain thoroughly in a sieve (strainer).

3 Heat the oil in a large pan. Add the onion, ginger, coriander seeds, cumin seeds, lemon grass and lime rind and fry over a low heat for 2–3 minutes.

4 Add the drained rice and cook for 1 minute, then pour in the stock and bring to the boil. Reduce the heat to very low and cover the pan. Cook gently for 30 minutes, then check the rice. If it is still crunchy, cover the pan and leave for 3–5 minutes more, until tender. Remove from the heat.

5 Stir in the fresh coriander, fluff up the grains, cover and leave for about 10 minutes. Garnish with spring onions and toasted coconut strips, and serve with lime wedges.

Nutritional information per portion: Energy 234kcal/992kJ; Protein 4.3g; Carbohydrate 47.2g, of which sugars 1.8g; Fat 4.5g, of which saturates 0.8g; Cholesterol 0mg; Calcium 29mg; Fibre 1.8g; Sodium 6mg.

Festive rice

This pretty Thai dish is traditionally shaped into a cone and surrounded by a variety of accompaniments before being served.

SERVES 8

450g/1lb/2¹/₃ cups Thai fragrant rice
60ml/4 tbsp oil
2 garlic cloves, crushed
2 onions, finely sliced
2.5ml/¹/₂ tsp ground turmeric
750ml/1¹/₄ pints/3 cups water
400ml/14fl oz can coconut milk
1–2 lemon grass stalks, bruised

FOR THE ACCOMPANIMENTS

omelette strips
2 fresh red chillies, shredded
cucumber chunks
tomato wedges
deep-fried onions
prawn crackers

1 Put the Thai fragrant rice in a sieve (strainer) and rinse thoroughly under cold water. Drain well.

2 Put the oil in a frying pan that has a lid and heat gently. Add the crushed garlic, finely sliced onions and the ground turmeric, and stir-fry over a low heat for a few minutes, until the onions are softened but not browned. Add the drained rice to the frying pan and stir well so that each rice grain is coated in oil.

3 Pour in the water and coconut milk and add the lemon grass stalks to the pan. Bring to the boil, stirring frequently. Cover the frying pan, reduce the heat and cook the mixture gently for about 12 minutes or until all the liquid has been absorbed.

4 Remove the pan from the heat and lift the lid. Cover with a clean dish towel, replace the lid and leave to stand in a warm place for 15 minutes. Remove the lemon grass, mound the rice mixture in a cone on a serving platter and garnish with the accompaniments. Serve immediately.

Nutritional information per portion: Energy 303kcal/1263kJ; Protein 6.4g; Carbohydrate 49.5g, of which sugars 4.2g; Fat 8.6g, of which saturates 2g; Cholesterol 53mg; Calcium 41mg; Fibre 0.5g; Sodium 212mg.

Thai fried rice

This dish is based on Thai fragrant rice, which is sometimes known as jasmine rice. Chicken, red pepper and corn add colour and extra flavour.

SERVES 4

475ml/17fl oz/2 cups water
50g/1³/₄oz/¹/₂ cup coconut milk powder
350g/12oz/1³/₄ cups Thai fragrant
   rice, rinsed
30ml/2 tbsp groundnut (peanut) oil
2 garlic cloves, chopped
1 small onion, finely chopped
2.5cm/1in piece of fresh root ginger, grated
225g/8oz skinless, boneless chicken
   breasts, cut into 1cm/¹/₂in dice

1 red (bell) pepper, seeded and sliced
115g/4oz/1 cup drained canned
   corn kernels
5ml/1 tsp chilli oil
5ml/1 tsp hot curry powder
2 eggs, beaten
salt
spring onion (scallion) shreds,
   to garnish

1 Pour the water into a large pan and whisk in the coconut milk powder. Add the rice and bring to the boil. Lower the heat, cover and cook for 12 minutes or until the rice is tender and the liquid has been absorbed. Spread the rice on a baking sheet and leave until cold.

2 Heat the oil in a wok, add the garlic, onion and ginger and stir-fry over a medium heat for 2 minutes.

3 Push the vegetables to the sides of the wok, add the chicken to the centre and stir-fry for 2 minutes. Add the rice and stir-fry over a high heat for about 3 minutes more.

4 Stir in the sliced red pepper, corn, chilli oil and curry powder, with salt to taste. Toss over the heat for 1 minute. Stir in the beaten eggs and cook for 1 minute more. Garnish with spring onion shreds and serve immediately.

Nutritional information per portion: Energy 508kcal/2127kJ; Protein 24.7g; Carbohydrate 83.9g, of which sugars 8.7g; Fat 8g, of which saturates 1.6g; Cholesterol 135mg; Calcium 57mg; Fibre 1.3g; Sodium 204mg.

Mushroom pilau

This dish is absolutely delicious but is simplicity itself to make, which makes it ideal if you are pressed for time. You can serve it with any Indian dish or with roast lamb or chicken.

SERVES 4

30ml/2 tbsp vegetable oil

2 shallots, finely chopped

1 garlic clove, crushed

3 green cardamom pods

25g/1oz/2 tbsp ghee or butter

175g/6oz/2¹⁄₂ cups button (white)
   mushrooms, sliced

225g/8oz/generous 1 cup basmati
   rice, soaked and drained

5ml/1 tsp grated fresh root ginger

good pinch of garam masala

450ml/³⁄₄ pint/scant 2 cups water

15ml/1 tbsp chopped fresh
   coriander (cilantro)

salt

1 Pour the vegetable oil into a large, heavy pan and heat it over a medium heat.

2 Add the finely chopped shallots, crushed garlic and green cardamom pods to the pan and cook, stirring frequently, for about 3–4 minutes until the shallots have softened and are beginning to brown.

3 Add the ghee or butter. When it has melted, add the mushrooms and fry for 2–3 minutes.

4 Add the rice, ginger and garam masala. Stir-fry over a low heat for 2–3 minutes, then stir in the water and a little salt. Bring to the boil, then cover tightly and simmer over a very low heat for 10 minutes.

5 Remove the pan from the heat and leave to stand, covered, for 5 minutes.

6 Add the chopped coriander and fork it through the rice. Spoon into a serving bowl and serve at once.

Nutritional information per portion: Energy 309kcal/1286kJ; Protein 5.2g; Carbohydrate 46.3g, of which sugars 1g; Fat 11.2g, of which saturates 4g; Cholesterol 13mg; Calcium 18mg; Fibre 0.7g; Sodium 41mg.

Sweet and sour rice

This popular Middle Eastern rice dish is flavoured with a mouthwatering combination of fruit and spices. It is often served with lamb or chicken.

SERVES 4

45g/1¹/₂oz/3 tbsp butter

50g/1³/₄oz/¹/₃ cup raisins

50g/1³/₄oz/¹/₂ cup *zereshk* (if these dried berries are unavailable, use fresh cranberries instead), thoroughly washed in cold water 4–5 times and drained to remove any grit

50g/1³/₄oz/¹/₄ cup sugar

5ml/1 tsp ground cinnamon

5ml/1 tsp ground cumin

350g/12oz/1³/₄ cups basmati rice, soaked

2–3 saffron strands, soaked in 15ml/ 1 tbsp boiling water

pinch of salt

1 Melt 15g/¹/₂oz/1 tbsp of the butter in a frying pan and fry the raisins for 1–2 minutes. Add the *zereshk*, fry for a few seconds. Add the sugar, with half of the cinnamon and cumin. Cook briefly and set aside. Drain the rice and put it in a pan of boiling, lightly salted water. Bring back to the boil, reduce the heat and simmer for 4 minutes. Drain and rinse.

2 Melt half the remaining butter in the clean pan and add 15ml/1 tbsp water. Stir in half the rice. Sprinkle with half the raisin mixture. Top with all but 45ml/3 tbsp of the rice. Top with the remaining raisin mixture.

3 Mix the remaining cinnamon and cumin with the reserved rice, and sprinkle evenly over the layered mixture. Melt the remaining butter, drizzle it over the surface, then cover the pan with a clean dish towel. Cover with a tight-fitting lid, lifting the corners of the cloth back over the lid. Steam the rice over a very low heat for 20–30 minutes, until tender.

4 Mix 45ml/3 tbsp of the rice with the saffron water. Spoon the sweet and sour rice on to a large, flat serving dish and sprinkle the saffron rice over the top. Serve immediately.

Nutritional information per portion: Energy 465kcal/1943kJ; Protein 7g; Carbohydrate 87g, of which sugars 17.2g; Fat 9.8g, of which saturates 5.9g; Cholesterol 24mg; Calcium 32mg; Fibre 0.6g; Sodium 77mg.

Savoury ground rice

An especially popular dish in West Africa, delicious savoury ground rice is often served as an accompaniment to soups and stews.

SERVES 4

300ml/¹/₂ pint/1¹/₄ cups water
300ml/¹/₂ pint/1¹/₄ cups milk
2.5ml/¹/₂ tsp salt
15ml/1 tbsp chopped fresh parsley
25g/1oz/2 tbsp butter or margarine
275g/9¹/₂oz/1²/₃ cups ground rice

1 Place the water in a large pan. Pour in the milk, bring to the boil and add the salt and parsley.

2 Add the butter or margarine and the ground rice, stirring with a wooden spoon to prevent the rice from becoming lumpy.

3 Cover the pan and cook over a low heat for about 15 minutes, beating the mixture every 2 minutes to prevent the formation of lumps.

4 To test if the rice is cooked, rub a pinch of the mixture between your fingers: if it feels smooth and fairly dry, it is ready. Serve hot.

Nutritional information per portion: Energy 329kcal/1374kJ; Protein 7.8g; Carbohydrate 58.5g, of which sugars 3.6g; Fat 6.8g, of which saturates 4.1g; Cholesterol 18mg; Calcium 109mg; Fibre 0.1g; Sodium 317mg.

Tanzanian vegetable rice

Serve this tasty dish with roast chicken or steamed fish. The vegetables are added near the end of cooking so that they remain crisp and flavoursome.

SERVES 4

350g/12oz/1¾ cups basmati rice
45ml/3 tbsp vegetable oil
1 onion, chopped
2 garlic cloves, crushed
750ml/1¼ pints/3 cups vegetable
   stock or water
115g/4oz/²⁄₃ cup fresh or drained
   canned corn kernels
½ red or green (bell) pepper, seeded
   and chopped
1 large carrot, grated
salt
fresh chervil sprigs, to garnish

1 Rinse the rice in a sieve (strainer) under cold water, then leave to drain thoroughly for about 15 minutes.

2 Heat the oil in a large, heavy pan and fry the onion for a few minutes over a medium heat until it starts to soften.

3 Add the rice and fry for 10 minutes, stirring constantly to prevent the rice sticking to the pan. Then stir in the crushed garlic.

4 Pour in the stock or water, season with salt if necessary, and stir well. Bring to the boil, then lower the heat, cover and simmer for 10 minutes.

5 Sprinkle the corn kernels, chopped pepper and grated carrot over the rice, then cover the pan tightly. Steam over a low heat for a few minutes, until the rice is tender, then mix together with a fork, pile on to a platter and garnish with chervil. Serve immediately.

Nutritional information per portion: Energy 455kcal/1902kJ; Protein 8.3g; Carbohydrate 84.2g, of which sugars 8.5g; Fat 9.3g, of which saturates 1.1g; Cholesterol 0mg; Calcium 34mg; Fibre 1.9g; Sodium 84mg.

Rice and beans

This is a popular dish on the islands of the eastern Caribbean. It is essential to boil the beans fast for ten minutes at the beginning of cooking them, as this destroys a toxin that they contain.

SERVES 4–6

175g/6oz/¾ cup red kidney beans
2 fresh thyme sprigs
50g/1¾oz piece of creamed coconut
    (see page 221)
2 bay leaves
1 onion, finely chopped
2 garlic cloves, crushed
2.5ml/½ tsp ground allspice
115g/4oz/⅔ cup chopped red
    (bell) pepper
475ml/16fl oz/2 cups cups water
450g/1lb/2⅓ cups white long grain rice
salt and ground black pepper

1 Place the red kidney beans in a large bowl. Cover with water and leave to soak overnight.

2 Drain the beans, place in a large pan and pour in enough water to cover them by 2.5cm/1in. Bring to the boil. Boil over a high heat for 10 minutes, then lower the heat and simmer for 1½ hours or until the beans are tender.

3 Add the thyme, coconut milk, bay leaves, onion, garlic, allspice and red pepper. Season well and stir in the measured water.

4 Bring to the boil and add the rice. Stir well, lower the heat and cover the pan. Simmer for 25–30 minutes, until all the liquid has been absorbed. Serve as an accompaniment to fish, meat or vegetarian dishes.

Nutritional information per portion: Energy 295kcal/1240kJ; Protein 10g; Carbohydrate 58.1g, of which sugars 6.7g; Fat 2.7g, of which saturates 0.4g; Cholesterol 0mg; Calcium 66mg; Fibre 4.6g; Sodium 79mg.

Tomato rice

This is proof positive that you don't always need elaborate ingredients or complicated cooking methods to make a delicious, irresistible dish.

SERVES 4

30ml/2 tbsp sunflower oil

2.5ml/¹/₂ tsp onion seeds

1 onion, sliced

2 tomatoes, chopped

1 orange (bell) pepper, seeded and sliced

5ml/1 tsp crushed fresh root ginger

1 garlic clove, crushed

5ml/1 tsp chilli powder

1 potato, diced

7.5ml/1¹/₂ tsp salt

400g/14oz/2 cups basmati rice, soaked

750ml/1¹/₄ pints/3 cups water

30–45ml/2–3 tbsp chopped fresh coriander (cilantro)

1 Heat the sunflower oil in a large, heavy pan and fry the onion seeds for about 30 seconds. Add the sliced onion and fry for about 5 minutes, until softened.

2 Stir in the chopped tomatoes, sliced orange or yellow pepper, and the ginger, garlic, chilli powder, potato and salt. Stir-fry over a medium heat for about 5 minutes.

3 Drain the rice and add to the pan, then stir for about 1 minute until the grains are well coated.

4 Pour in the water and bring to the boil, then lower the heat, cover and simmer for about 12–15 minutes, until just tender. Remove from the heat and leave to stand, still covered, for 5 minutes. Stir in the chopped coriander and serve.

Nutritional information per portion: Energy 463kcal/1940kJ; Protein 10g; Carbohydrate 96.2g, of which sugars 7.6g; Fat 4.1g, of which saturates 0.5g; Cholesterol 0mg; Calcium 57mg; Fibre 3g; Sodium 21mg.

Roasted red pepper salad

This Mediterranean-flavoured dish makes an excellent accompaniment to sausages or fish.

SERVES 4

225g/8oz/generous 1 cup Camargue red rice
vegetable stock, chicken stock or water (see step 1)
45ml/3 tbsp olive oil
3 red (bell) peppers, seeded and sliced into strips
4–5 sun-dried tomatoes
4–5 whole garlic cloves, unpeeled
1 onion, chopped
30ml/2 tbsp chopped fresh parsley, plus extra to garnish
15ml/1 tbsp chopped fresh coriander (cilantro)
10ml/2 tsp balsamic vinegar
salt and ground black pepper

1 Cook the rice in stock or water, following the instructions on the packet. Heat the oil in a frying pan and add the red peppers. Cook over a medium heat for 4 minutes, shaking occasionally.

2 Lower the heat, add the sun-dried tomatoes, whole garlic cloves and onion, cover the pan and cook for about 8–10 minutes more, stirring occasionally. Remove the lid and cook for 3 minutes more.

3 Off the heat, stir in the parsley, coriander and vinegar, and season. Spread the rice out on a serving dish and spoon the pepper mixture on top. Peel the whole garlic cloves, cut the flesh into slices and sprinkle these over the salad. Serve at room temperature, garnished with more fresh parsley.

Nutritional information per portion: Energy 344kcal/1436kJ; Protein 6.7g; Carbohydrate 57.9g, of which sugars 12.2g; Fat 9.5g, of which saturates 1.4g; Cholesterol 0mg; Calcium 54mg; Fibre 3.8g; Sodium 17mg.

Creamy fish pilau

This dish is inspired by a fusion of cuisines – it uses Indian basmati rice and a French sauce.

SERVES 4–6

450g/1lb fresh mussels, scrubbed
350ml/12fl oz/1¹/₂ cups white wine
fresh parsley sprig, plus extra to garnish
225g/8oz scallops, corals detached
40g/1¹/₂oz/3 tbsp butter
15ml/1 tbsp olive oil
2 shallots, finely chopped
225g/8oz/3 cups button (white) mushrooms, halved if large
275g/9¹/₂oz/1¹/₂ cups basmati rice, soaked
300ml/¹/₂ pint/1¹/₄ cups fish stock
150ml/¹/₄ pint/²/₃ cup double (heavy) cream
15ml/1 tbsp chopped fresh parsley
675g/1¹/₂lb salmon, cut into bitesize pieces
225g/8oz large cooked prawns (shrimp), peeled and deveined
salt and ground black peppers

1 Preheat the oven to 160°C/325°F/Gas 3. In a heavy pan, boil the mussels, 90ml/6 tbsp of the wine and the parsley sprig, covered, for 5 minutes. Drain, reserving the liquid. Discard any mussels that remain closed; shell the rest. Cut the scallops into pieces. Fry the shallots and mushrooms in the butter and half the oil for 3–4 minutes. Transfer to a bowl. Fry the rice in the remaining oil for 2 minutes, stirring. Transfer to a casserole.

2 Bring the stock, remaining wine and mussel liquid to the boil in a pan. Add the cream, parsley and seasoning. Pour over the rice. Stir in the salmon, scallop flesh and mushroom mixture. Cover and bake for 3 minutes. Add the corals, cover and cook for 4 minutes. Add the mussels and prawns, cover and cook for 3 minutes. Garnish with parsley.

Nutritional information per portion: Energy 428kcal/1787kJ; Protein 24.2g; Carbohydrate 39g, of which sugars 1.1g; Fat 15.2g, of which saturates 8.7g; Cholesterol 134mg; Calcium 130mg; Fibre 0.8g; Sodium 200mg.

Red rice salad niçoise

Red rice, with its sweet nuttiness, goes well in this classic salad. The tuna or swordfish could be barbecued or pan-fried but take care that it does not overcook.

SERVES 6

675g/1¹/₂lb fresh tuna or swordfish,
   sliced into 2cm/³/₄in thick steaks
350g/12oz/1³/₄ cups Camargue red rice
fish or vegetable stock or water
450g/1lb green beans
450g/1lb shelled broad (fava) beans
1 cos or romaine lettuce
450g/1lb cherry tomatoes, halved unless
   very tiny
30ml/2 tbsp coarsely chopped fresh
   coriander (cilantro)
3 hard-boiled eggs
175g/6oz/1¹/₂ cups pitted black olives
salt and ground black pepper
olive oil, for brushing

FOR THE MARINADE

1 red onion, roughly chopped
2 garlic cloves
¹/₂ bunch fresh parsley
¹/₂ bunch fresh coriander
10ml/2 tsp paprika
45ml/3 tbsp olive oil
45ml/3 tbsp water
30ml/2 tbsp white wine vinegar
15ml/1 tbsp fresh lime or lemon juice

FOR THE DRESSING

30ml/2 tbsp fresh lime or lemon juice
5ml/1 tsp Dijon mustard
¹/₂ garlic clove, crushed (optional)
60ml/4 tbsp olive oil
60ml/4 tbsp sunflower oil

1 Make the marinade by mixing all the ingredients, with salt and pepper, in a food processor and processing them for 30–40 seconds until the vegetables and herbs are finely chopped.

2 Prick the tuna or swordfish steaks all over with a fork, lay them side by side in a shallow dish and pour over the marinade, turning to coat well. Cover with clear film (plastic wrap) and leave in a cool place for 2–4 hours.

3 Cook the rice in stock or water, following the instructions on the packet, then drain, place in a bowl and set aside.

4 Make the dressing. Mix the citrus juice and mustard, and garlic if using, in a bowl. Whisk in the oils, then add salt and ground black pepper to taste. Stir 60ml/4 tbsp of the dressing into the rice, then spoon the rice into the centre of a large serving dish.

5 Cook the green beans and broad beans in boiling salted water until tender. Drain, refresh under cold water and drain again. Remove the skin from the broad beans and add them to the rice.

6 Discard the outer leaves from the lettuce and tear the inner leaves into pieces. Add to the salad with the tomatoes and coriander. Shell the hard-boiled eggs and cut into sixths. Preheat the grill (broiler).

7 Arrange the tuna or swordfish steaks on a grill pan. Brush with the marinade and a little extra olive oil. Grill for 3–4 minutes on each side, until the fish is tender and flakes easily when tested with the tip of a sharp knife. Brush with marinade and more olive oil when turning the fish over.

8 Allow the fish to cool a little, then break the steaks into large pieces. Toss into the salad with the olives and the remaining dressing. Decorate with the eggs and serve.

Nutritional information per portion: Energy 726kcal/3041kJ; Protein 42.2g; Carbohydrate 62.3g, of which sugars 6.9g; Fat 36g, of which saturates 6.3g; Cholesterol 127mg; Calcium 142mg; Fibre 9.7g; Sodium 760mg.

Spanish rice salad

Rice and a choice of chopped salad vegetables are served here in a well-flavoured dressing.

SERVES 6

275g/9¹/₂oz/1¹/₂ cups white long grain rice
1 bunch spring onions (scallions), finely sliced
1 green (bell) pepper, seeded and finely diced
1 yellow (bell) pepper, seeded and finely diced
225g/8oz tomatoes, peeled, seeded and chopped
30ml/2 tbsp chopped fresh coriander (cilantro)
salt and ground black pepper

OPTIONAL EXTRA INGREDIENTS
cooked garden peas
cooked carrots, diced
canned corn kernels, drained

FOR THE DRESSING
75ml/5 tbsp mixed sunflower oil and olive oil
15ml/1 tbsp rice vinegar
5ml/1 tsp Dijon mustard

1 Cook the rice in boiling salted water for 10–12 minutes until tender but still firm to the bite. Drain, rinse under cold water and drain again. Leave to cool completely, then transfer the rice to a large serving bowl. Add the spring onions, peppers, tomatoes and coriander. If using, add any or all of the optional extra ingredients.

2 Make the dressing. Mix all the ingredients, with salt and pepper, in a screw-top jar and shake vigorously. Stir 60–75ml/4–5 tbsp of the dressing into the rice and adjust the seasoning. Cover and chill for 1 hour before serving. Offer the remaining dressing separately.

Nutritional information per portion: Energy 246kcal/1028kJ; Protein 4.7g; Carbohydrate 42.4g, of which sugars 5.6g; Fat 6.3g, of which saturates 0.8g; Cholesterol 0mg; Calcium 24mg; Fibre 1.7g; Sodium 33mg.

Prawn, melon and chorizo salad

This is a rich and colourful salad. It tastes best when made with fresh prawns.

SERVES 4

450g/1lb/4 cups cooked white long grain rice
1 avocado
15ml/1 tbsp lemon juice
¹/₂ small melon, seeded and cut into wedges
15g/¹/₂oz/1 tbsp butter
¹/₂ garlic clove, chopped
115g/4oz raw prawns (shrimp), peeled and deveined
25g/1oz chorizo sausage, finely sliced
flat leaf parsley sprigs, to garnish

FOR THE DRESSING
75ml/5 tbsp natural (plain) yogurt
45ml/3 tbsp mayonnaise
15ml/1 tbsp olive oil
3 fresh tarragon sprigs
ground black pepper

1 Put the rice in a large salad bowl. Peel the avocado, cut into chunks and toss with the lemon juice in a bowl. Slice the melon off the rind, cut the flesh into chunks and add to the avocado.

2 Melt the butter and fry the garlic for 30 seconds. Add the prawns and cook for 3 minutes. Add the chorizo and stir-fry for 1 minute, then mix into the bowl with the avocado and melon. Cool. Mix the dressing ingredients in a food processor; stir half into the rice and the remainder into the prawn mixture. Pile the salad on to the rice. Chill for 30 minutes, garnish with flat leaf parsley and serve.

Nutritional information per portion: Energy 414kcal/1734kJ; Protein 10.8g; Carbohydrate 44.6g, of which sugars 8.8g; Fat 22.6g, of which saturates 5.8g; Cholesterol 75mg; Calcium 102mg; Fibre 1.5g; Sodium 236mg.

Orange chicken salad

With their tangy flavour, orange segments are the perfect partner for tender chicken in this tasty rice salad. To appreciate all the flavours fully, serve it at room temperature.

SERVES 4

3 large seedless oranges
175g/6oz/scant 1 cup white long grain rice
475ml/16fl oz/2 cups water
10ml/2 tsp Dijon mustard
2.5ml/¹⁄₂ tsp caster (superfine) sugar
45ml/3 tbsp red wine vinegar
90ml/6 tbsp corn oil
60ml/4 tbsp olive oil
450g/1lb cooked chicken, diced
45ml/3 tbsp chopped fresh chives
75g/2³⁄₄oz/³⁄₄ cup cashew nuts, toasted
salt and ground black pepper
mixed salad leaves, to serve

1 Pare one of the oranges thinly, taking care to remove only the coloured part of the rind and avoiding the bitter pith.

2 Put the orange rind in a large, heavy pan and add the rice. Pour in the water, add a pinch of salt and bring to the boil. Cover and steam over a very low heat for 15 minutes, or until the rice is tender and all the water has been absorbed. Meanwhile, peel all the oranges. Working over a plate to catch the juice, cut them into segments.

3 To make the dressing, whisk together the orange juice, mustard, sugar, vinegar, corn oil and olive oil in a bowl, and season to taste. When the rice is cooked, remove from the heat and discard the orange rind. Spoon the rice into a bowl, let it cool slightly, then add half the dressing. Toss well and cool completely.

4 Add the chicken, chives, cashew nuts and orange segments to the rice in the bowl. Add the remaining dressing and toss gently. Serve on a bed of mixed salad leaves.

Nutritional information per portion: Energy 382kcal/1607kJ; Protein 42.5g; Carbohydrate 27.7g, of which sugars 24.6g; Fat 12g, of which saturates 2.5g; Cholesterol 110mg; Calcium 42mg; Fibre 2.6g; Sodium 279mg.

Peruvian salad

This is a spectacular salad. It could be served as a side dish or would make a delicious light lunch. In Peru, white rice would be used, but brown rice adds an interesting texture and flavour.

SERVES 4

1 garlic clove, crushed
75ml/5 tbsp olive oil
45ml/3 tbsp sunflower oil
45ml/3 tbsp lemon juice
45ml/3 tbsp natural (plain) yogurt
2.5ml/¹/₂ tsp mustard
2.5ml/¹/₂ tsp sugar
225g/8oz/2 cups cooked long grain
    brown or white rice
15ml/1 tbsp chopped fresh parsley
1 red (bell) pepper, halved and seeded
1 small onion, sliced
115g/4oz green beans, halved
50g/1³/₄oz/¹/₂ cup baby corn
4 quail's eggs, hard-boiled
25–50g/1–1³/₄oz Spanish ham,
    cut into thin slices (optional)
1 small avocado
75g/2³/₄oz mixed salad leaves
15ml/1 tbsp capers
10 stuffed olives, halved
salt and ground black pepper

1 Whisk the garlic, 60ml/4 tbsp olive oil, sunflower oil, 30ml/2 tbsp lemon juice, yogurt, mustard, sugar and seasoning in a bowl. Put the rice into a salad bowl, add half the dressing and the parsley and stir.

2 Preheat the grill (broiler). Put the red pepper, cut sides down, in a roasting pan with the onion rings. Sprinkle with olive oil and grill (broil) for 5–6 minutes, stirring occasionally, until the pepper blackens and the onion is golden. Stir the onion into the rice. Put the pepper in a plastic bag, tie the top and leave for 15 minutes, then peel and cut the flesh into thin strips.

3 Boil the green beans for 2 minutes, add the corn and cook for 1–2 minutes more, until tender. Drain, refresh under cold water, then drain again. Place in a large bowl and mix in the red pepper strips and quail's eggs, and ham if using.

4 Peel the avocado, remove the stone (pit), and cut the flesh into slices or chunks. Sprinkle with the lemon juice. Put the salad leaves in a separate mixing bowl, add the avocado and mix lightly. Arrange the salad on top of the rice. Stir about 45ml/3 tbsp of the remaining dressing into the green bean and pepper mixture. Pile this on top of the salad. Sprinkle the capers and stuffed olives on top and serve the salad with the remaining dressing.

Nutritional information per portion: Energy 415kcal/1726kJ; Protein 9.1g; Carbohydrate 52.8g, of which sugars 6.6g; Fat 18.5g, of which saturates 3.2g; Cholesterol 48mg; Calcium 77mg; Fibre 3.3g; Sodium 417mg.

Chicken and mango salad with orange rice

Contemporary cuisine draws its inspiration from all over the world. This beautifully flavoured dish has both British and Indian influences and is ideal for informal entertaining.

SERVES 4

75ml/5 tbsp sunflower oil
1 onion, chopped
2 garlic cloves, crushed
30ml/2 tbsp red curry paste
10ml/2 tsp apricot jam
30ml/2 tbsp chicken stock
450g/1lb cooked chicken, chopped
175g/6oz/scant 1 cup white long grain rice
225g/8oz carrots, grated (1¹/₃ cups)
1 large orange, cut into segments
40g/1¹/₂oz/¹/₃ cup roasted flaked
   (sliced) almonds
45ml/3 tbsp olive oil
45ml/3 tbsp lemon juice
15ml/1 tbsp chopped mixed fresh herbs
   (tarragon, parsley, chives)
150ml/¹/₄ pint/²/₃ cup natural
   (plain) yogurt
60–75ml/4–5 tbsp mayonnaise
1 large mango, cut into 1cm/¹/₂in dice
salt and ground black pepper
fresh flat leaf parsley sprigs, to garnish
poppadums, to serve

1 Heat 15ml/1 tbsp sunflower oil in a frying pan and fry the onion and half the garlic for 3–4 minutes until soft. Stir in the curry paste, cook for about 1 minute, then lower the heat and stir in the apricot jam and stock. Mix well, add the chopped chicken and stir until the chicken is thoroughly coated in the paste. Spoon the mixture into a large bowl and leave to cool.

2 Boil the rice in lightly salted water for 15-20 minutes, until just tender. Drain, rinse under cold water and drain again. When cool, place in a bowl with the grated carrots, orange segments and flaked almonds, and mix well.

3 For the dressing, whisk the remaining sunflower oil and garlic in a bowl with the olive oil, lemon juice, mixed herbs and seasoning.

4 When the chicken mixture is cool, stir in the yogurt and mayonnaise, then add the mango, stirring it in carefully so as not to break the flesh. Chill for about 30 minutes.

5 When ready to serve, pour the dressing into the rice salad and mix well. Spoon on to a platter and mound the cold curried chicken on top. Garnish with flat leaf parsley and serve with poppadums.

Nutritional information per portion: Energy 776kcal/3245kJ; Protein 35.9g; Carbohydrate 60.2g, of which sugars 21.1g; Fat 45.3g, of which saturates 6.4g; Cholesterol 93mg; Calcium 172mg; Fibre 4.5g; Sodium 206mg.

Californian citrus fried rice

As with all fried rice dishes, the important thing here is to make sure the rice is cold before frying. Add it after cooking all the other ingredients, and stir to heat it through completely.

SERVES 4–6

4 eggs
10ml/2 tsp Japanese rice vinegar
30ml/2 tbsp light soy sauce
45ml/3 tbsp groundnut (peanut) oil
50g/1³/₄oz/¹/₂ cup cashew nuts
2 garlic cloves, crushed
6 spring onions (scallions), diagonally sliced
2 small carrots, cut into julienne strips
225g/8oz asparagus, quartered
175g/6oz/2¹/₄ cups button (white)
    mushrooms, halved
30ml/2 tbsp rice wine
30ml/2 tbsp water
450g/1lb/4 cups cooked white
    long grain rice
5ml/1 tsp grated orange rind
45ml/3 tbsp oyster sauce
30ml/2 tbsp freshly squeezed orange juice
5ml/1 tsp medium or hot chilli sauce
1 orange
10ml/2 tsp sesame oil

1 Beat the eggs with the vinegar and 10ml/2 tsp of the soy sauce. Heat 15ml/1 tbsp of the oil in a wok and cook the eggs, stirring, until lightly scrambled. Transfer to a plate and set aside. Add the cashew nuts to the wok and stir-fry for 1–2 minutes. Set aside.

2 Heat the remaining oil and add the garlic and spring onions. Cook over a medium heat for 1–2 minutes until the onions begin to soften, then add the carrots and stir-fry for 4 minutes.

3 Add the asparagus and cook for 2–3 minutes, then add the mushrooms and stir-fry for 1 minute. Stir in half the rice wine, the remaining soy sauce and water. Simmer for a few minutes until the vegetables are just tender but still firm. In a bowl, mix the grated orange rind, remaining rice wine, oyster sauce, orange juice and chilli sauce.

4 Add the dressing to the wok, stir and bring to the boil. Add the rice, scrambled eggs and cashew nuts. Toss over a low heat for 3–4 minutes, until the rice is heated through. Just before serving, pare thin strips of rind from the orange and segment the flesh. Stir the segments into the rice with the sesame oil, garnish with strips of orange rind and serve.

Nutritional information per portion: Energy 264kcal/1107kJ; Protein 6.5g; Carbohydrate 32.3g, of which sugars 7.7g; Fat 12.6g, of which saturates 2.1g; Cholesterol 13mg; Calcium 48mg; Fibre 2.3g; Sodium 517mg.

Waldorf rice salad

Waldorf Salad takes its name from the Waldorf Hotel in New York, where it was first made.

SERVES 2–4

1 red apple
1 green apple
60ml/4 tbsp lemon juice
2–3 slices thick cooked ham, rolled up and finely sliced
3 celery stalks, cut into thin strips
115g/4oz/generous 1/2 cup cooked white long grain rice
90ml/6 tbsp mayonnaise, preferably home-made
60ml/4 tbsp sour cream
generous pinch of saffron, dissolved in 15ml/1 tbsp hot water
10ml/2 tsp chopped fresh basil
15ml/1 tbsp chopped fresh parsley
several cos or iceberg lettuce leaves
50g/1³/₄oz/1/2 cup walnuts, roughly chopped
salt and ground black pepper

1 Core and quarter the apples, and finely slice one red and one green quarter. Toss the slices in a bowl with half the lemon juice and reserve for the garnish. Peel the remaining quarters and cut into julienne strips. Place in a separate bowl and toss with 15ml/1 tbsp of the lemon juice. Add the ham and celery to the apple sticks.

2 Mix the mayonnaise, sour cream and saffron water in a large bowl. Add the rice, apple and celery mixture, remaining lemon juice and seasoning. Mix well.

3 Arrange the lettuce leaves around a salad bowl and pile the rice and apple mixture into the centre. Sprinkle with the chopped walnuts and serve.

Nutritional information per portion: Energy 414kcal/1717kJ; Protein 8.7g; Carbohydrate 28.4g, of which sugars 5.2g; Fat 29.6g, of which saturates 5.4g; Cholesterol 37mg; Calcium 68mg; Fibre 1.9g; Sodium 351mg.

Smoked salmon and rice salad parcels

Feta cheese, cucumber and tomatoes give a Greek flavour to the salad in these parcels.

SERVES 4

175g/6oz/scant 1 cup mixed wild rice and basmati rice, cooked according to the packet instructions, drained and cooled
8 slices smoked salmon, total weight about 350g/12oz
10cm/4in piece of cucumber, finely diced
225g/8oz feta cheese, cubed
8 cherry tomatoes, quartered
30ml/2 tbsp mayonnaise
10ml/2 tsp fresh lime juice
15ml/1 tbsp chopped fresh chervil
salt and ground black pepper
lime slices and fresh chervil, to garnish

1 Put the rice in a bowl. Line four ramekins with clear film (plastic wrap), then line each with two slices of smoked salmon. Reserve any extra pieces for the tops. Add the cucumber, feta and tomatoes to the rice, and stir in the mayonnaise, lime juice and chervil. Mix together well. Season to taste.

2 Spoon the mixture into the salmon-lined ramekins. Place any extra pieces of smoked salmon on top, then fold over the overlapping pieces of fish so that the rice mixture is completely encased.

3 Chill for 30–60 minutes, then invert each parcel on to a plate, using the clear film to ease them out of the ramekins. Peel off the clear film, garnish each parcel with slices of lime and a sprig of fresh chervil and serve.

Nutritional information per portion: Energy 479kcal/2000kJ; Protein 34.6g; Carbohydrate 36.9g, of which sugars 1.9g; Fat 21.3g, of which saturates 9.3g; Cholesterol 76mg; Calcium 232mg; Fibre 0.3g; Sodium 2491mg.

Desserts

Rice pudding is one of the world's favourite desserts and this chapter boasts some wonderful variations from many different countries. However, if you are in the mood for a different kind of treat, there are other dishes to choose from, whether you prefer something sweet, chocolatey and tempting, or fresh, tangy and fruity.

Pear, almond and ground rice flan

Ground rice gives a distinctive, slightly grainy texture to puddings that goes particularly well with autumn fruit. Pears and almonds are a divine combination.

SERVES 6

4 ripe pears

30ml/2 tbsp soft light brown sugar

115g/4oz/¹/₂ cup unsalted (sweet) butter

115g/4oz/generous ¹/₂ cup caster (superfine) sugar

2 eggs

a few drops of almond extract

75g/2³/₄oz/²/₃ cup self-raising (self-rising) flour

50g/1³/₄oz/¹/₃ cup ground rice

25g/1oz/¹/₄ cup flaked (sliced) almonds

custard or crème fraîche, to serve

1 Preheat the oven to 180°C/350°F/ Gas 4. Grease a shallow 25cm/10in flan dish. Peel and quarter the pears and arrange them in the flan dish. Sprinkle with the brown sugar.

2 Cream the butter and caster sugar until light and fluffy, then beat in the eggs and almond extract. Fold in the flour and ground rice.

3 Carefully spoon the almond-flavoured egg and ground rice mixture over the quartered pears and level the surface with a metal spatula.

4 Sprinkle the top with the flaked almonds, then transfer to the oven and bake the flan for 30–35 minutes until the topping is golden. Serve with custard or crème fraîche.

Nutritional information per portion: Energy 396kcal/1656kJ; Protein 5.2g; Carbohydrate 50.9g, of which sugars 34.8g; Fat 20.2g, of which saturates 10.7g; Cholesterol 104mg; Calcium 92mg; Fibre 2.9g; Sodium 190mg.

South-western rice pudding

Coconut is the secret ingredient in this unusual Mexican rice pudding. Do not overcook the rice or it will become stodgy. Fresh fruits, such as strawberries, make the ideal partner.

SERVES 4

40g/1¹/₂oz/¹/₄ cup raisins
about 475ml/17fl oz/2 cups water
200g/7oz/1 cup short grain pudding rice
1 cinnamon stick
30ml/2 tbsp sugar
475ml/17fl oz/2 cups milk
250ml/8fl oz/1 cup canned sweetened
    coconut cream
2.5ml/¹/₂ tsp vanilla extract
15g/¹/₂oz/1 tbsp butter
25g/1oz/¹/₃ cup shredded coconut
ground cinnamon, for sprinkling

1 Put the raisins in a small bowl and pour over enough water to cover. Leave the raisins to soak.

2 Pour the measured water into a heavy or non-stick pan and bring to the boil. Add the rice, cinnamon and sugar, and stir. Return to the boil, lower the heat, cover and simmer for 15–20 minutes until the liquid has been absorbed.

3 Remove and discard the cinnamon stick. Drain the raisins and add them to the rice.

4 Stir in the milk, coconut cream and vanilla extract. Replace the lid and then cook the mixture for about 20 minutes more, until it is just thick. Do not overcook the rice. Preheat the grill (broiler).

5 Transfer the mixture to a flameproof serving dish. Dot with the butter and sprinkle shredded coconut evenly over the surface. Grill (broil) about 13cm/5in from the heat until the top is just browned. Sprinkle with cinnamon. Serve warm or cold.

Nutritional information per portion: Energy 259kcal/1087kJ; Protein 5.8g; Carbohydrate 34g, of which sugars 19.9g; Fat 11.6g, of which saturates 8.2g; Cholesterol 19mg; Calcium 153mg; Fibre 1g; Sodium 153mg.

Strawberry shortcake

Ground rice is widely used for baking. It adds a light, fine texture to this shortbread.

SERVES 8

350g/12oz/3 cups strawberries
300ml/¹/₂ pint/1¹/₄ cups double (heavy) cream
115g/4oz/1 cup plain (all-purpose) flour
50g/1³/₄oz/1/₃ cup ground rice
105g/3¹/₂oz/¹/₂ cup caster (superfine) sugar
115g/4oz/¹/₂ cup unsalted (sweet) butter
1 egg yolk
about 15ml/1 tbsp milk

1 Preheat the oven to 180°C/350°F/Gas 4. Sift the flour and rice into a bowl. Stir in 75g/2³/₄oz/6 tbsp of the caster sugar, rub in the butter, stir in the egg yolk and milk, and mix to a dough.

2 Knead lightly, halve, and roll each half into a 20cm/8in round. Place on greased fluted flan tins (pans). Mark one of the rounds into eight wedges. Bake for 15–20 minutes until golden, then place the tins on a wire rack to cool slightly. Cut the marked round into wedges, remove both rounds from the tins and cool on the rack.

3 Reserve a strawberry for decoration; hull and slice the rest, reserving eight slices. Whip the cream until thick. Stir in the remaining caster sugar. Spoon one-third of the cream into a piping (pastry) bag. Spread the rest over the whole shortbread base. Top with sliced strawberries and shortbread wedges at an angle. Pipe cream between them. Slice the whole strawberry almost through into a fan and place in the centre.

Nutritional information per portion: Energy 436kcal/1811kJ; Protein 3.2g; Carbohydrate 33.2g, of which sugars 17.3g; Fat 32.9g, of which saturates 20.2g; Cholesterol 107mg; Calcium 60mg; Fibre 1.1g; Sodium 101mg.

English rice pudding

A proper rice pudding is smooth, creamy and a little spicy. Try serving with thick cherry jam.

SERVES 4

600ml/1 pint/2¹/₂ cups creamy milk
1 vanilla pod (bean)
50g/1³/₄oz/generous ¹/₄ cup short grain pudding rice
45ml/3 tbsp caster (superfine) sugar
25g/1oz/2 tbsp butter
freshly grated nutmeg

1 Pour the milk into a pan. If possible, always use a non-stick pan when heating milk, otherwise it is likely to stick to the bottom of the pan and burn.

2 Add the vanilla pod. Bring to simmering point, then remove from the heat, cover and leave to infuse (steep) for about 1 hour.

3 Preheat the oven to 150°C/300°F/Gas 2. Put the rice and sugar in an ovenproof dish. Strain the milk over the rice, discarding the vanilla pod. Stir to mix, then dot the surface with the butter.

4 Bake in the preheated oven, uncovered, for 2 hours. After about 40 minutes, stir the surface skin into the pudding, and repeat this after a further 40 minutes. At this point, sprinkle the surface of the pudding with grated nutmeg. Allow the pudding to finish cooking without stirring.

Nutritional information per portion: Energy 433kcal/1829kJ; Protein 5.8g; Carbohydrate 85.6g, of which sugars 65.7g; Fat 6.9g, of which saturates 3.3g; Cholesterol 112mg; Calcium 113mg; Fibre 0.5g; Sodium 68mg.

Souffléd rice pudding

Using skimmed milk to make this pudding is a healthy option. However, if you prefer a creamier taste, you could use whole milk instead.

SERVES 4

65g/2¹/₂oz/¹/₃ cup short grain
   pudding rice
45ml/3 tbsp clear honey
750ml/1¹/₄ pints/3 cups skimmed milk
1 vanilla pod (bean) or 2.5ml/¹/₂ tsp
   vanilla extract
butter, for greasing
2 egg whites
5ml/1 tsp freshly grated nutmeg
dessert biscuits (cookies),
   to serve (optional)

1 Place the rice, honey and milk in a heavy or non-stick pan, and bring the milk to just below boiling point, watching it closely to prevent it from boiling over. Add the vanilla pod, if using.

2 Reduce the heat to the lowest setting and cover the pan. Leave to cook for about 1–1¹/₄ hours, stirring occasionally to prevent sticking, until most of the liquid has been absorbed.

3 Remove the vanilla pod or, if using vanilla extract, add this to the rice mixture now. Preheat the oven to 220°C/425°F/Gas 7. Grease a 1 litre/1³/₄ pint/4 cup baking dish with butter.

4 Place the egg whites in a large grease-free bowl and whisk them until they hold soft peaks. Using either a large metal spoon or a spatula, carefully fold the egg whites evenly into the rice and milk mixture. Turn into the baking dish.

5 Sprinkle with grated nutmeg and bake in the oven for 15–20 minutes, until the rice pudding has risen well and the surface is golden brown. Serve the pudding hot, with dessert biscuits, if you like.

Nutritional information per portion: Energy 183kcal/773kJ; Protein 9.1g; Carbohydrate 30.4g, of which sugars 17.4g; Fat 3.3g, of which saturates 2g; Cholesterol 11mg; Calcium 230mg; Fibre 0g; Sodium 112mg.

Caramel rice pudding

This rice pudding is delicious served with crunchy fresh fruit. Fresh baby pineapples and figs have been used in this recipe, but you can vary it by serving it with other fresh fruits of your choice.

SERVES 4

15g/¹/₂oz/1 tbsp butter
50g/³/₄oz/¹/₄ cup short grain
    pudding rice
75ml/5 tbsp demerara (raw) sugar
400g/14oz can evaporated milk made up
    to 600ml/1 pint/2¹/₂ cups with water
2 fresh baby pineapples
2 figs
1 crisp eating apple
10ml/2 tsp lemon juice
salt

1 Preheat the oven to 150°C/300°F/Gas 2. Grease a flameproof baking dish lightly with a little of the butter. Put the rice in a sieve (strainer) and wash it thoroughly under cold water. Drain well and put into the baking dish.

2 Add 30ml/2 tbsp of the sugar to the dish, with a pinch of salt. Pour on the diluted evaporated milk and stir gently.

3 Dot the surface of the rice with butter. Bake for 2 hours, then leave to cool for 30 minutes.

4 Meanwhile, quarter the pineapples and the figs. Cut the apple into segments and toss in the lemon juice. Preheat the grill (broiler).

5 Sprinkle the remaining sugar evenly over the rice. Grill (broil) for 5 minutes or until the sugar has caramelized. Leave the rice to stand for 5 minutes to allow the caramel to harden, then serve with the fresh fruit.

Nutritional information per portion: Energy 313kcal/1321kJ; Protein 9.6g; Carbohydrate 54.3g, of which sugars 44.3g; Fat 7.6g, of which saturates 4.5g; Cholesterol 25mg; Calcium 312mg; Fibre 1.9g; Sodium 147mg.

Fruity rice pudding custard

This delicious variation on rice pudding hails from Latin America. The rum – or brandy, depending on your preference – gives it that extra kick.

SERVES 4–6

60ml/4 tbsp rum or brandy

75g/2³/₄oz/¹/₂ cup sultanas
   (golden raisins)

75g/2³/₄oz/scant ¹/₂ cup short grain
   pudding rice

600ml/1 pint/2¹/₂ cups creamy milk

1 strip pared lemon rind

¹/₂ cinnamon stick

115g/4oz/scant ¹/₂ cup caster
   (superfine) sugar

butter, for greasing

150ml/¹/₄ pint/²/₃ cup single
   (light) cream

2 eggs, plus 1 egg yolk

almond biscuits (cookies),
   to serve (optional)

1 Warm the rum or brandy in a small pan, then pour it over the sultanas. Soak for 3–4 hours or overnight.

2 Cook the rice in boiling water for 10 minutes. Drain and return to the pan. Stir in 300ml/¹/₂ pint/1¹/₄ cups of milk. Add the lemon rind and cinnamon, bring to the boil, lower the heat and simmer for 5 minutes. Remove from the heat and stir in half the sugar. Cover with a damp dish towel held in place with the pan lid. Leave to cool for 1–2 hours.

3 Preheat the oven to 180°C/350°F/ Gas 4. Butter a baking dish. Sprinkle the sultanas over the bottom, with any rum or brandy left over.

4 Stir the rice, which should by now be thick and creamy, most of the liquid having been absorbed. Discard the cinnamon and lemon rind. Spoon the rice over the sultanas.

5 Heat the remaining milk with the cream until it is just boiling. Meanwhile, mix the eggs and egg yolk in a jug (pitcher). Whisk in the remaining sugar, then the hot milk, then pour over the rice.

6 Stand the dish in a roasting pan, then pour in hot water to halfway up the sides of the dish and bake for 1–1¹/₄ hours until the top is firm. Serve hot, with almond biscuits, if you like.

Nutritional information per portion: Energy 326kcal/1366kJ; Protein 8.1g; Carbohydrate 43.7g, of which sugars 33.8g; Fat 11.6g, of which saturates 6.3g; Cholesterol 125mg; Calcium 174mg; Fibre 0.3g; Sodium 79mg.

Orange rice pudding

In Morocco, as in Spain, Greece and Italy, thick, creamy rice puddings are very popular, especially when sweetened with honey and flavoured with orange.

SERVES 4

50g/1³/₄oz/generous ¹/₄ cup short grain
  pudding rice
600ml/1 pint/2¹/₂ cups milk
finely grated rind of ¹/₂ small orange
30–45ml/2–3 tbsp clear honey
150ml/¹/₄ pint/²/₃ cup double
  (heavy) cream
15ml/1 tbsp chopped pistachio nuts,
  toasted (optional)
grated orange rind, to garnish

1 Mix the pudding rice with the milk and finely grated orange rind in a large, heavy pan. Stir the honey into the rice and milk.

2 Bring to the boil, then lower the heat, cover with a lid and simmer very gently for about 1¹/₄ hours, stirring frequently.

3 Remove the lid and continue cooking and stirring the rice for 15–20 minutes, until creamy.

4 Stir in the cream, then simmer for 5–8 minutes more. Spoon into warmed individual bowls. Sprinkle with the pistachio nuts, if using, and grated orange rind. Serve.

Nutritional information per portion: Energy 355kcal/1477kJ; Protein 7.4g; Carbohydrate 26.6g, of which sugars 16.5g; Fat 24.8g, of which saturates 14.4g; Cholesterol 60mg; Calcium 206mg; Fibre 0.2g; Sodium 94mg.

Portuguese rice pudding

This variation on rice pudding is popular all over Portugal, so if you visit that country, you're likely to find it on most menus. Traditionally, it is served cold, but it is also delicious warm.

SERVES 4–6

175g/6oz/scant 1 cup short grain
   pudding rice
600ml/1 pint/2¹/₂ cups creamy milk
2 or 3 strips pared lemon rind
65g/2¹/₂oz/5 tbsp butter, in pieces

115g/4oz/¹/₂ cup caster (superfine) sugar
4 egg yolks
salt
ground cinnamon, for dusting
lemon wedges, to serve

1 Cook the rice in plenty of lightly salted boiling water for about 5 minutes, by which time it will have lost its brittleness.

2 Drain well, then return to the clean pan. Add the milk, lemon rind and butter. Bring to the boil over a moderately low heat, then cover, reduce the heat to the lowest setting and simmer for about 20 minutes or until the rice is thick and creamy.

3 Remove the pan from the heat and allow the rice to cool a little. Remove and discard the lemon rind, then stir in the sugar and the egg yolks. Mix well.

4 Divide among four to six serving bowls and dust with ground cinnamon. Serve cool, with lemon wedges for squeezing.

Nutritional information per portion: Energy 368kcal/1534kJ; Protein 7.6g; Carbohydrate 47.9g, of which sugars 24.6g; Fat 16.6g, of which saturates 9.2g; Cholesterol 172mg; Calcium 151mg; Fibre 0g; Sodium 116mg.

Calas

These sweet rice fritters are a Creole speciality, sold by "Calas" women on the streets of the French quarter of New Orleans. They make a popular and tasty breakfast.

MAKES OVER 40

115g/4oz/generous ¹/₂ cup short
    grain pudding rice
900ml/1¹/₂ pints/3³/₄ cups mixed
    milk and water
30ml/2 tbsp caster (superfine) sugar
50g/1³/₄oz/¹/₂ cup plain
    (all-purpose) flour
7.5ml/1¹/₂ tsp baking powder
5ml/1 tsp grated lemon rind
2.5ml/¹/₂ tsp ground cinnamon
1.5ml/¹/₄ tsp ground ginger
generous pinch of grated nutmeg
2 eggs
vegetable oil, for deep-frying
salt
icing (confectioners') sugar, for dusting
cherry or strawberry jam and thick
    cream, to serve

1 Put the rice in a large, heavy pan and pour in the milk and water. Add a pinch of salt and bring to the boil. Stir, then cover and simmer over a very gentle heat for 15–20 minutes until the rice is tender.

2 Remove from the heat, then add the sugar. Stir well, cover and leave until completely cool, by which time the rice should have absorbed all the liquid and become very soft.

3 Put the rice in a food processor or blender and add the flour, baking powder, lemon rind, spices and eggs. Process for 20–30 seconds to a thick batter.

4 Heat the oil in a large pan to 160°C/325°F. Scoop up a generous teaspoon of the rice batter and, using a second spoon, push this off carefully into the hot oil. Add four or five more and fry for 3–4 minutes, turning them occasionally, until the calas are a deep golden brown. Drain on kitchen paper and keep warm while cooking successive batches.

5 Dust the calas with icing sugar and serve them warm with fruit jam and thick cream.

Nutritional information per portion: Energy 50kcal/206kJ; Protein 0.9g; Carbohydrate 3.5g, of which sugars 1.3g; Fat 3.6g, of which saturates 0.6g; Cholesterol 10mg; Calcium 16mg; Fibre 0g; Sodium 8mg.

Apple and lemon risotto with poached plums

Although it's possible to cook this by the conventional risotto method – by adding the liquid slowly – it makes more sense to cook the rice with the milk, in the same way as for a rice pudding.

SERVES 4

1 cooking apple
15g/¹/₂oz/1 tbsp butter
175g/6oz/scant 1 cup risotto rice
600ml/1 pint/2¹/₂ cups creamy milk
about 50g/1³/₄oz/¹/₄ cup caster
   (superfine) sugar
1.5ml/¹/₄ tsp ground cinnamon
30ml/2 tbsp lemon juice
45ml/3 tbsp double (heavy) cream
grated rind of 1 lemon, to decorate

FOR THE POACHED PLUMS

50g/1³/₄oz/¹/₄ cup light muscovado
   (brown) sugar
200ml/7fl oz/scant 1 cup apple juice
3 star anise
1 cinnamon stick
6 plums, halved and sliced

1 Peel and core the cooking apple, then cut it into large chunks. Put the apple chunks into a large, heavy pan and add the butter. Heat gently until the butter melts.

2 Add the risotto rice and the milk and stir together well. Bring the mixture to the boil over a medium heat, then reduce the heat and simmer very gently for 20–25 minutes, stirring occasionally. If the apple is very sharp (acidic), the milk may curdle. There is no need to worry about this – it won't affect the look or taste of the risotto.

3 To make the poached plums, dissolve the light muscovado sugar in 150ml/¹/₄ pints/²/₃ cup of the apple juice in a pan. Add the spices and bring to the boil. Boil for 2 minutes. Add the plums and simmer for 2 minutes. Add the remaining apple juice, heat through, then set aside and keep warm.

4 Stir the caster sugar, ground cinnamon and lemon juice into the risotto. Cook for 2 minutes, stirring all the time, then stir in the cream. Taste and add more sugar, if necessary. Decorate with the lemon rind and serve with the poached plums.

Nutritional information per portion: Energy 479kcal/2010kJ; Protein 8.9g; Carbohydrate 78.4g, of which sugars 43.5g; Fat 15.3g, of which saturates 9.5g; Cholesterol 44mg; Calcium 215mg; Fibre 1g; Sodium 94mg.

Chocolate risotto

If you've never tasted a sweet chocolate risotto, there's a treat in store. Chocolate risotto is delectable, and children of all ages love it.

SERVES 4–6

175g/6oz/scant 1 cup risotto rice
600ml/1 pint/2½ cups creamy milk
75g/2¾oz plain (semisweet) chocolate, broken into pieces
25g/1oz/2 tbsp butter
about 50g/1¾oz/¼ cup caster (superfine) sugar
pinch of ground cinnamon
60ml/4 tbsp double (heavy) cream
fresh raspberries and chocolate caraque, to decorate
chocolate sauce, to serve

1 Put the rice in a large, heavy pan. Pour in the milk and bring to the boil over a low to medium heat. Reduce the heat and simmer very gently for about 20 minutes, stirring occasionally, until the rice is very soft.

2 Stir in the chocolate, butter and sugar. Cook, stirring all the time, over a very gentle heat for 1–2 minutes, until the chocolate has melted.

3 Remove the pan from the heat and stir in the ground cinnamon and the double cream. Cover the pan with a lid and leave to stand for a few minutes.

4 Spoon the chocolate risotto into individual dishes or dessert plates, and decorate with fresh raspberries and chocolate caraque. Serve the risotto immediately, with chocolate sauce.

Nutritional information per portion: Energy 348kcal/1451kJ; Protein 6.3g; Carbohydrate 44.6g, of which sugars 21.2g; Fat 16.3g, of which saturates 10.1g; Cholesterol 37mg; Calcium 138mg; Fibre 0.3g; Sodium 72mg.

Rice conde sundae

Cooking rice pudding on top of the hob instead of in the oven gives it a light, creamy texture. It is particularly good served cold with a topping of fruit and toasted nuts or hot chocolate sauce.

SERVES 4

50g/1³/₄oz/generous ¼ cup short
   grain pudding rice
5ml/1 tsp vanilla extract
2.5ml/¹/₂ tsp ground cinnamon
45ml/3 tbsp sugar
600ml/1 pint/2¹/₂ cups milk
soft berry fruits such as strawberries,
   raspberries and cherries
toasted chocolate sauce and flaked
   (sliced) almonds (optional)

1 Mix the pudding rice, vanilla extract, cinnamon and sugar in a large, heavy pan. Pour in the milk. Bring to the boil, stirring constantly, then reduce the heat so that the mixture barely simmers.

2 Cook the rice over a low heat for 30–40 minutes, stirring frequently. Add extra milk to the rice if it begins to dry out.

3 When the rice grains are soft, remove the pan from the heat, then allow the rice to cool, stirring it occasionally. When cooled, cover and chill in the refrigerator.

4 Before serving, stir the rice pudding and spoon it into four sundae dishes. Top with soft berries, and with chocolate sauce and toasted flaked almonds if using.

Nutritional information per portion: Energy 185kcal/782kJ; Protein 6.9g; Carbohydrate 34.8g, of which sugars 24.8g; Fat 2.7g, of which saturates 1.6g; Cholesterol 9mg; Calcium 204mg; Fibre 1.1g; Sodium 71mg.

Coconut cream dessert

For this dish, use Thai fragrant rice. Although commercially ground rice can be used, grinding the rice yourself – in a food processor – gives a much better result.

SERVES 4–6

75g/2³/₄oz/scant ¹/₂ cup Thai fragrant
    rice, soaked overnight in 175ml/6fl oz/
    ³/₄ cup water
350ml/12fl oz/1¹/₂ cups coconut milk
150ml/¹/₄ pint/²/₃ cup single (light) cream
50g//1³/₄oz/¹/₄ cup caster
    (superfine) sugar
fresh raspberries and mint leaves,
    to decorate

FOR THE COULIS

75g/2³/₄oz/³/₄ cup blackcurrants,
    stalks removed
about 30ml/2 tbsp caster
    (superfine) sugar
75g/2³/₄oz/¹/₂ cup fresh or
    frozen raspberries

1 Put the rice and its soaking water into a food processor and process for a few minutes until the mixture is soupy.

2 Heat the coconut milk and cream in a large, heavy pan. When the mixture is on the point of boiling, stir in the rice mixture.

3 Cook over a very gentle heat for 10 minutes, stirring constantly, then stir in the sugar and continue cooking for 10–15 minutes more, or until the mixture is thick and creamy.

4 Pour the rice mixture into a rectangular pan that has been lined with a baking parchment. Cool, then chill in the refrigerator until the pudding is firm.

5 To make the coulis, put the blackcurrants in a bowl and sprinkle with the sugar. Set aside for about 30 minutes. Turn into a wire sieve (strainer) with the raspberries and use the back of a spoon to press the fruit against the sides of the sieve so that the juices collect in a bowl underneath. Taste and add more sugar if necessary. Discard the pulp remaining in the sieve.

6 Carefully cut the coconut cream into diamonds. Spoon a little of the coulis on to each dessert plate, arrange the coconut cream diamonds on top and decorate with fresh raspberries and mint leaves.

Nutritional information per portion: Energy 165kcal/696kJ; Protein 2.3g; Carbohydrate 28.7g, of which sugars 18.8g; Fat 5.1g, of which saturates 3.2g; Cholesterol 14mg; Calcium 59mg; Fibre 0.8g; Sodium 73mg.

Rice and risotto basics

The following chapter offers a comprehensive guide to the assorted varieties of rice, and the equipment and utensils needed for cooking and serving rice and risotto dishes. As well as introducing a range of essential rice products for your store cupboard, it also covers the techniques for producing perfect rice, paella and sushi, classic stocks and rice pudding.

The rice field

Throughout the world, rice fields continue to produce the nutritious food staple that has been vital to the survival of many millions of people for thousands of years.

CLASSIFICATION

There are numerous varieties of rice, although all of them stem from a single species. In simple terms, each of these varieties of rice can be classified as one of three main types of grain: indica, japonica and javonica.

Indica, as the name suggests, is the rice of India. The grains are long and tend to remain separate after cooking.

Japonica, which is grown in other parts of Asia, has short grains that are sticky or glutinous when cooked.

The third group, javonica, is long grained but has sticky properties.

CULTIVATION

Rice is the only important cereal to grow in water. Water brings nutrients to the plant, insulates it against extreme heat and cold and, some believe, helps to keep down weeds, although some weeding is still required.

In America, the rice checks (rice fields) are flooded through a system of canals, which introduce fresh water from a nearby river wherever needed. In much of South-east Asia, water for the paddy fields flows constantly, but relying on Nature for the supply can be tricky. Either there is too much or too little, or the water flows too quickly or not at all. The plant will survive wet or dry periods, and can grow in still water, but ideally the paddy should be flooded after the plant has flowered, and drained dry before harvest.

The biggest rice-producing area in the world is South-east Asia, from Pakistan in the west, to Japan and the Philippines in the east. Outside South-east Asia the principal regions are the southern United States, Brazil, Egypt, Spain and Italy.

In the West, mechanization has taken over the jobs that are still carried out manually in Asia. The rice fields of Texas and Louisiana look very different from those of Bali or Thailand. Only in

ABOVE: *The combine harvester has a central role to play in the modern-day rice harvest.*

Asia will you see the traditional images associated with rice growing: water buffalo harrowing the paddy fields, men hoeing the flooded fields before planting, and women in conical hats, planting rice seeds.

In many parts of Asia, farmers aim for two crops a year. The first job is to prepare the land. A hoe is used to break up the soil, which is then flooded prior to planting. In mountainous areas, rice is planted in the highest fields first. Water then flows downhill to the lower terraces. Oxen or water buffalo may be used for harrowing the flooded field, which is then planted by women. It can take several days to plant a paddy field. During the growing season all family members help to add fertilizers and pesticides, and to do the weeding.

HARVESTING

In many Asian countries, come harvest, the women once again move back into the fields to cut the rice

LEFT: *In South-east Asia, labourers work on a terraced rice field as they have done for thousands of years.*

stalks, using a small, sharp knife. Once they have been cut, the rice stalks are stacked in bundles and threshed – beaten over hard ground with flails or drawn over spikes to release the rice grains. Mechanization is creeping in, predominantly in the developed world, but you may still see hand threshing in parts of Java and Bali. Here, the grain is manually husked and winnowed to dispel the straw and chaff before being stored in the traditional family rice barn, the highly elaborate shrine to the rice spirit.

MILLING

Unless it has been threshed and husked manually, paddy, once cut, is taken to the mill, where the bran and husk are removed to give fully milled or "polished" white rice. Unmilled rice that has had only the husk removed is known as cargo rice. This is the form that is imported into Europe from both Asia and America, so that the milling process can be completed.

In Europe, milling is a mechanized procedure, although the basic principle is much the same as in the

small, noisy mills of Asia. The brown rice passes between rubber rollers that rub away the brown outer skin, leaving the white grain. Once fully milled, this is known as "polished" rice, and while once implied that the grain had been treated with glycerine or talc to make the grains glossy, this operation is now fairly rare.

MARKETING

Even until very recently, all the rice grown on a typical Asian plot would have been for the family's own consumption, and even today less than 4 per cent is traded between countries. Demand for rice is growing worldwide, however, and as agriculture and jobs diversify, a greater proportion of the rice farmer's annual crop will be sold either for the local market or for export.

Europe is the biggest importer of rice, followed by Brazil and the Middle East. Many rice-growing countries import rice to supplement their own crop, as in the case of Brazil, or so that the home-grown rice can be exported. In order to earn foreign currency, China exports the greater part of its high-grade rice and imports a low-grade rice for its own population. In parts of the Punjab where basmati rice is grown, almost the entire crop is exported. The price that basmati can fetch means that there is a huge incentive to sell this quality rice. Paradoxically, within the region, bread is more commonly eaten than rice.

LEFT: *Rice labourers at work in a rice paddy field in Hiroshima, Japan*

NUTRITION

Rice is a non-allergenic food, rich in complex carbohydrates and low in salts and fats. Since brown rice retains the bran, it has twice the nutritional content of white rice and is therefore considered the healthier choice, but all rice is good for you.

Starch/complex carbohydrate Rice contains two main starches, which determine how sticky or glutinous a rice is. Both provide slow-release energy, a healthier form of carbohydrate than sugar.

Protein Brown and white rice both contain a small amount of easily digestible protein.

Minerals Rice contains small amounts of phosphorus, magnesium, zinc and potassium. They are mostly found in the bran part of brown rice and, to a lesser extent, in par-boiled rice, the production of which involves a process that "glues" nutrients into the grain.

Fibre The bran in brown rice provides some fibre, but little remains in white rice after the bran has been taken out.

Vitamins Rice contains small amounts of vitamin E, and B vitamins, including thiamine, riboflavin, niacin, vitamin B6 and folic acid, although since most of the vitamins are contained in the bran, brown rice is a richer source of these nutrients. Par-boiled rice also contains a higher proportion of vitamins than ordinary white rice.

Equipment

It may be a simple foodstuff but to cook rice perfectly for a variety of dishes, and to serve it stylishly to impress friends and family, you will still need a range of kitchen essentials.

ELECTRIC RICE COOKER

In Japan and other more affluent rice-eating countries, electric rice cookers have now replaced more conventional means of cooking rice. In the West they are also becoming increasingly popular, and cooks who use them often say they are indispensable. The cookers cook rice perfectly and have the added advantage of keeping it warm throughout the meal, without it drying or becoming soggy. Another bonus of the rice cooker is that it frees hob space.

PANS

Even if you have invested in a rice cooker, you will always need pans. For plain boiled rice and for risottos, a heavy pan is the best choice – the actual size will depend on the quantities you are likely to be making, but bigger is definitely better; small amounts of rice can be cooked in a large pan but you'll run into difficulties if you try cooking lots of rice in a pan that is too small. For risottos, some cooks prefer to use a deep frying pan. A small frying pan or crêpe pan will also be useful for frying the omelettes often used to garnish Oriental rice dishes.

COLANDERS AND SIEVES

A colander or sieve (strainer) is essential for draining boiled rice. Buy a good-quality colander with a long handle, so that you can stand well back in order to pour the steaming rice out of the pan.

MEASURING JUGS AND SCALES

It is important to measure rice accurately, and to add the correct quantity of water or other liquid, as specified in the recipe or on the packet, especially when cooking by the absorption method. In most recipes the rice is measured by weight, although it can also be measured by volume. When adding stocks and other liquids, use a measuring jug.

ABOVE: Large pans are essential for rice and risotto dishes.

BELOW: Colander and sieve

FLAMEPROOF CASSEROLE

Many rice dishes are started off on the hob, then finished in the oven. A flameproof casserole is perfect for this, and will also prove useful for dishes that are entirely oven-baked. Casseroles should have well-fitting lids; if lids are at all loose, cover the casserole with foil before fitting the lid in place.

EARTHENWARE CASSEROLE

These cannot be used on the hob, but are very useful for oven-cooked pilaffs. It is essential for the casserole to have a well-fitting lid.

PARMESAN GRATER

Freshly grated Parmesan cheese is essential in risottos. Although many supermarkets now stock it freshly grated, it is fairly expensive. Buying it whole and grating it yourself is a better option. Small metal Parmesan graters are available, but the graters where you put the cheese in the top and turn the handle allow you to grate only the amount you need.

MORTAR AND PESTLE

It is not necessary to use spices when cooking rice, but for many dishes, particularly those with an Oriental flavour, they are essential. The advantage of grinding your own spices is that you can be sure they are absolutely fresh; you'll notice the difference at once compared with ready-ground spices. A mortar and pestle is the traditional piece of equipment for grinding spices, and has the advantage that you can grind very small quantities. The mortar is the container, while the pestle is used to pulverize spices, seeds, garlic or herbs. Mortar and pestle sets can be made of stone, wood or marble.

SPICE MILL

A spice mill can be used instead of a mortar and pestle. It will grind spices very finely with very little effort.

COOKING KNIVES

Though they are not specifically required for cooking rice, good-quality kitchen knives in a range of sizes and weights are essential for preparing other ingredients.

ABOVE: *Bamboo steamer*

ABOVE: *Chopsticks and chopstick stand*

PAELLA PAN

If you are likely to make paella on a regular basis – or fancy bringing back a souvenir of your visit to Spain – do invest in a paella pan. Bigger pans obviously make bigger paellas, but very large pans will probably turn out to be bigger than your gas or electric rings, which will mean the food will cook unevenly.

WOK

You will need a wok for any stir-fried rice dish and will also find one useful for making a wide variety of sauces and stir-fries to accompany rice dishes. Buy the appropriate wok for your hob. Round-bottomed woks can only be used on gas hobs; a flat-bottomed wok should be used on an electric hob.

STEAMERS

You can use a rice steamer to cook rice and for "finishing" rice if you do not have an electric rice cooker.

JAPANESE BAMBOO ROLLING MAT

Essential for rolling rice when making sushi, this simple but very useful piece of equipment is flexible in one direction but rigid in the other.

MUSLIN (CHEESECLOTH) BAG

This is useful for making your own lontong (compressed rice). If you don't have a bamboo steamer, you can fill a bag with rice and put it in a pan of boiling water. Make a bag by cutting two 25cm/10in squares of muslin: sew them together around three sides, leaving one edge open.

CHOPSTICKS AND CHOPSTICK STANDS

Oriental cooks use long chopsticks for manipulating foods when stir-frying. Using good-quality chopsticks when serving a Chinese or Thai meal also adds authenticity. Provide stands for chopsticks at the table; less elaborate ones can be used when cooking.

RICE BOWLS

Chinese or Japanese rice bowls are attractive to use for an Oriental meal. Buy genuine sets from Oriental markets or when travelling, for use on special occasions.

BELOW: *Bowls*

Types of rice

There are thousands of varieties of rice. In the world's major rice-growing areas, it is not unknown for each field to yield its own strain. However, roughly two-thirds of the rice grown is eaten very close to where it is grown, so the many varieties are not widely known.

There are several ways of classifying rice: by region, by colour, by cooking properties, even by price. But the most common classification, and the one most supermarkets favour, is by the length of the grain. As a general rule, long and medium grain rices are used for savoury dishes, while short grain is used for desserts, although there are exceptions: risotto is only ever made with special short grain rices, for example. In America, the terms Patna, rose and pearl are used by millers to describe long, medium and short grain rice respectively.

ABOVE: *Organic rice is grown entirely free of chemicals.*

ORGANIC RICE
This is rice that has been grown without the use of pesticides or chemical fertilizers. It can be long, medium or short grain.

LONG GRAIN RICE
This rice is three or four times as long as it is wide. When it is cooked, the individual grains separate. Long grain rice can be used in a variety of recipes.

White long grain rice
This is the most commonly available white rice and may come from any of a number of countries. America is the most significant producer of long grain rice sold in Europe. China, India, Malaysia and Thailand, among others, produce far greater amounts of this rice than does America, but their production is principally used for the home market and is not exported.

In China, long grain rice is called simply *xian* or *indica* (*Oryza indica* is the generic name for all long grain rice). In the main rice-eating regions of China, this type is the cheapest and most widely available rice for everyday consumption.

The white variety of long grain rice has been milled, and all of the bran and outer coating has been removed. The grains are white and slightly shiny, a feature often described by the expression "polished", although, strictly speaking, this would mean that glycerine or talc has been used to polish the grains, giving them a

ABOVE: *From left, white and brown long grain rice*

smooth and glossy appearance. This practice is relatively rare these days, although the term "polished rice" still persists in some quarters. While white rice hasn't the flavour of basmati or Thai fragrant rice, it is still a firm favourite and is a good choice for a large number of Western-style and Oriental dishes.

Brown long grain rice
Sometimes called "wholegrain rice", this is the whole of the grain with bran – the rice equivalent of wholemeal (whole-wheat) bread. In countries where rice is a staple food, brown rice is generally disliked and is seldom eaten. Most brown rice is consumed in the West, where it is considered a healthier alternative to white rice, and is enjoyed for its pleasant texture and nutty flavour. Almost all brown rice is long or medium grain. Short grain rice, perhaps because it is mainly used for sweet puddings and desserts, is

almost always milled to remove the bran, but you can buy brown short grain rice from health stores.

MEDIUM GRAIN RICE

Medium grain rice is about twice as long as it is wide. After cooking, the grains are moist and tender, and tend to cling together more than long grain rice.

Medium grain rice is sold in both brown and white varieties. In Spain, white medium grain rice is often used for making paella.

SHORT GRAIN RICE

Mention short grain rice and most people will either think of risotto or creamy, slow-cooked puddings. Both these dishes owe their success to the ability of short grain rice to absorb liquid, becoming soft and sticky in the process. Short grain rice is almost as broad as it is long and is sometimes described as round grain. The grains stick together when cooked.

Pudding rice

This is a catch-all name for any short grain rice. Virtually all pudding rice is white, with short, plump grains.

ABOVE: *White and brown basmati rices, admired for their fragrance and slender grains, provide a unique texture.*

ABOVE: *Short grain pudding rice*

Carolina rice, the original name for American short grain rice, is derived from the state where it was first grown. The name is seldom used today, although occasionally some cookbooks do call for it to be used.

INDIAN RICE
Basmati rice

This rice is grown in northern India, in the Punjab, in parts of Pakistan adjacent to West Punjab, and in the foothills of the Himalayas. The particular soil and climate of this region of northern India is thought to account for basmati's unique taste and texture.

The word "basmati" means "the fragrant one" in Hindi, and this grain is rightly considered by most rice lovers around the world to be the prince of rice. Basmati rice has a fine aromatic flavour. The grains are long and slender and become even longer during cooking, which partly accounts for its wonderful texture. There are various grades of basmati, but it is impossible for the shopper to differentiate between them except by trying different brands to discover the variety with the best fragrance and flavour. Basmati is excellent in almost any savoury rice dish and is perfect for pilaffs or with curries. It is also an essential ingredient in biryani.

Brown basmati rice

Like all types of brown rice, brown basmati comes with the bran. It has all the flavour of white basmati with the texture typical of brown rice. It would not be used in Indian dishes but is superb in any number of Western-style meals.

Dehra dun

This is a long grain, non-sticky Indian rice. It is not generally available outside India, but you can buy it in some specialist shops.

Patna rice

At one time, most of the long grain rice sold in Europe came from Patna in India, and the term was used loosely to mean any long grain rice. The custom persists in parts of America today, but elsewhere the term Patna is used to describe a specific variety of long grain rice that comes from the Bihar region of India.

JAPANESE RICE

In Japan, two basic types of rice are eaten: a glutinous rice called *mochigome*, which is used for special occasions and to make snacks and sweets (candy), and a plump, short grained, non-glutinous rice called *uruchimai*, which is often sold simply as Japanese rice. This is the ordinary rice that is usually served with meals.

Although it is not a glutinous rice, even the ordinary rice has sticky properties, which makes it easier to eat with chopsticks.

Sushi rice

In the West, a packet labelled sushi rice will almost inevitably contain a short grain rice that will need to be cooked before you can use it to make sushi. Typical examples are Japanese rose, kokuho rose and calrose.

In Japan, however, sushi rice has usually been cooked with vinegar, sugar and salt, ready for making sushi.

ABOVE: *With its clingy texture when cooked, Thai fragrant rice goes very well with fiery hot red or green Thai curries.*

Shinmai

This is a highly esteemed rice that is usually sold in Japan in late summer. It is the first rice of the season. It has a high moisture content, and thus needs less water for cooking.

THAI RICE
Thai fragrant rice or jasmine rice

This fragrant long grain rice is grown in Thailand. It is widely used in South-east Asian and Oriental cooking. It has a faintly scented, almost milky aroma that is a perfect match for the exotic flavours of Oriental cuisine. Once cooked, the grains are slightly sticky. Thai fragrant rice is excellent both for savoury dishes and for sweet ones. To fully appreciate its fragrance, it is best cooked by the absorption method.

ITALIAN RICE

Italy produces more rice, and in greater variety, than any other country in Europe. Most is grown in

LEFT: *Three different types of sushi rice as sold in the West, all of which need to be cooked before making sushi.*

the north, in the Po Valley around Piedmont. Italian rice is classified by size, ranging from the shortest grain, *ordinario*, to *semi-fino*, *fino* and *superfino*. Most varieties of risotto rice are either *fino* or *superfino*.

Arborio

This is one of the best-known varieties of Italian risotto rice and takes its name from a town in the Vercelli region of north-west Italy. Unlike the finer risotto rices such as carnaroli (see below), arborio has a comparatively large plump grain with a high proportion of amylopectin. This is one of the components of starch that dissolves during cooking to give risotto its creamy texture. However, because it contains less amylose (the firm inner starch), it is easy to overcook. Recipes often recommend removing from the heat when almost cooked and "resting" it for a few minutes. The rice will continue to cook in its own heat, without becoming pappy.

Vialone nano

This is another popular risotto rice. It has a plump grain. Vialone nano contains less amylopectin than arborio does and a higher proportion of amylose, so it retains a firm "bite" at the centre of the grain when the rest of the rice has cooked to a creamy consistency. Risottos made using this rice tend to be of a rippling consistency, which is described in Italian as *all'onda*. Vialone nano is especially popular in Venetian- and Veronese-style risottos.

Carnaroli

This is considered the premium risotto rice. It was developed by a Milanese rice grower who crossed vialone nano with a Japanese rice. The outer part of the grain is made up of a soft starch that dissolves during cooking to leave the inner grain, which has a satisfying, firm "bite".

SPANISH RICE

Rice is grown extensively in Spain, particularly in the swampy regions outside Valencia. The most common rice grown is a medium grain variety that has a slightly sticky consistency when cooked. It is particularly popular for making paella. A longer type of rice grain is also grown and this is generally added to soups.

ABOVE: *Italian risotto rices. Clockwise from top, as follows: arborio, carnaroli and vialone nano*

Categoria extra, uno and dos

Within Spain, rice is graded by the amount of whole grains included in the weight: *Categoria extra* (red label) is the finest rice, with 95 per cent whole grains; *Categoria uno* (green label) has 87 per cent whole grains; while *Categoria dos* (yellow label) has 80 per cent whole grains.

Calasparra

This top-quality short grain rice is quite easy to locate outside Spain, unlike most Spanish rices, which must be bought from specialist shops.

Grano largo or variedad Americana

A long grain white rice. The brown equivalent is called *arroz integral*.

Bahia

A medium grain rice used in paella.

Bomba

Another paella rice, this plump grain absorbs a lot of liquid.

AMERICAN AROMATIC RICE

America grows several familiar aromatic rices, and has developed several of its own. Texmati, an American version of basmati, is generally not sold outside the United States.

GIANT CANADIAN WILD RICE

Canadian wild rice is similar to the variety from the United States, but the grains are longer and are considered to have a superior flavour. It is grown on lakes in the north and

ABOVE: *Canadian wild rice*

on the west coast of Canada. It is harvested by local indigenous people, who beat the overhanging stems with canoe paddles and keep the grain that falls into their canoes. Like all wild rice, Giant Canadian wild rice should be soaked in water for several hours and then rinsed and drained, before being cooked for at least 40 minutes, until the tough outer husk has burst open.

OTHER RICES
Domsiah rice

This is a fine grained Persian rice, which is available from Middle-Eastern stores.

Wild rice

This is not a true rice at all, but a grass that grows in the marshy areas around the American Great Lakes.

Wild rice was once a favourite food of the Native Americans. Today, through various treaty agreements, they harvest much of North America's wild rice.

Wild rice needs to be soaked for several hours before cooking, and must be cooked for about 40 minutes until the inner grain breaks through the husk. Wild rice has acquired a fashionable status throughout the West, but its greatest popularity is still in the United States. It is used at Thanksgiving for stuffing the turkey. Wild rice was important for early settlers when their wheat and barley failed to thrive in the New World.

Wild rice and basmati

This is simply a mixture of two popular and well-flavoured grains, wild rice and basmati rice.

GLUTINOUS RICE

There are several types of glutinous rice. The name is misleading – the grains contain no gluten – but they are renowned for the way they stick together after cooking. Often known as sticky or sweet rice, glutinous rice is not usually eaten with savoury dishes, but is sweetened and served, hot or cold, with fruit as a dessert.

Japanese glutinous rice

This short grained rice is sticky when cooked, which makes it perfect for shaping. It has a slightly sweet taste.

Chinese glutinous rice

In China, glutinous rice is called *geng* rice. It is also known by the generic name for short grain rice (*Oryza japonica*).

There are white and black varieties of this rice, and also a pinkish-red rice that grows along the Yangtze river. Glutinous rice is used for puddings and dim sum.

Thai glutinous rice

This rice is also available in white and black grains. Thai glutinous rice is very popular in puddings and

ABOVE: *Chinese short grained white glutinous rice*

desserts. When cooked, the Thai glutinous black rice grain is really a deep blue-purple colour.

Since wild rice normally takes much longer to cook than plain basmati rice, the manufacturers of this product use a par-boiled basmati rice, which has a longer cooking time, matching it with a particular strain of wild rice that requires less cooking than most varieties. This ensures that they take the same amount of time to cook. Check the packet for exact cooking times.

ABOVE: *Wild rice and basmati*

Par-boiled or easy-cook rice

In spite of its name, par-boiled rice (sometimes labelled "easy-cook") takes almost half as long again to cook as most long grain varieties. Par-boiling is an ancient technique that was developed in India. The whole-grain rice is soaked in water, then steamed, locking the nutrients in the bran layer. For white rice, the bran is then removed.

In India and the Middle East, par-boiled rice is very popular. In the West it is mainly – and mistakenly – perceived to be an easy-to-cook rice. However, a more accurate description might be "difficult to ruin", because par-boiled rice can stand quite a bit of abuse during cooking.

The par-boiled rice grains are more yellow than those of normal rice, although this coloration disappears during cooking; when fully cooked, par-boiled white rice is a brilliant white. Par-boiled rice does take longer to cook than normal rice, but the advantage, for those people who enjoy this rice, is that the rice grains stay noticeably separate and slightly chewy. However, some people dislike the over-assertive texture and complain that the flavour is bland.

If you are unsure, try both types for comparison. There are par-boiled versions of white and brown basmati, and white and brown long grain rice.

Red rice

Though not unheard of in rice-growing areas, red rice's presence is not always welcome because it means the rice is reverting to a wild strain, and is likely to be brittle, shatter easily and prove difficult to harvest.

In the Camargue region of France, however, a red rice has been developed that is the result of cross-pollination between the local white rice and an indigenous wild red rice. The uncooked grain is a reddish brown, and as it cooks the colour intensifies and the water turns a distinct shade of red. Like most wholegrain rice, red rice needs to be cooked for longer than white rice. It has a nutty flavour and a good firm texture. Use it in place of brown rice or long grain white rice.

QUICK-COOK RICE
Boil-in-the-bag rice

This is a called a convenience rice, although it takes just as long to cook as regular rice; the main convenience is that the pan doesn't have to be washed afterwards. Most varieties of boil-in-the-bag rice are prepared with par-boiled (easy-cook) rice.

Pre-cooked and quick-cook rice

Not to be confused with par-boiled rice, pre-cooked rice is just that – rice that has been fully cooked in advance and only needs to be rehydrated and heated in order to be ready to serve. There are a number of different brands of pre-cooked rice available, each with different rehydrating and reheating instructions, so it is important to check the packet carefully before cooking.

Frozen rice

This is a pre-cooked rice and needs only to be thawed and reheated. This can often be done in the microwave; check the instructions on the packet.

Canned rice

This type of rice really couldn't be simpler to use; just open the can, turn it into a bowl and reheat in the microwave or in a conventional oven. For single people with little time for cooking, canned rice may be a handy standby, but it is a hugely expensive way to eat rice, and the flavour is severely diminished, so it's not something to rely on regularly.

Rice products

In addition to the many varieties of rice available, there are also many products derived from rice for both sweet and savoury dishes.

BELOW: *Flaked rice and ground rice. Both cook quickly and evenly, which makes them good for puddings, desserts and baking.*

FLAKED RICE

This rice is commonly used in Chinese, Thai and Vietnamese cooking for stuffings and desserts. The par-boiled rice is flattened with heavy rollers, so the rice cooks quickly and evenly. In the West, flaked rice is used by the food trade for breakfast cereals and snacks but it is seldom used in recipes. Flaked rice is available from Oriental shops.

GROUND RICE

More granulated than rice flour, this rice is used for milk puddings, and was once particularly popular in England.

Ground rice is also widely used for biscuits (cookies) and baking. It makes a good substitute for wheat flour, especially for those people who find it difficult to tolerate gluten.

BELOW: *Types of glutinous rice flour. The top product is made from cooked glutinous rice.*

RICE FLOUR

Finer than ground rice, this flour is also used in both Oriental and Western cooking for cakes, biscuits and desserts.

GLUTINOUS RICE FLOUR

This is made from glutinous rice and is normally labelled "rice powder". It is used for sweet puddings.

SHIRATAMO-KO

This is a Japanese version of glutinous rice flour.

WHITE RICE VINEGAR

Made from glutinous rice, Japanese rice wine vinegar has a subtle, delicate flavour. It is excellent not only in Oriental cooking but for any dressing where you need a mild, unassuming flavour. Chinese rice wine vinegar is not as delicate but it makes a good alternative to wine vinegar.

BLACK RICE VINEGAR

Though dark in colour, black rice vinegar has a surprisingly mild taste. It can be used for Oriental soups and for dipping sauces.

RED RICE VINEGAR

Much spicier than other rice vinegars, Chinese red rice vinegar is used mainly in hot dipping sauces to be served with seafood.

SHAOXING

This Chinese rice wine, which is made from glutinous rice, yeast and water, has a rich, mellow flavour. It is popular throughout China for cooking and drinking, and is available in Chinese groceries and some wine stores. Although both are rice wines, do not confuse Shaoxing with sake, which has a completely different taste altogether.

SAKE

This Japanese rice wine is quite sweet with a mild flavour that belies its potency. It is served

RIGHT: *Shaoxing rice wine*

in small cups – about the size of egg cups – and can be chilled but is more often served warm. Nowadays, sake is often drunk with a meal, which is a shift in emphasis; traditionally, sake was the central attraction, and the small portions of food that accompanied it were there to enhance the flavour of this celebrated drink.

ABOVE: *Sake*

MIRIN

This is a sweet cooking sake with a delicate flavour. Mirin is normally stirred into Japanese dishes during the final stages of cooking. It adds a mild sweetness to sauces or dips. Combined with soy sauce, it is the basis of teriyaki sauce, which is popular for basting grilled (broiled) foods. Mirin is available from any Japanese food store and from many of the larger supermarkets.

RICE-STICK NOODLES

These flat noodles vary in thickness; each is roughly the same length as a chopstick. To cook rice-stick noodles, soak them in warm water or stock for 20 minutes to soften before draining. The noodles are used to thicken soups and casseroles, and for stir-fries.

RICE VERMICELLI NOODLES

These hair-like noodles are very popular in Thai, Vietnamese and Indonesian cooking. Don't confuse them with bean thread noodles (which look similar and are confusingly called vermicelli noodles) because these are made from ground mung beans. Soak rice vermicelli noodles in warm water for about 5–10 minutes to soften them, then use them according to the recipe.

JAPANESE HARUSAME NOODLES

Similar to rice vermicelli noodles and prepared in the same way, these are also made from ground rice and sold in fragile-looking loops.

RICE PAPER

Sometimes called rice wrappers, these wafer-thin papers are made from rice flour, salt and water. They can be round or triangular in shape. Before use, soften them in hot water for a few seconds. They are used in Vietnamese cooking to make spring

ABOVE: *Chinese and Thai rice-stick and rice vermicelli noodles*

rolls, and are popular in some Chinese dishes. Don't confuse them with spring roll wrappers, which are made from wheat flour and water, or with the edible rice paper used for lining baking sheets.

BELOW: *Round and triangular rice papers. Clockwise from top: Thai, Chinese and Vietnamese varieties*

Cooking perfect rice

Sometimes, only a specific type of rice will do – risottos, for example, can only be made with risotto rice. In general, however, providing you know a little about the qualities of the rice, there are no hard and fast rules for cooking perfect rice.

Quantities

The following quantities of uncooked rice apply to basmati rice, Thai fragrant rice and brown and white long grain rice.
• Side dishes: 50–75g/1³/₄–2³/₄oz rice per person or 225–350g/8–12oz rice to serve four.
• Pilaffs: 50g/1³/₄oz rice per person or 225g/8oz to serve four.
• Salads: 25–40g/1–1¹/₂oz per person or 115–175g/4–6oz to serve four.
• Short grain rice puddings: 15–20g/¹/₂–³/₄oz per person or 50–75g/2–3oz to serve four.
As a basic rule, when a recipe calls for cooked rice, use just under half the weight in uncooked rice.

Rinsing

Though not essential to rinse rice before cooking, it does help to remove excess starch and any dust. Most types of rice benefit from being rinsed, but do not rinse risotto rice.

1 Cover the rice with cold water and swirl the grains between your fingers. The water will become slightly cloudy.

2 Allow the rice to settle, then tilt the bowl so that the water drains away. Cover the rice once more with cold water, then rinse. Repeat several times until the water runs clear.

Soaking

Though seldom essential to soak rice for cooking, it does increase the moisture content of the grains, which means the rice will cook more quickly and will be less sticky. Risotto rice must not be soaked. Occasionally, rice that has been soaked will be fried; if this is the case, drain it thoroughly first.

1 To soak rice, simply place it in a large bowl and cover with double the volume of cold water.

2 Leave the rice in the bowl for about 30 minutes or for the time suggested in the recipe, then drain it thoroughly.

PERFECT BOILED RICE
Pan-of-water method

This method of cooking rice is suitable for most types of rice. It is not, however, appropriate for Thai fragrant rice.

In Asia, cooks often add a few drops of vegetable oil as well as salt when cooking rice by this method.

1 Put the rice in a large, heavy pan and add about 1.2 litres/2 pints/5 cups of boiling water or stock for every 200g/7oz/1 cup of rice. Add a pinch of salt. Bring back to the boil, then lower the heat and simmer, uncovered, for the time indicated on the packet, until the rice is just tender.

2 Strain in a sieve (strainer) or colander and rinse well with hot water, then return the rice to the pan or set a sieve over the pan. Cover with a lid or dish towel and leave to stand for 5 minutes. Fork through thoroughly before serving, adding butter or oil, if you like.

Flavourings Stock can be used instead of water (see page 211), and flavourings such as bay leaves, curry leaves or whole spices can be added, especially if the rice is to be used in a salad.

Absorption method

This is suitable for basmati, Thai fragrant rice, long and short grain rice and glutinous rice.

1 Put the rice in a pan and pour in a measured quantity of liquid (as stated in the recipe). Bring to the boil. Reduce the heat to the lowest possible setting.

2 Cover and cook until the liquid has been absorbed (up to 25 minutes, depending on the type of rice).

3 Remove from the heat and leave, covered, for 5 minutes until steam holes appear on the surface of the rice. If the grains are not completely tender, replace the cover tightly and leave for 5 more minutes.

Flavourings If you want to flavour the rice, the absorption method provides the perfect opportunity. Lemon grass, curry leaves and whole spices can be added with the liquid, which can be water, stock, coconut milk or a mixture. This method of cooking rice is the basis of several pilaff-style dishes, where onions, garlic and other ingredients, such as spices, are fried before the rice and liquid are added.

Microwave method

This is suitable for basmati, brown basmati, Thai fragrant rice, and white and brown long grain rice.

1 Put the rice in a deep, heatproof glass bowl or microwave container and stir in the quantity of boiling water or stock stated in the recipe.

2 Cover with a lid or microwave-proof clear film (plastic wrap) and cook on 100% Full Power. Check your microwave instruction book for timings. Leave to stand for 10 minutes before using.

Flavourings Cooking in a microwave is essentially the same as the absorption method and simple flavourings can be added. If using a large number of additional ingredients, consult your microwave instruction book, because the cooking times may differ.

Oven method

This is suitable for basmati, brown basmati, American long grain, brown long grain and red Camargue rice.

This is a combination of two methods: the rice is partially cooked first in a pan on the hob (stovetop), before being finished in the oven. This produces a slightly dry rice, with separate grains.

1 Cook the rice by the pan-of-water method or by the absorption method for three-quarters of the normal cooking time.

2 Drain, if necessary, then spoon the rice into a baking dish. Dot with butter or ghee and cover tightly.

3 Cook in the oven for about 10–20 minutes. The oven temperature can be between 160°C/325°F/Gas 3 and 190°C/375°F/Gas 5 but the cooking time will need to be adjusted.

Flavourings These can be added to the rice during the first stage of cooking, or part of the cooked rice can be coloured and flavoured with saffron or spice. Fried onions, garlic or cardamoms can be dotted over the rice before it is placed in the oven.

Steaming

Use this for white basmati, American long grain and Thai fragrant rice.

1 Cook the rice by the pan-of-water method or the absorption method for about three-quarters of the normal cooking time. Turn the part-cooked rice into a sieve (strainer) or colander.

2 Transfer the rice to a muslin (cheesecloth) bag set inside a pan of simmering water. Cover and steam for 5–10 minutes for white rice; 15 minutes for brown rice. If the grains still feel hard, steam for a little longer.

Flavourings Add these during the first stage of cooking, in the same way as for the pan-of-water or absorption methods. Replace the cooking water with stock, coconut milk or a mixture, and add bay leaves, curry leaves, lemon grass or whole spices.

OTHER COOKING METHODS
Electric rice cooker

This method is suitable for all types of rice.

1 Put the rice into the cooker and add the amount of water indicated in your instruction booklet. Do not add salt.

2 Cover with the lid and switch on. It switches off automatically when the rice is ready, and keeps the rice hot.

Quick-cook method

Rice can be soaked in boiling water and then quickly cooked at the last minute, which is useful when entertaining.

1 Put the rice into a large bowl. Cover with boiling water. Leave to stand, uncovered, for 30 minutes to 1 hour.

2 Bring a pan of lightly salted stock or water to the boil. Drain the rice, add it to the pan and cook for 3–4 minutes until tender.

Flavourings These can be added in the same way as for boiled rice.

Cooking brown rice

Brown rice takes longer to cook than white rice, so check the packet instructions. Soaking softens the rice but will not shorten the cooking time.

Cooking glutinous rice

Soak glutinous rice for 1–4 hours before cooking, then drain. It can then be simmered with coconut milk and sugar for a dessert. For a savoury dish, steam for 10–15 minutes until tender.

Cooking wild rice

Although this is not strictly a rice, wild rice can be treated in the same way. It takes a lot of cooking and, for best results, should be soaked in water for 1 hour before being boiled in lightly salted water for 45–60 minutes. Check the instructions on the packet because cooking times differ according to the size of the grains. It is cooked when the inner white grain bursts out of the black husk.

Cooking par-boiled or easy-cook rice

Par-boiled rice can be cooked by the pan-of-water or by the absorption method. Always check the packet for instructions. It can also be cooked in the microwave or in a rice cooker. This rice is fine for accompanying a meal, but is not as good for fried rice dishes.

Storing rice

Raw (uncooked) rice can be kept in a cool, dark place for up to three years in the unopened packet or in an airtight container. Keep it perfectly dry or it will turn mouldy. If it is old, it may need more water or longer cooking. Check the packet for "best before" dates.

Cooked rice can be stored for up to 24 hours if cooled, covered and kept in the refrigerator. You can also freeze the cooled rice; reheat it in a covered casserole in the oven or thaw it and use for fried rice or in a salad. Reheated rice should be piping hot all the way through.

Making stocks

The foundation of many a tasty rice dish is a good, savoury stock. Here are recipes for three of the most commonly used – fish, chicken and vegetable.

FISH STOCK
MAKES ABOUT 2.5 LITRES/ 4½ PINTS/10 CUPS

900g/2lb white fish bones and trimmings, but not gills
2.5 litres/4½ pints/10 cups water
1 onion, roughly chopped
1 celery stick, chopped
1 carrot, chopped
1 bay leaf
3 fresh parsley sprigs
6 peppercorns
5cm/2in piece of pared lemon rind
75ml/5 tbsp/⅓ cup dry white wine

1 Put the fish bones and fish heads in a large, heavy pan. Pour in the water. Bring to the boil; skim off any scum with a spoon. Add the remaining ingredients.

2 Lower the heat, cover and simmer for 20–30 minutes, then cool. Strain through a muslin (cheesecloth) bag into a clean bowl. Keep in the refrigerator for up to 2 days or freeze for up to 3 months.

CHICKEN STOCK
MAKES ABOUT 1.5 LITRES/ 2¾ PINTS/6¼ CUPS

1 onion, quartered
2 celery sticks, chopped
1 carrot, roughly chopped
675g/1½lb fresh chicken, either
    ½ whole chicken or 2–3 chicken quarters
1 fresh thyme or marjoram sprig
2 fresh parsley sprigs
8 whole peppercorns
salt

1 Put the vegetables in a large, heavy pan. Lay the chicken on top, then cover with cold water (about 1.5 litres/2¾ pints/6¼ cups).

2 Bring to the boil slowly, uncovered, then carefully skim off any fat from the surface.

3 Add the herbs, peppercorns and a pinch of salt. Lower the heat, cover and simmer gently for 2–2½ hours.

4 Using a slotted spoon, transfer the chicken to a plate. Remove any skin or bones; reserve the chicken for another recipe. Strain the stock into a clean bowl, cool, then chill. Remove any fat from the surface before use. Store in the refrigerator for up to 3 days or freeze for up to 6 months.

VEGETABLE STOCK
MAKES ABOUT 1.2 LITRES/ 2 PINTS/5 CUPS

3–4 shallots, halved
2 celery sticks or 75g/2¾oz celeriac, chopped
2 carrots, roughly chopped
3 tomatoes, halved
3 fresh parsley stalks
1 fresh tarragon sprig
1 fresh marjoram or thyme sprig
2.5cm/1in piece of pared orange rind
6 peppercorns
2 allspice berries
1.5 litres/2¾ pints/6¼ cups water

1 Put all the ingredients into a large, heavy pan. Bring the liquid to the boil, then lower the heat and simmer gently for 30 minutes. Leave to cool completely.

2 Strain the vegetable stock through a sieve (strainer) into a large bowl. Then, using the back of a spoon, press all of the liquid from the cooked vegetables through the mesh.

3 Cover the bowl with clear film (plastic wrap), then transfer to the refrigerator and store for up to 3 days. Alternatively, you can keep the stock in a container in the freezer for up to 6 months.

Risotto

What could be simpler than a risotto? Though there are elaborate versions, some of the best risottos are made simply using rice, a good stock and a few fresh herbs or cheeses.

The method of cooking rice in stock may have been influenced by cooking styles in France and Spain. It is usually eaten as a separate course before the meat and vegetables. Rice and stock are the only essentials, but choose them carefully. The stock must be home-made (or the best you can afford) and the rice must be one recommended for the purpose.

Have the stock simmering in a pan adjacent to the risotto pan, and add it slowly. Observe the standing time at the end, to allow the rice to rest and reach perfection. Do all this, and you'll find risotto one of the most simple and rewarding of all rice dishes.

TYPES OF RISOTTO RICE

It is essential to use a risotto rice, but which one is up to you. Named risotto rices are becoming widely available, but you will often find packets labelled simply "Italian risotto rice". Of the named varieties, arborio is most widely available, with carnaroli and vialone nano becoming easier to find. Others include baldo, vialone nano gigante and roma. Each has its own qualities. Some recipes call for a named risotto rice, but most are non-specific and any risotto rice will give a good result.

MAKING PERFECT RISOTTO

1 Put some extra virgin olive oil into a large, deep, heavy pan and heat gently. Add the onion, garlic and any other vegetable(s) and then fry them over a medium heat for a few minutes, stirring all the time. Unless the recipe specifies otherwise, the onion and any other vegetables you are using in the risotto should be softened but not browned.

2 If you are using uncooked meat or poultry, add it to the onions, unless the recipe specifies otherwise. Turn the heat up to high and cook, stirring frequently, until the meat is browned on all sides.

3 Stir in the rice. Fry over a high heat, stirring constantly, for 3–4 minutes. The grains become transparent as they are stirred in the hot oil, but their centres remain opaque.

4 Add a little wine, or a ladleful of hot stock. Stir the rice until all the liquid has been absorbed.

5 Lower the heat to medium, then stir in another ladleful of hot stock. Keep the pan over a medium heat so that the liquid bubbles but the rice does not burn. Stir frequently. Add the remaining stock gradually, using each ladleful before adding the next. This should take about 20 minutes. The grains will soften and merge together.

6 When the risotto begins to look creamy, grate in the cheese or add butter. The rice should be almost tender, but still a little firm in the centre. Remove the pan from the heat, cover with a dish towel and leave for 5 minutes for it to cook to perfection in the residual heat.

ADDITIONAL INGREDIENTS

Use this guide to help you decide when to add other ingredients.

Vegetables

Fry onions and garlic until soft, before adding the rice. Fry vegetables, such as carrots, aubergines (eggplant), courgettes (zucchini), mushrooms and (bell) peppers, with the onions. Vegetables that require little cooking, such as spinach and asparagus, can be stirred in towards the end of cooking.

Fish and shellfish

Cook these first. Fish fillets, such as salmon, plaice or sea bass, are usually poached, then flaked. Scallops should be lightly cooked, then sliced. Stir fish or shellfish into the risotto three-quarters of the way through cooking.

Meat and poultry

If you are using raw meat or poultry, you should cook these first, with the onions. The rice is added later, so that they cook together. Stir cooked meats, such as sausage or ham, into the risotto towards the end of the cooking time.

Herbs

Robust herbs may be cooked first with the onions, but more delicate herbs, such as parsley or coriander (cilantro), are usually added at the end of cooking the risotto, with the Parmesan cheese or butter.

Cheese

Where cheese is the dominant flavouring, add it halfway through cooking; otherwise, add Parmesan just before the risotto is left to rest.

RISOTTO TIPS

• Add any wine or sherry to the risotto before adding stock. The alcohol will evaporate, but the flavour will remain.
• Use a good-quality, home-made stock for your risotto. Alternatively, buy cartons of fresh stock, which are available from large supermarkets.
• The stock must always be hot. Have it simmering in a separate pan adjacent to the pan in which you are cooking the risotto. Add it slowly, making sure each ladleful has been absorbed before adding the next.
• Avoid overcooking. Remove the pan from the heat while the rice is still slightly undercooked.
• For best results, season after cooking but before leaving it to rest. Stock, salted butter and Parmesan cheese will all contribute saltiness, so always taste before adding any extra salt.
• Don't use ready-grated Parmesan. For the best flavour, always buy good-quality Parmesan in one piece and grate it.

Instant risottos

There are several instant risottos on the market, available from supermarkets and delicatessens. They are easy to make – all you need to do is add water, heat and stir. Packets give simple instructions and recommend simmering for about 10 minutes – roughly half the time required for making a classic risotto. Instant risottos come in several flavours, including four cheeses, spinach, saffron, tomato and black cuttlefish. They are handy for a quick meal, and the colours supplied by the flavourings make them pretty to serve. More importantly, these risottos taste surprisingly good.

ABOVE: *Clockwise from top, instant risottos flavoured with cuttlefish, tomatoes, saffron and spinach*

Equipment

Only four pieces of equipment are essential for making a risotto, and with any luck you'll have most of them already:
• A large, heavy pan. Ideally, this should be a wide, straight-sided pot, deep enough to contain the cooked risotto. A deep frying pan can be used for smaller quantities.
• A pan for the simmering stock.
• A ladle.
• A wooden spoon.

Paella

In Spain, paella is not just a meal, it is an occasion. The ingredients can be many and varied. Short grain rice is an obvious essential, but saffron, garlic and olive oil will inevitably feature too.

Traditionally, men cook the paella out of doors, over a wood fire. Everyone will help to gather wood and light a fire, after which one of the men will prepare and cook the paella. Other men will doubtless make their contribution. There will be advice for the chef on when to add the rice, how much stock to use and whether to add herbs early or late. The indoor version, cooked over a stove by a woman, is known as an *arroz* – a rice.

Short-grain rice and saffron are essential ingredients. Purists believe that an authentic paella should also contain only eels, snails and beans, as in the original Valencian paella, but most Spanish people today are fairly relaxed about using other ingredients. Fish, shellfish, meat and poultry are routinely used, sometimes together.

For the Spanish, paella is the epitome of convivial eating: it is served with generous amounts of wine and is made for a large party of people. The paella dish – the paellera – is a spectacular centrepiece on the table, and everyone helps themselves to the food, while the conversation, lubricated by wine, is, in true Spanish fashion, lively and convivial.

MAKING PERFECT PAELLA
You can vary the combination of meat, poultry, fish and shellfish to suit your taste, your pocket and the occasion.

1 Cut the meat or joint the poultry into large pieces; season to taste, if the recipe requires it.

2 Fry the meat or poultry in olive oil in a paella pan or large frying pan until deep golden-brown. Transfer the cooked meat or poultry to a plate. Slice the sausage.

3 Prepare any fish and shellfish: steam mussels (make sure always to discard any that fail to open), prepare squid and peel prawns (shrimp). Fry all of these ingredients briefly, if required by the recipe, and transfer to a plate.

4 In a paella pan, fry the onions in olive oil until golden brown. Then add the garlic, tomatoes and any firm vegetables that you are using. Stir in cooked dried beans, if using. Stir briefly, then add water or stock and any seasonings. Bring to the boil.

5 Add in the rice, stirring so that it is evenly distributed, then add the meat or poultry, and any sausage. Cook, uncovered, over a medium heat (so that the liquid simmers nicely) for 15 minutes.

6 Lower the heat, and add any softer vegetables that you are using, plus the fish or shellfish. Add saffron to give the paella its distinctive colour. Cook over a low heat for 10 minutes until the liquid has been absorbed, then cover and leave to rest for 5–10 minutes.

PAELLA TIPS

• For a perfect paella, always use fresh ingredients, especially the fish and shellfish. Paella is not a dish for cooked leftovers.

• Cook other ingredients carefully before you start to cook the paella. Meats should be cooked until golden brown, as should onions, because this will add flavour to the dish.

• Fish should be seared lightly, and added to the rice towards the end of cooking, to avoid overcooking it. Less tender cuts of meat or larger pieces of poultry may require longer cooking. Always check instructions in the recipe for timings.

• Use a well-flavoured stock, preferably home-made chicken, meat, fish or vegetable. Bring the stock or other liquid to a fierce boil before adding in the rice.

• This method is the opposite of the technique used when making a risotto, where the stock is added slowly to the rice.

BELOW: *The width and shallow depth of the paella pan allow an even distribution of heat when the rice is cooking.*

A GUIDE TO PAELLA QUANTITIES

Individual paella recipes will usually specify quantities of rice, liquid and other ingredients, although the following can be used as a rough guide.

Amount of rice	Amount of liquid	Servings
200g/7oz/1 cup	550ml/19fl oz/2^1/$_4$ cups	2–3
350g/12oz/1^3/$_4$ cups	900ml/1^1/$_2$ pints/3^3/$_4$ cups	4–6
450g/1lb/2^1^{1}/$_3$ cups	1.2 litres/2 pints/5 cups	6
500g/1lb 2oz/3 cups	1.3 litres/2^1/$_4$ pints/5^1/$_2$ cups	8

Allow between 65–75g/about 2^1/$_2$–3oz/^{1}/$_3$–^{1}/$_2$ cup rice per person

Once the liquid has been absorbed by the rice, cover the paella with a dampened dish towel and allow it to rest for a few minutes before serving, to complete the cooking.

It is essential to use the right type of rice. The Spanish will occasionally use a medium grain rice, although the traditional choice is a short grain rice that absorbs liquid well. The round grained and stubby Spanish rice called Calasparra would be ideal.

If an authentic Spanish rice is unavailable, use arborio rice instead. However, try to use saffron rather than turmeric or any other colouring.

The rice needs to be cooked in a shallow layer with plenty of room to spread out so, if possible, use a paella pan (called a paellera). This is a wide, flat, metal pan. If you don't have a paella pan, you can use a frying pan – use the largest one you have – but even this will, most likley, only be large enough for a paella for three or four people.

To stir or not to stir

Read any guide to making paella and you'll be told that the paella mustn't be stirred or disturbed in any way. This is fine advice for a true paella – cooked over an open fire so that the heat is distributed evenly over the base of the pan. However, if you're using a gas or electric heat source, the uneven heat distribution will mean that the centre will cook quicker than the outside. To get around this, you can either break the rules and stir occasionally, or cook the paella in the oven. That way it will cook evenly, although technically, in Spain, it would be a "rice" (*arroz*) and not a paella.

Sushi

Sushi is wonderful food. The little snacks are superb, easy to prepare at home, surprisingly filling and also make great appetizers.

A Japanese short grain rice should be used for sushi. Some supermarkets and delicatessens sell a rice labelled "sushi rice", which happily takes the guesswork out of the process. Japanese short grain rice is slightly sticky, which makes it easy to pick up with chopsticks and ideal for sushi, because the grains of rice cling together. Glutinous rice is not suitable for making sushi, however, because it is too sticky.

The rice should be rinsed and left to drain for 30 minutes before cooking it by the absorption method. You can use an electric rice cooker, but the pan-of-water method will not work for sushi rice.

Accompaniments

Nori This dried seaweed is sold in paper-thin sheets. It is dark green to black in colour and almost transparent in places. Some comes ready-toasted (*yaki-nori*), seasoned with soy sauce and sesame oil. If not, toast it under a hot grill (broiler).
Gari Pale pink ginger pickles, which are excellent for serving with sushi.
Shoyu A mild Japanese soy sauce. Serve with sushi.
Wasabi A hot green horseradish to serve with fish. It is sold as a paste or as a powder, to which water is added.

MAKING PERFECT SUSHI

1 Rinse the rice, then drain it for 30–60 minutes. Put it in a heavy pan and add a piece of dried kelp (*kombu*) and measured water. Bring to the boil, remove the kelp, cover the pan and cook gently over a low heat for 15 minutes. Increase to high for 10 seconds, then remove from the heat. Leave to stand for about 10 minutes. Lift the lid. Steam holes will have appeared in the rice and it will be tender.

2 Prepare the sushi vinegar. For every 450g/1lb/2⅓ cups rice, mix together 60ml/4 tbsp rice vinegar, 15ml/1 tbsp sugar and 2.5ml/½ tsp salt.

3 Stir the vinegar into the rice, cover with a damp cloth and leave to cool. Do not put in the refrigerator or it will go hard.

QUANTITIES

Use between 600ml/1 pint/2½ cups and 750ml/1¼ pints/3 cups water for every 450g/1lb/2⅓ cups sushi rice, depending on the type of rice; always check the instructions on the packet. If you prefer, you could use sake instead of 30ml/2 tbsp of the water.

ROLLED SUSHI WITH NORI AND FILLING
MAKES 24 SLICES

To make this sushi, you will need sheets of yaki-nori (toasted seaweed). Two sheets will be enough to make four long rolls.

1 Cut the yaki-nori in half lengthways and place a half-sheet, shiny side down, on the bamboo sushi mat.

2 Spread a layer of the dressed rice over the yaki-nori, leaving a 1cm/½in clear edge at the top and bottom.

3 Arrange a line of filling horizontally across the middle of the rice. This could be raw salmon or raw tuna, cut into 1cm/½in square long sticks, sliced raw scallops, Japanese omelette, roasted (bell) pepper, spring onions (scallions), cucumber or a selection of two or three of these.

4 Using the rolling mat as a guide, and working from the nearest edge of yaki-nori, roll up the yaki-nori and rice into a cigar (do not include the mat in the roll). Roll the mat in your palms so that the edges stick together.

5 Wrap the rolls in clear film (plastic wrap) and chill in the refrigerator for 10 minutes, then unwrap the rolls. Using a wet knife, cut each roll into six slices.

SHAPED SUSHI

1 Wet your hands. Take 15–20g/ 1/2–3/4oz/2–3 tbsp dressed sushi rice and shape into a rectangle measuring 2 x 5cm/3/4 x 2in and 1cm/1/2in high.

2 Repeat this process until all the rice is used up. Spread a little wasabi paste in the middle of each rectangle of rice, then add your chosen topping.

ROLLED SUSHI WITH SMOKED SALMON

1 Line a bamboo mat with clear film (plastic wrap). Place smoked salmon on it, overlapping if needed. Top generously with dressed rice.

2 Roll the mat so the salmon rolls around the rice, keeping the film outside the roll. Then, make more the same way.

3 Chill for 10 minutes. Unwrap. Use a wet knife to cut each roll into six slices. Cover with a damp cloth. Keep cool.

SUSHI TOPPINGS
Make plain rolled sushi and top them with any one of these suggestions.

Raw sushi-grade salmon, raw sushi-grade tuna, salmon roe or other fish roe Cut the salmon and tuna into pieces that are roughly the same size as the rice portions.

Peeled raw prawn (shrimp) tails Cook for 1 minute in simmering water. Drain. Slit each prawn along the belly, remove the vein, then open out. Mix 15ml/ 1 tbsp rice vinegar and 5ml/1 tsp sugar in a bowl. Add the prawns and marinate in a cool place for 10 minutes.

Blanched squid and boiled octopus Slice the squid and octopus into strips that are roughly the same size as the rice portions.

Rolled omelette slices Beat together 1 egg, 15ml/1 tbsp sake, 15ml/1 tbsp sugar, 15ml/1 tbsp water and a pinch of salt. Heat a little groundnut (peanut) oil in a frying pan, pour in the mixture and fry over a medium to high heat until just set but not browned. Roll up the omelette and slice.

GARNISHES
Fish sushi can be garnished with fresh chives, fresh coriander (cilantro) or toasted sesame seeds.
    Omelette sushi can be decorated by wrapping strips of yaki-nori around the moulded rice.

Other Asian dishes

Most regions of Asia have their own favourite rice dishes, many of which are now popular worldwide.

BIRYANI

This is one of India's most famous rice dishes. Use basmati rice: soak it for 3 hours in lightly salted water. You can use lamb, chicken or beef, and duck and game also work well. Vegetarian biryanis are popular too.

Perfect chicken biryani

1 Crumble 5ml/1 tsp of saffron strands into 30ml/2 tbsp of warm milk in a small bowl. Stir, then soak for 3 hours.

2 Meanwhile, wash 275g/9½oz/1½ cups basmati rice in cold water. Drain thoroughly and place in a large bowl. Cover with cold water. Stir in 10ml/ 2 tsp salt. Soak for 3 hours.

3 Heat 45ml/3 tbsp oil in a frying pan. Add 3 sliced onions. Cook until soft. Add 175g/6oz cubed chicken breasts, and any spices. Stir. Add 2.5ml/½ tsp salt, 2–3 chopped garlic cloves and lemon juice to taste. Stir-fry for 5 minutes.

4 Drain the rice. Boil in salted water for 4–5 minutes. Spoon enough drained rice into an ovenproof dish to cover the bottom, then add the curry.

5 Spoon 150ml/¼ pint/⅔ cup natural (plain) yogurt evenly on top. Preheat the oven to 150°C/300°F/Gas 2. Pile on the remaining rice, then use the handle of a wooden spoon to make a 2.5cm/1in hole from top to bottom.

6 Dribble the saffron milk and 150ml/ ¼ pint/⅔ cup hot chicken stock over the rice, and dot with butter or ghee. Sprinkle over fried onions, sultanas (golden raisins) and toasted almonds. Cover tightly with a double piece of foil, then the lid. Bake for 40 minutes.

Chicken biryani spices

For 175g/6oz chicken use 10 green cardamom pods, 1.5ml/¼ tsp ground cloves, 2–3 whole cloves, 5cm/2in cinnamon stick, 5ml/1 tsp ground cumin, 2.5ml/½ tsp ground black pepper, 5ml/1 tsp ground coriander, 5ml/1 tsp finely chopped fresh root ginger and 1.5ml/¼ tsp chilli powder.

LONTONG

This compressed rice dish is a speciality of Indonesia and Malaysia. It is eaten cold, usually with salads and satay, and other spicy sauces.

Lontong is traditionally cooked in a banana leaf, but a muslin (cheesecloth) bag is generally easier to use. You can use Thai fragrant rice, basmati or any other long grain variety except parboiled (easy-cook) rice because it will not form a solid mass.

Making perfect lontong

1 You will need several muslin bags, each 15cm/6in square. Fill each bag one-third full with long grain rice (about 115g/4oz/generous ½ cup), then sew the top of each bag closed.

2 Bring a pan of salted water to the boil, add the bags of rice and simmer gently, uncovered, for 75 minutes, making sure the pan doesn't boil dry and adding more water if necessary.

3 Drain thoroughly. Each bag should feel like a rather hard and solid lump.

4 When totally cold, open the bags, remove the blocks and cut into squares or oblongs with a wet, sharp knife.

FRIED RICE

There are several classic fried rice dishes, such as Nasi Goreng from Indonesia, and Egg Fried Rice from China. Here is a guide to some popular ingredients.

Aromatics Use sliced spring onions (scallions) or shallots, sliced red or yellow onions, and sliced or crushed garlic. Stir-fry in oil for 3–4 minutes, then add the meat, fish, vegetables and/or eggs. If choosing two or more different ingredients, stir-fry them individually before stirring together.

Meat Use any tender cut of chicken, duck, beef, lamb or pork fillet. Slice it thinly to cook quickly. Marinate for 30

minutes before cooking. Stir-fry with onions until cooked. Cooked meats only require heating through.

Fish Raw fish and shellfish should always be stir-fried after any meat. Cooked fish or prawns (shrimp) can be added last.

Vegetables Choose colourful vegetables, such as carrots and (bell) peppers. Cut into julienne strips and stir-fry until just tender.

Eggs Beat the eggs together and scramble with the onions, or use them to make an omelette: roll it up, cut into slices and use to garnish the rice.

Making perfect fried rice

1 Stir-fry any uncooked meat in oil in a wok or large, deep frying pan, then add onions. Transfer the mixture to a plate.

2 Add beaten egg to the pan and scramble with sliced spring onions.

3 Add spices and flavourings such as soy sauce, rice wine, fresh chillies, tomato purée (paste) or spices.

4 Add the cold, cooked rice to the mixture and mix with the scrambled egg. Stir together well.

5 Return any cooked meats, cooked fish or cooked vegetables to the pan, or add chopped herbs. Cook the mixture over a low heat, stirring occasionally, to warm the rice through completely.

Fried rice tips
Rice must be cooked and completely cold before frying. Warm rice will become soggy and oily if fried. If you are preparing rice for frying, then first spread it on a baking sheet as soon as it has been cooked so that it cools rapidly. Leave it for at least 2–3 hours.

• Use long grain white or brown rice for frying.

• Other ingredients should be cooked before the rice is added.

• Always cook the rice over a low heat. It is important to heat the rice through completely, but take care not to overcook it.

Rice pudding

Rice pudding is enjoyed all over the world. In particular, it is England's best-known rice dish, and most other European and Asian countries have at least one version of their own.

Rice pudding may owe its popularity to the fact that it is difficult to overcook. In the 18th century, food was often overcooked, and rice pudding was one of the few foods that could stand up to such abuse. Its tender grains cooked in creamy milk quickly became a favourite.

Traditionally, English rice pudding is made with short grain rice. If short grain rice is unavailable, you can substitute the same quantity of Thai fragrant rice or basmati rice for the short grain rice. In Asia, stickier glutinous rice is used.

ENGLISH RICE PUDDING
Oven method

1 Preheat the oven to 150°C/300°F/ Gas 2. Following your chosen recipe, put the rice and sugar in a shallow baking dish and pour in cold milk. Stir well to mix and then dot the surface with a little butter.

2 Bake for about 45 minutes, by which time a thick skin will have formed on top of the pudding.

3 Stir in the skin and bake for about 1¼ hours more, until the rice is tender, stirring once or twice.

Pan method

1 Place the rice in a large, heavy pan. Add the quantity of milk and sugar as specified in the recipe and stir to mix.

2 Bring the mixture to the boil, then lower the heat, cover the pan and simmer very gently for 1¼ hours, stirring frequently.

3 Remove the lid and simmer the mixture for about 15–20 minutes until the rice is thick and creamy. You can also stir a little cream into the rice before serving.

Combination method

1 Partly cook the rice by the absorption method. Put it in a pan and add a third of the measured liquid. Simmer gently.

2 When absorbed, stir in half the remaining liquid. Simmer for 6 minutes.

3 Stir in the sugar, flavourings and remaining milk, then pour into a buttered baking dish. Dot with butter. Bake for 1–1½ hours at between 150°C/300°F/Gas 2 and 180°C/350°F/ Gas 4.

PERFECT GLUTINOUS RICE PUDDING

1 Place the rice in a large bowl, add cold water to cover and leave to soak for 3–4 hours.

2 Drain the rice thoroughly, then put it in a large, heavy pan and pour in coconut milk or cow's milk. Bring the milk to the boil, then lower the heat, cover the pan and simmer gently for about 25–30 minutes, stirring frequently.

3 Add sugar, creamed coconut and any flavourings of choice, and then cook for a further 5–10 minutes, with the pan uncovered, until the rice reaches the required consistency. Then remove from the heat and serve with slices of exotic fruits such as mango, papaya and pineapple, if you like.

PERFECT THAI RICE PUDDING

This dish is quick, easy and, most of all, completely delicious. Cook Thai fragrant rice in boiling water using the absorption method. Leave it to stand for a few minutes, then stir in milk and sugar to taste, and creamed coconut, if you like. Serve hot, with fresh fruit.

QUANTITIES FOR 4 PEOPLE

For short grain rice pudding:
600ml/1 pint/2½ cups milk
50g/1¾oz/generous ¼ cup rice, then stir in 45ml/3 tbsp sugar.
For a glutinous rice pudding:
300ml/½ pint/1¼ cups of liquid
75g/2¾oz/scant ½ cup of rice.
For a Thai rice pudding:
475ml/17fl oz/2 cups of water,
125ml/4fl oz/½ cup milk and 60ml/4 tbsp of creamed coconut and
50g/1¾oz/generous ¼ cup rice.

If creamed coconut (in solid blocks) is not available, replace every 50g/2oz of creamed coconut with 150ml/¼ pint/⅔ cup coconut milk, and reduce the water by 100ml/3fl oz/scant ½ cup.

FLAVOURINGS

Vanilla Give the milk a delicate flavour by heating it with a vanilla pod (bean) until the milk is hot but not boiling. Remove from the heat and leave to infuse for 1–2 hours. Strain the flavoured milk over the rice.

Nutmeg This is another very popular flavouring. Either grate it over the surface of a rice pudding that is to be baked, or stir grated nutmeg into the mixture in the pan. Ground cinnamon can be used as an alternative, if you prefer.

Raisins or sultanas (golden raisins) Stir into the rice or sprinkle over the bottom of the dish.

Spices Add lemon grass, cardamom pods, or pared orange, lemon or lime rind to the rice as it is cooking.

Nuts Add chopped pistachio nuts or almonds to a rice pudding that is being cooked by the combination or pan method.

ABOVE: *Pistachios stirred into the dessert with shreds of fresh mint will provide texture and a slightly sweet flavour.*

Index